Birth Rights and Wrongs

Birth Rights and Wrongs

How Medicine and Technology are Remaking Reproduction and the Law

DOV FOX

OXFORD
UNIVERSITY PRESS

OXFORD
UNIVERSITY PRESS

Oxford University Press is a department of the University of Oxford. It furthers the University's
objective of excellence in research, scholarship, and education by publishing worldwide. Oxford is
a registered trademark of Oxford University Press in the UK and certain other countries.

Published in the United States of America by Oxford University Press
198 Madison Avenue, New York, NY 10016, United States of America.

Library of Congress Cataloging-in-Publication Data
Names: Fox, Dov, author.
Title: Birth rights and wrongs : how medicine and technology are remaking reproduction
and the law / Dov Fox.
Description: New York : Oxford University Press, 2019. | Includes bibliographical references
and index.
Identifiers: LCCN 2018060423 | ISBN 9780190675721 ((hardback) : alk. paper)
Subjects: LCSH: Human reproduction—Law and legislation—United States. |
Medical personnel—Malpractice—United States. | Liability (Law)—United States.
Classification: LCC KF3760 .F69 2019 | DDC 342.7308/5—dc23
LC record available at https://lccn.loc.gov/2018060423

1 3 5 7 9 8 6 4 2

Printed by Sheridan Books, Inc., United States of America

Note to Readers
This publication is designed to provide accurate and authoritative information in regard to
the subject matter covered. It is based upon sources believed to be accurate and reliable and
is intended to be current as of the time it was written. It is sold with the understanding that
the publisher is not engaged in rendering legal, accounting, or other professional services.
If legal advice or other expert assistance is required, the services of a competent professional
person should be sought. Also, to confirm that the information has not been affected or
changed by recent developments, traditional legal research techniques should be used,
including checking primary sources where appropriate.

*(Based on the Declaration of Principles jointly adopted by a Committee of the
American Bar Association and a Committee of Publishers and Associations.)*

Contents

III. TO ERR IS TOO HUMAN

Foreword

People's reproductive choices improve and define their lives like few other decisions they make in a lifetime. Some want biological children, more likely to develop into their likes and keep their genes alive. Others are looking to limit their family size, or to avoid having any kids at all. Many seek help from reproductive medicines and technologies like birth control and abortion, surrogacy and in vitro fertilization, embryo screening and fetal diagnosis. The proliferation of these interventions has shored up their efficacy, driven down their costs, and made them accessible to millions. But they do not always work how they were supposed to. It is not just that unavoidable failures let patients down, upend their plans, and cause them emotional distress. Sometimes, professionals are to blame for accidents that result in unwanted pregnancies, genetic mismatches, birth defects, and mass destruction of eggs or embryos. These errors generate deep puzzles and practical challenges for divided democracies and modern systems of law.

Reproductive negligence does not translate comfortably into conventional notions of injury, damages, or causation. Consider the straight white couple who conceives a baby through artificial insemination when a donor switch gives them a healthy non-Caucasian baby. Did the couple incur an "injury" in the way that tort law recognizes this concept? If not, can the couple sue the sperm bank or egg vendor for a breach of contract? Or would contractual assurance to produce a particular offspring race be unenforceable or noncompensable on public policy or other grounds? Or take the woman who undergoes a tubal ligation procedure to prevent future pregnancies only to find herself with a baby she could not support after her physician left one of her tubes untied. Even if a court were willing to call her child a legal injury, can she recover "damages" for the cost of raising him? And if so, can the hospital offset from that total the value of parenting's inevitable prides and joys? Then there is the wife and husband whose doctor gave them too many fertility drugs. The resulting quadruplets are born dangerously premature, one gravely infirm. Is the misadministered medicine what "caused" the ailment? Their sick baby could not have been any healthier herself. Had it not been for the overdose, the couple would have had altogether different children instead, if they got any at all.

These are among the many hundreds of real-life cases that require a special legal toolset to vindicate interests in procreation. *Birth Rights and Wrongs* examines these cases and develops this much-needed toolset. The book is that rare masterwork: beautifully written, astoundingly erudite, comprehensively researched, and meticulously analyzed. It must be read by anyone who wants to understand how the law treats emotions, love, race, identity, and family, and how it grapples with controversies born of technological change. This book is also for every practitioner, policymaker, scholar, or student of law, medicine, or science who is interested in navigating the complexities of reproductive negligence, the concept that Professor Dov Fox coined in his acclaimed article of that name. Months after it appeared in the *Columbia Law Review*, my counterparts on the highest court of Singapore relied on it in their unanimous judgment setting forth a new right of "genetic affinity." This book answers the questions that article had posed.

More than a century ago, the legal system stood on the cusp of a similar revolution to protect individual privacy. In generations past, even the most intimate images and sensitive facts were fair game for scandalmongering tabloids, armed with click-camera advances of the day. The law gave no refuge to victims who had their pictures unwittingly used in business ads or humiliating stories. Then Samuel Warren and future U.S. Supreme Court Justice Louis Brandeis published among the most influential articles of all time, in the 1890 *Harvard Law Review*, awakening courts to the urgency of that lasting problem and their common law power to do something about it. Just as invasions by prying Kodaks dramatized crucial interests in being let alone, today's reproductive mix-ups lay bare the centrality and richness of interests in matters of procreation. This book is *The Right to Privacy* for the twenty-first century. It deserves to achieve what Warren and Brandeis did.

Alex Stein is a Justice of the Supreme Court of Israel. He is the author of four academic books, including Foundations of Evidence Law *and* Tort Liability under Uncertainty, *and scores of law review articles, including* "A Theory of Medical Malpractice" *and* "The Domain of Torts."

Preface

I was born a few days before Elizabeth Carr, the first American baby conceived by in vitro fertilization (IVF). Her parents—Judy and Roger—desperately wanted a child, one who'd share their genes. But they couldn't reproduce on their own. A decade of failed attempts left Judy with pregnancy complications that required removing her fallopian tubes. That made it impossible for any fertilized egg to get from her ovaries to the uterus, where it develops. The couple put their faith in the country's first fertility clinic. A team of pioneering doctors and scientists made an end run around Judy's missing tubes by surgically removing her eggs and then combining them with Roger's sperm in a laboratory, before implanting the resulting embryo back into Judy's uterus. In December 1981, this technological breakthrough gave the Carrs the child they had longed for. Critics decried Elizabeth's arrival for defying nature and playing God. "The others have their opinions," Judy said. "We have our baby."[1]

Many aspiring parents aren't so lucky, even a million IVF babies later. One fateful weekend in March 2018, hundreds of couples like the Carrs had their hopes for biological parenthood crushed when high-capacity freezers failed at two major medical facilities, University Hospital of Cleveland and Pacific Fertility Center in San Francisco. These subzero containers aren't regulated any better than kitchen appliances or farm tools. The livestock industry developed the bulk vats in the 1960s to store animal semen for breeding. Now they're used by almost five hundred fertility clinics nationwide to cryopreserve people's eggs and embryos at a constant $-196°C$. Tank temperatures at the two facilities began rising on the same unstaffed Saturday, after remote alarms had inexplicably been turned off. By the time lab technicians returned on Monday morning, everything inside was destroyed.

Investigations are ongoing. So far, only coordinated cyberattacks have been ruled out. Center operators are pointing the finger at defective equipment, while the manufacturers have blamed laboratory staff for "forget[ting] to refill" the liquid nitrogen chambers in these "ever-dependable vessels."[2] The medical centers also could have used more reliable monitoring systems that measure nitrogen levels with a specialized scale that can detect tiny fluctuations of even a few hundred grams. These weight-based methods can identify early signs of dangerous warming weeks sooner than the thermometer-based sensors that give mere hours' warning before people's reproductive materials are thawed beyond rescue or repair.[3]

The incidents devastated thousands of cancer survivors, injured veterans, and other would-be parents who now won't be. Sacramento residents Megan and Jonathan Bauer had made plans to transfer the first of their eight embryos the very next month when they got word that every one had been lost forever. The couple grieved over their stolen "dreams of having children together." Breast cancer survivor Rachel Mehl of Pittsburgh couldn't imagine a future without kids. She had delayed urgent, life-saving chemotherapy—that would take her fertility—until she could freeze her eggs for later use. All nineteen were irrevocably damaged, dashing her only chance of genetic offspring—"that light at the end of a very dark tunnel. . . . has been extinguished."[4] Katelynn Gurbach lives in Wickliffe, Ohio. An only child, she lost her mother at thirteen and was diagnosed with ovarian cancer at twenty-three. The freezer failure took each of the four embryos she and her boyfriend had created before cancer treatment left her sterile. "I wanted nothing more than to be a mom," she posted on Facebook the next day. "The unthinkable, the unimaginable, the unbelievable has happened. My worst fears and deepest nightmares made a reality."[5]

An engraved bench now sits beneath an ash tree in the Woodvale Cemetery outside Cleveland: "Our Hopes and Dreams Lost: In Memory of the Unborn."

National media called the recent malfunctions "inconceivable" and "utterly unprecedented."[6] They were neither. In October 2005, a mechanical crash at the University of Florida Health Center destroyed the reproductive materials that sixty men had saved before undergoing chemotherapy or deploying overseas. Technicians didn't even notice the casualties until August of the following year.[7] An April 2012 breakdown affected two hundred fifty patients and troops at Northwestern Memorial Hospital who had put their sperm samples on ice.[8] Forty of the men filed a class-action lawsuit that took over six years to settle behind closed doors in October 2018.[9] Legal proceedings against University Hospital and Pacific Fertility Center have only just gotten off the ground as this book goes to press. These catastrophic losses point to a larger phenomenon of procreation gone awry.

IVF isn't the only reproductive innovation that came of age as I did—so did abortion pills (e.g., RU-486), long-lasting birth control (e.g., Norplant), and non-invasive blood tests (e.g., AFP Plus) that screen for fetal risks of neural tube defects.

Today, tens of millions of Americans rely on these advances to help them carry out decisions more personal and far-reaching than almost any other they'll ever make. They use birth control or abortion to delay or avoid having children; surrogacy or tissue donation to start or grow a family; and genetic diagnosis or embryo selection to have offspring who survive and flourish. Two in seven American women of childbearing age undergo surgical sterilization or long-term contraception to prevent pregnancy—one in four have an abortion by forty-five.[10] One in nine adults are treated for fertility problems like blocked fallopian tubes or low sperm counts.[11] And 62,000 babies—nearly 2 percent born in the United States each year—are conceived using reproductive technologies.[12] Surrogates carry three thousand annually to term. Many thousands more are screened—even before pregnancy—for conditions like Tay-Sachs, cystic fibrosis, and sickle cell disease. This is no less than the medicine of miracles. It fills empty cradles; frees families from debilitating maladies; and empowers them to plan a life that doesn't include parenthood. But accidents happen.

Embryologists miss ailments. Egg vendors switch donors. Obstetricians tell pregnant women that their healthy fetuses will be stillborn. The aftermaths can last a lifetime. Yet political and economic forces conspire against regulation to prevent negligence from happening in the first place. After the fact, social stigma and lawyers' fees stave off lawsuits. And legal relief is a long shot. Judges and juries are reluctant to designate reproductive losses as worthy of redress when mix-ups foist parenthood on patients who didn't want it, or childlessness on those who did. Some courts insist that even unplanned babies are blessings, and shrug over the fact that infertile couples weren't assured offspring anyway. Others are resigned that these tragedies are just part of modern life, like the "betrayal, brutal words, and heartless disregard" that lie beyond "the power of any judicial system" to do anything about.[13] The result is a society that lets badly behaving specialists off the hook and leaves broken victims to pick up the pieces. Failed abortions, switched donors, and lost embryos may be First World problems. But these aren't innocent lapses or harmless errors. They're wrongs in need of rights.

This book is about the fragility of family planning and the promise of law to vindicate its expression. I have profited from opportunities to present these ideas at the American Law and Economics Association Conference, the Clifford Symposium on Civil Justice, the International Baby Markets Congress, and the World Life Sciences Convention, and with faculty and students at Harvard Law School, NYU School of Law, Pennsylvania Law School, and Stanford Law School. Portions of Part I appeared in much earlier form in "Reproductive Negligence," 117 *Columbia Law Review* 149 (2017). So did a section of Part II in "Making Things Right When Reproductive Medicine Goes Wrong: Reply to Robert Rabin, Carol Sanger, and Gregory Keating," 118 *Columbia Law Review Online* 94 (2018). I thank the *Columbia Law Review* for permission to incorporate these pieces, and Professors Rabin, Sanger, and Keating for their searching engagement in the pages of that journal and beyond.

My colleagues at the University of San Diego (USD) have been steady sources of camaraderie and conversation. I owe special thanks to Larry Alexander, Jonathan Anomaly, Jordan Barry, Laurie Claus, Margaret Dalton, Miranda Perry Fleischer, Vic Fleischer, Adam Hirsch, Bert Lazerow, Miranda McGowan, Frank Partnoy, Ted Sichelman, Steve Smith, Mila Sohoni, Ed Ursin, Mary Jo Wiggins, and Matt Zwolinski. I am particularly indebted to my Dean, Stephen Ferruolo. I received exceptional support from USD law librarians Jane Larrington, Melissa Abernathy, Dan Kimmons, Ruth Levor, Sasha Orman, and Liz Parker. I've been fortunate for superlative research assistants during their legal studies at USD: Lauren Friedenberg, Thang Hoang, Veneeta Jaswal, Alex Niebling, Thomas Rainey, and David Rao. It was a pleasure to explore these themes with the law students and medical residents in my courses on "Medical Malpractice" and "Health Law and Reproduction."

Fellow travelers provided uncommonly generous comments: Paula Abrams, Rene Almeling, Susan Appleton, Russell Blackford, Michael Boucai, Khiara Bridges, Naomi Cahn, Steve Calandrillo, June Carbone, Andrew Coan, Glenn Cohen, Mary Crossley, Judy Daar, Teun Dekker, Bernard Dickens, Carter Dillard, Janet Dolgin, Richard Epstein, Martha Ertman, Colin Gavaghan, Michelle Goodwin, Adam Grant, Michael Green, Jessie Hill, Karla Holloway, Lisa Ikemoto, Josh Kleinfeld, Wendy Kramer, Saul Levmore, Kristen Loveland, Jody Lyneé Madeira, Kaipo Matsumura, Elaine Tyler May, Max Mehlman, Jennifer Mnookin, Seema Mohapatra, Lyria Bennett Moses, Doug NeJaime, Lars Noah, Christine Overall, David

Partlett, Philip Peters, Nicky Priaulx, Dara Purvis, Natalie Ram, Richard Re, Rachel Rebouché, John Robertson, Liz Sepper, Jane Stapleton, Steve Sugarman, Sonia Suter, David Wasserman, Ellen Wertheimer, Jonathan Will, Mary Ziegler, and Ben Zipursky.

My editors at Oxford University Press, Jamie Berezin, and David Lipp, believed in this project from its earliest stirrings and infused it with their insight. Balamurugan Rajendran at Newgen Knowledge Works Pvt. Ltd. managed an impossibly smooth production process, dynamic and obliging at every turn. My teachers made philosophy, science, and the law come alive—Christine Jolls, Michael Sandel, Julian Savulescu, Peter Schuck, Reva Siegel, and Alex Stein, currently a justice on the Israeli Supreme Court. G.A. (Jerry) Cohen and (Judge) Stephen Reinhardt were more than mentors to me. At key moments in my life, Jerry and the Judge were the father I needed. My greatest disappointment about this project is that they didn't live to see it finished.

My deepest thanks go to my family: To my mom, who raised three boys while working multiple jobs, and never let us want for love. To my brothers, my best friends. To my grandparents, who took us in and lit our way. To my in-laws, who treat me as their own. To my kids, who filled these seasons of writing with joy. And finally, to my wife, who did more than anyone to shape this book, which I dedicate to her with love.

Introduction

How many little girls dream of being a nun? "I always wanted to be a mother, but the marriage part didn't appeal to me," Angie Collins explains. "I thought if I was a nun, I could live at an orphanage, and those could be my kids." It wasn't the life of solemn contemplation that appealed to her. Sisterhood fit two things she knew about herself from an early age: She wanted children, and she wasn't attracted to men. She ended up trading a religious habit for phys ed sweats. At thirty-two, the spry gym instructor fell in love with a soft-spoken music teacher named Beth Hanson. The couple made a home in Port Hope, Ontario, and decided to start a family together. They looked into adoption, but worried that lesbians like them would have trouble gaining legal recognition as parents. Besides, Collins wanted to experience pregnancy and give birth. What they needed was a man, or at least his sperm.[1]

"I didn't have a friend in mind," Collins recalls, "and my doctor was actually discouraging of using a known donor."[2] It turns out asking a relative or social contact can risk unwelcome involvement in the couple's parenting. Known donors have even sued for legal custody based on a genetic connection to the child. Transacting at arm's length "seemed simpler, more clear-cut."[3] But Canadian donors are in short supply, in part because the country makes it a crime to exchange reproductive samples for money. So Collins and Hanson looked to the United States, where sperm banks pay. The couple settled on Georgia-based Xytex. Its catalog features over five hundred donors, recruited with the promise of an "easy, anonymous way to make some serious money—up to $1,800 a month, so you can say goodbye to ramen and hello to steak."[4]

Despite its dystopian name, Xytex projects itself as more community clinic than multinational conglomerate. A cheery representative told Collins over the phone that donors complete an extensive personal and family history and undergo physical exams every six months. The company's website boasts: "You can rest easy knowing right up front, every Xytex donor ranks in the top 1% of the population in health and wellness." The sperm bank prides itself on being "an industry leader in reproductive services with a commitment to unsurpassed quality controls." The screening process was so thorough, the rep assured Collins, they'd learn more about any Xytex donor than they ever could about an acquaintance—or even each other. They were sold.[5]

After poring over hundreds of profiles, they found The One. Donor 9623 had everything they were looking for: He was fit, gifted, and easy on the eyes. His lean frame, warm smile, and fetching eyes reminded Collins of the "male version of my partner." Xytex said his "celebrity lookalike" was Tom Cruise, but a foot taller. Donor 9623 also shared Hanson's love of literature and music and Collins's for sports and hiking. The Renaissance Man was an "internationally acclaimed" drummer who spoke five languages and read four books a month ("non-fiction mostly"). The couple knew hobbies aren't inherited—still, DNA might give them a nudge. And lots of medical conditions have a stronger genetic component. Donor 9623's six-page family questionnaire checked "no" for all 143 diseases or disorders but one. His father was colorblind.[6] It wasn't just the donor's diverse talents and clean bill of health.

His 160 IQ placed him in the company of Albert Einstein and Stephen Hawking among the top 0.1 percent of the world's population. The thirty-year-old had earned his bachelor's degree in neuroscience and master's in artificial intelligence. He was currently studying for a Ph.D. in neuroscience engineering, on his way to become a professor of biomedical robotics. A Xytex counselor referred to him as the "perfect donor." Hanson recalls, "All the other donors vanished as soon as we saw his profile." The couple wired the company $3,000 for six units of sperm from Donor 9623. Two weeks later, frozen samples arrived in the mail. Collins got pregnant on the first try. She and Hanson were elated to welcome a son. Seven years passed.

As he grew from baby to boy, his parents took Xytex up on its offer to join a "sibling group" of families who'd selected the same donor to have children. They were hardly the only ones charmed by Donor 9623. Twenty-five families had used his genetic material to have thirty-six offspring by 2014.[7] That June is when Collins and Hanson got a Facebook message from a woman in the sibling group. It said that Xytex had inadvertently revealed Donor 9623's email address in a correspondence with her. It's company policy to keep donor contacts and identities a secret. Donors supply their sperm to the bank on the condition of anonymity. The leaked address for Donor 9623 also included the man's last name: Aggeles. A social media profile linked his email to a James Christian Aggeles, who goes by Chris. His plump frame and facial mole looked nothing like the Top Gun features of his donor photograph. Okay, the couple thought, so what. But other discrepancies took them aback.

A Google search turned up documents from a Georgia court that had convicted Aggeles of burglary in 2005, shortly before Collins and Hanson had picked his profile from the catalog. He'd broken into a home and stolen musical instruments. Aggeles pled guilty and spent eight months in jail, another ten on probation. That wasn't his first run-in with the law either. He'd been arrested several times before for offenses including trespassing, drunk driving, and disorderly conduct.[8] His educational career had started out promising, but he never enrolled in the touted doctoral program, or even finished college. Aggeles graduated high school as an honor student and got a full scholarship to the University of Georgia. But he dropped out a few months in, at age nineteen. That was when his psychotic breaks began.

Medical evidence in the burglary case revealed diagnoses of schizophrenia, bipolar disorder, and narcissistic personality disorder with "significant grandiose delusions." Collins also found an online comment Aggeles had posted in 2012 to a YouTube video of a young woman describing her struggles with schizophrenia. Aggeles wrote: "It's like my thought gets interrupted by a voice that tells me something that usually has nothing to do with what I was just thinking. It's usually mean, and will say things that are derogatory and demeaning to me."[9] Collins and Hanson learned that having one parent with schizophrenia gives a boy a 12 percent chance of developing it by the time he can drive. That's when the average affected male starts hallucinating. Half of young men with schizophrenia try to kill themselves—one in twenty succeed.[10]

"[M]y heart s[a]nk like a lead ball into my stomach," Collins recalled.[11] She wouldn't have bought sperm that she knew came from a convicted felon with mental illness: "[A] hitchhiker on the side of the road would have been a [] more responsible option."[12]

Aggeles is doing better today, with the help of medication and therapy. He made it back to college, got married, and even drums in an indie-rock band. Collins and Hanson don't hold it against him that his donor profile was a lie. Aggeles had fallen on hard times that left him desperate for cash. "He's not a bad man," Collins says. "He's a person who has an illness." The couple would support their son if he wanted to reach out to Aggeles.[13] It's Xytex they blame.

The corporation got rich by looking the other way on the truth about donors whose reproductive material it hawked to thousands of families. Its don't-ask-don't-tell policy exploited a lax regulatory regime to profit off of families who banked their futures on its false representations about Donor 9623. That's how Collins saw it. "I didn't feel they were selling perfection"— just "due diligence. Who would have thought that an industry that makes people would be like this?" she asked in April 2016.[14] Two months later, the *New York Times* profiled "a new wave of lawsuits" against U.S. sperm banks, labeling the industry "buyer-beware."[15] A November 2018 story in the *Washington Post* detailed a slew of yet more recent cases ranging from "babies sired by the 'wrong' father" to "children who inherit serious, undisclosed medical issues."[16]

Professional societies that oversee the fertility industry recommend screening donors for infectious diseases like HIV, hepatitis, and syphilis. The largest banks like Xytex also test samples for genes known to cause Tay-Sachs, cystic fibrosis, and cerebral palsy—these are recessive disorders that offspring can inherit from people who don't suffer from the condition themselves, and usually don't find out that they carry it in their DNA until they have a child who does. But no public body or private organization requires that sperm banks conduct such analysis or reporting.[17] And even the most scrupulous ones rely heavily on unverified information provided by donors themselves. Few ask for so much as a student ID or college diploma to back up their self-professed credentials, let alone run a background check or drug test. "If a donor says his Aunt Pearl died of a heart attack, we take him at his word," a Xytex representative told *Self* magazine in 2006.[18]

People who reproduce the old-fashioned way can also pass along dangers lurking in their genetics. But sperm banks like Xytex multiply that risk to potentially scores of offspring. In 2011, news broke that one donor's samples had been used to conceive over one hundred fifty children. None of the families had been warned that those genetic siblings could end up sleeping with each other or falling in love.[19]

Collins is open with her son, now ten, about where he came from. "I told him, 'The man who helped create you and all your half-siblings has something wrong with his brain.'"[20] The boy loves handball and geography—he knows all the street names in Port Hope and the shape of every American state. And he plays drums like Aggeles. Collins and Hanson are monitoring his mental health closely and will do what they can to steer him clear of the drugs that could trigger psychotic episodes. "He's the love of our lives."[21]

Dozens of parents like Collins and Hanson sued the sperm bank. The final pages of this book take stock of how things played out for them in court. For now, it'll do to remark just how unremarkable their story is. "In households across the country," another *New York Times* exposé began, "children conceived with donated sperm are struggling with serious genetic conditions inherited from men they have never met."[22] New examples make their way into peer-reviewed scientific journals every few years.

A 2012 report in *Human Reproduction* uncovered a nameless donor who transmitted to five offspring a genetic condition that significantly increases the risk of brain tumors, leukemia, and other cancers.[23] In 2009, the *Journal of the American Medical Association* published the case study of a Virginia donor with a heart disorder that he passed on to at least eight of his twenty-two offspring, including a toddler who died from cardiac failure.[24] In 2006, the *Journal of Pediatrics* chronicled a network of half-siblings conceived from the same popular donor, all of whom inherited a rare blood disease known to cause cancer, seizures, and developmental delays. Affected families had notified the bank about these health problems years earlier, but it didn't deactivate the donor or even red-flag his profile.[25] Court documents in a 2003 case revealed that a sperm bank sold hundreds of vials from a donor with a family history of kidney disease—*after* it learned that at least one girl conceived from his material had already inherited the disorder, which threatens renal failure.[26] The sperm bank settled the lawsuit to avoid further investigation into the unknown number of other children who came from the same donor.[27]

It's not just sperm banks. A 2008 survey of half of all U.S. fertility clinics found that more than one in five misdiagnosed, mislabeled, or mishandled reproductive materials.[28] A 2014 study reported that hundreds of women each year are persuaded to end pregnancies they'd wanted to keep, based on dire test results that sound "a false alarm half of the time."[29] And in 2016, a national ratings website found that 18–24 percent of fertility patients reported miscues including dropped embryos, switched donors, and contaminated samples.[30] These failures can't be chalked up to reasonable slips of hand or lapses in judgment as often as deficient quality controls.[31] Just *how* often is hard to pin down.

In other areas of health care, most states make hospitals monitor and report any major avoidable errors, like mismatched blood transfusions or surgery on the wrong body part. But no one tracks similar "never events" in matters of procreation—at least not in the United States. Most developed countries take reproductive negligence far more seriously.[32] In the United Kingdom, the Human Fertilisation and Embryology Authority enforces rigorous and regular inspections of all fertility clinics "in line with the latest evidence."[33] Even under this strict oversight regime, the regulatory body reports that over five hundred procedures each year misplace, damage, or destroy people's sperm, eggs, and embryos.[34]

In the United States, victims who take procreation specialists to court almost always lose. This puzzle has gone all but unnoticed in the case reports and academic literature.[35] The only book that's addressed it at all observes that policymakers and judges respond to "the startling consequences" of reproductive advances "with confusion and ambivalence."[36] Among legal texts, just one gives these controversies more than passing reference.[37] Beyond government regulation of abortion or IVF, law and ethics scholarship has attended to different kinds of disputes: between former couples about whether or not to use their frozen embryos,[38] or between children and parents whose prenatal decisions led them to be born with health complications.[39] These questions about embryo disposition and offspring disability have crowded out broader inquiry into matters of procreation.

This book develops a new way to think and talk about reproductive wrongdoing writ large. Some of these wrongs *deprive* people of the pregnancy or parenthood they want. Others *impose* those roles on people seeking to avoid them. Others still *confound* plans for not just any child, but for one born with certain traits. Recent cases illustrate each:

Case 1: "Procreation Deprived." Justin Hollman was diagnosed with testicular cancer at twenty. He needed chemotherapy and surgical removal of a testicle that would leave him sterile. He knew he wanted kids one day, so he deposited sperm with a fertility clinic and made regular payments to keep it safely stored. But when he returned for the sample a decade later, happily married and eager to start a family, it had been destroyed.[40]

Case 2: "Procreation Imposed." Shelby Nell, a young single mother, had found a job she liked and a man she loved. Nell wanted a healthy sex life, one that wouldn't risk another child she couldn't afford to raise. She got a prescription for birth control pills, but the pharmacist gave her prenatal vitamins instead. Her relationship couldn't bear the

weight of the resulting pregnancy. Nell was forced on welfare to support and raise her toddler and infant on her own.[41]

Case 3: "Procreation Confounded." Eve Rubell's eye exam revealed a
swirling pattern. It was a sign that she carried Fabry disease, a condition that's debilitating for boys. Rubell didn't suffer any symptoms
herself, but any male child she had would. It's a risk that she and her
husband sought to avoid. They created six embryos in a lab, enough to
get two females. But the hospital implanted one of the other four instead. Rubell gave birth to a baby boy afflicted by the disease.[42]

Hollman, Nell, and Rubell all sued. Each lost. Never mind that negligence
was to blame. However egregious the transgression, no statute or doctrine
says that their injuries matter, legally speaking. As one court put it, the "law
does not recognize disruption of family planning either as an independent
cause of action or element of damages."[43]

Take procreation deprived. When misconduct shatters people's dreams
of parenthood, victims can't point to any physical or financial harm they've
suffered. And fertility patients were never assured biological children.
Hollman, the cancer survivor, might not have been able to conceive, even if
the clinic had kept his tissues safe. But since it was still altogether possible
that his sample could have yielded offspring, shouldn't he be compensated
for whatever chance that he did have—before the clinic's misconduct took
that chance from him, when it lost his only samples, making reproduction
impossible? Proportional recourse is the norm when medical malpractice
reduces a patient's odds of recovery or survival, even if he (or his estate)
can't prove that a doctor's misconduct is what led him to deteriorate or die,
or that his preexisting condition wouldn't have caused that outcome anyway. But courts don't compensate for lost chances to reproduce. Some are
content that adoption and other paths to parenthood remain open. Others
worry that reproductive plans are too easy to contrive and too hard to verify.

Courts harbor similar suspicions against allegations of procreation
imposed. The judge in Nell's case expressed a similar concern that people
might "invent an intent to prevent pregnancy." It would "open the door to
fraud," she explained, were courts to credit "claims of inadequate directions,
wrong pills or any ineffectiveness of the chosen contraceptive method."
However sincere Nell's allegations, affirming them would invite sham suits
by people trying to make someone else pay for their failure "to exercise restraint or take responsibility."[44] Besides, if Nell had really wanted to avoid

reproducing, why did she keep the baby? And having declined abortion or adoption, didn't she nonetheless come to appreciate his birth as a gift, even if not one she'd asked for?[45] Even though that arrival might disrupt her life plans, courts insist that those trade-offs are bound to be outweighed by "the intangible but all-important, incalculable but invaluable 'benefits' of parenthood."[46]

Finally are thwarted efforts to choose a child's sex, health, heredity, or some other feature that's meaningfully influenced by the genetics he's born with. Courts resist finding for plaintiffs like Rubell when professional misconduct confounds their offspring preferences. Donor switches, embryo mix-ups, and fetal misdiagnoses don't produce unwitting parents, judges point out. These are people who'd set out to have a child, and got one—even if the experience of raising that child departs from their reasonable expectations. Courts refuse to rubber-stamp parental disappointment for fear of sending the intolerable message that any mother or father wishes a child hadn't been born, or loves the child less than some other one who's different. Most states are "unwilling to say that life, even life with severe [impairments], may ever amount to a legal injury."[47] The American legal system treats confounded procreation less like mischief than misfortune, closer to a star-crossed romance or a losing ticket in the natural lottery—the kind of adversity that, however fateful, you have no choice but to steel yourself against and move on from. You can't always get what you want.

This indifference is surprising in a country that's constitutionalized rights to abortion and birth control. In the 1960s and 1970s, the U.S. Supreme Court designated "decisions whether to accomplish or to prevent conception" as "among the most private and sensitive" that a person makes over the course of a life.[48] But even this "fundamental rights" status hasn't kept states from aggressively restricting access to abortion and contraception.[49] And the Court hasn't extended these reproductive freedoms to practices that introduce donors or surrogates into the mix. Besides, constitutional privacy applies only to misconduct by government actors. It offers no protection against wrongdoing by any nonstate clinic, pharmacy, or hospital.[50]

PART I

REPRODUCTIVE FRONTIERS

Reproductive advances have profoundly affected American life, transforming families, workplaces, and health care. But they've never been well regulated, and accidents are pervasive—accidents that upend plans to avoid or pursue or shape procreation. Chapter 1 distinguishes three core interests—in pregnancy, parenthood, and offspring particulars—and explains how their frustration harms people in distinct ways. Chapter 2 examines why federal and state lawmakers fail to protect those interests against negligence, and how social stigma and trial risks leave negligence victims reluctant to stand up for their own interests in court. Chapter 3 explores the limits of existing law to redress reproductive injuries—including contract enforcement and personal-injury doctrines like "wrongful birth" and "wrongful death."

1

"Basic Civil Rights"

Nature, that great tragic dramatist, knits us together by bone and muscle, and divides us by the subtler web of our brains; blends yearning and repulsion; and ties us by our heart-strings to the beings that jar us at every movement.
—George Eliot, *Adam Bede* (1859)

Judicial pronouncements about the centrality of reproductive life predate the privacy landmarks of the sexual revolution.[1] In 1942, the U.S. Supreme Court struck down a state law that said people convicted of certain crimes could be surgically prevented from producing offspring. In *Skinner v. Oklahoma*, the justices referred to "procreation" as "fundamental to the very existence and survival of the race," calling it one of "the basic civil rights of man."[2] But this lofty rhetoric came in simpler reproductive times—when sex plus fertility equaled offspring: nothing more, nothing less. And that language has never carried formal authority as binding precedent. Besides, *Skinner* emerged from a eugenic past that today evokes horror and shame.

A. One Family Tree

In the decades before World War II, thirty-three states forcibly sterilized their citizens. Policymakers urged these laws as a genetic solution to social problems like unemployment, promiscuity, and "feeblemindedness," a catch-all for unexplained low achievement. The most explicit targets were the sick, poor, and unpopular—from "indigents" and "epileptics" to "paupers" and "perverts."[3] Women, immigrants, and African Americans were disproportionately sterilized too, especially after state programs reached beyond the racially segregated walls of prisons, psychiatric hospitals, and residential institutions.[4] Jack Skinner was sentenced under an Oklahoma statute that singled out "habitual criminals," defined as people convicted of three

Birth Rights and Wrongs. Dov Fox.
© Dov Fox 2019. Published 2019 by Oxford University Press.

crimes "involving moral turpitude." This three-strikes law empowered the government to sterilize repeat low-level offenders like Skinner, a one-footed chicken thief.[5] He contested his sentence as unconstitutional, but faced an uphill battle—his legal challenge flew in the face of a popular movement to improve the social welfare through conscientious control over human breeding.

"Progressive eugenics," as it was called, held broad political, cultural, and religious appeal in early twentieth-century America.[6] This ideal assumed that human differences in intelligence, character, and temperament owed largely to differences in heredity—and it argued that those differences were too important to leave to the clumsy workings of natural selection. The father of eugenics, Sir Francis Galton, proclaimed that "what Nature does blindly, slowly and ruthlessly, man may do providently, quickly and kindly."[7] In 1916, activist Margaret Sanger opened the first U.S. birth control clinic in part to "limit and discourage the overfertility of the mentally and physically defective."[8] By 1920, three hundred fifty colleges and universities offered eugenics courses instructing students how to make wise reproductive decisions. And from 1918 to 1927, the American Eugenics Society sponsored state-fair competitions for the finest genetic histories and highest scores on medical, psychological, and IQ tests.[9] But it wasn't all "Fitter Family" contests.

Compulsory sterilization regimes cloaked Nazi eugenics in the legitimacy of democratic government. "What we racial hygienists promote is not at all new or unheard of," a German health director affirmed in 1923, just before the publication of Adolf Hitler's *Mein Kampf*. "In a cultural nation of the first order, the United States of America, that which we strive toward was introduced long ago."[10] A California sterilization report was the first English-language book the Führer translated into German. The Third Reich cited it widely to justify mass-sterilization as an effective and humane means of achieving what the report termed "Human Betterment."[11] Mainstream American commentators returned the praise for Nazi-style eugenics right up until the war. In 1935, the *Los Angeles Times* held up Hitler's more aggressive sterilization program as "an aspect of the new Germany that America, with the rest of the world, can little afford to criticize."[12] Progressive eugenics was championed by diverse causes, from family planning to population control, and across the ideological spectrum, from liberal Democrats like Woodrow Wilson to conservative Republicans like Calvin Coolidge. Teddy Roosevelt declared it the "inescapable duty" of every "citizen of the right type to leave his or her blood behind him in the world" and prevent "the perpetuation of the citizens of the wrong type."[13]

Public support for eugenics buoyed *Buck v. Bell*, a case so notorious it's been banished to U.S. constitutional law's "anti-canon," though never formally overturned.[14] That 1927 decision upheld Virginia's sterilization of Carrie Buck, a poor white teenager who had a child after she was raped. The state law authorizing the forced procedure purported to go after Buck as a "mental defective," but actually because she, like her mother, had given birth out of wedlock. "Three generations of imbeciles are enough," is how the Supreme Court justified making Buck forever childless—her only other child died at eight of infections related to measles. The girl's teachers had called her bright. Justice Oliver Wendell Holmes, Jr. wrote for the Court:

> It is better for all the world, if instead of waiting to execute degenerate offspring for crime, or to let them starve for their imbecility, society can prevent those who are manifestly unfit from continuing their kind.[15]

Justice Pierce Butler, the lone holdout, didn't even write a dissenting opinion. And he died before Oklahoma's sterilization law came before the Court fifteen years later.[16] With *Buck* squarely on the books, little wonder Skinner didn't bother arguing that compelled vasectomy infringed on his reproductive rights.

Skinner objected on the ground that Oklahoma treated him worse than people who'd committed similar crimes. The sterilization statute exploited the weasel term "moral turpitude," he objected, to go after him for petty larceny, while exempting the corruption, embezzlement, and treason of "the Capones, the Ponzis and the Benedict Arnolds."[17] The Supreme Court agreed that Skinner had been denied equal protection of law, guaranteed under the Fourteenth Amendment of the U.S. Constitution. When the law "sterilizes one" person who has committed the same quality of offense "and not the other," Justice William Douglas wrote for a near-unanimous Court,

> it has made as invidious a discrimination as if it had selected a particular race or nationality for oppressive treatment. Sterilization of those who have thrice committed grand larceny with immunity for those who are embezzlers is a clear, pointed, unmistakable discrimination.... Embezzlers are forever free. Those who steal or take in other ways are not.[18]

All but Chief Justice Harlan Stone agreed on what the problem was not: that the state had "forever deprived" its citizens "of a basic liberty" against their will. Every other justice signed off on forced sterilization as a general matter. The only constitutional flaw, the majority held, was that Oklahoma had treated white-collar criminals differently than similarly situated blue-collar ones. So the sterilization mandate would have passed muster if only it had it applied the same to Capones as it did to Skinners. For the Supreme Court, the reproductive nature of the punishment exacted was almost beside the point.

Most states stopped sterilizing people after World War II. But a few kept right on operating, mostly fixing their aim on poor immigrants and women of color. In one state, the procedure was compelled so often through the 1960s that it was known as a "Mississippi appendectomy."[19] The following decade, medical staff at the Los Angeles County Medical Center were credibly accused of having misled hundreds of Spanish-speaking mothers into signing English-consent forms to sterilize them as they underwent caesarian sections.[20] And from 2006 to 2012, two California prisons paid doctors to tie the tubes of at least 144 black and brown inmates while sedated for post-partum surgery.[21] In total, there were at least 60,000 Carrie Bucks nationwide. North Carolina is the only state that's compensated even a fraction of its victims: In 2018, its lawmakers paid out the last of $45,000 in reparations to each of 220 survivors, among 7,380 others the state sterilized from 1929 to 1974.[22]

The American legal system doesn't recognize any general right to make decisions about having children, not aside from narrow limits against severe government restrictions on access to abortion and birth control. Family planning deserves greater protection. It goes to the heart of autonomy, well-being, and equality. These vital human goods give distinct reasons to care that individuals be able to choose whether, when, and how to reproduce. Let me explain each value in turn. Autonomy here refers to a person's reproductive freedom—not just to choose for or against conception, gestation, and childrearing in any perfunctory sense but also to undertake meaningful efforts to carry those choices out. This liberty interest gives a woman the satisfaction that her family life is of her own making and wasn't forced on her, not even in the name of her putatively "authentic" values or "higher-order" goals. Real reproductive autonomy is about clearing away barriers to choice, whether legal (e.g., state restrictions), economic (e.g., insurance coverage), or social (e.g., group pressure). These obstacles can often vary based on a person's sex, age, race, class, sexual orientation, and immigration or relationship status.[23]

Reproductive autonomy commands authority from its distinctive place in the U.S. constitutional doctrine of abortion and birth control. Though this line of cases tends to indulge a more formalistic sense of autonomy— one that bars government from blocking individual decisions as "private and sensitive"[24] as whether to initiate a pregnancy, and as "intimate and personal" as whether to keep it.[25] This conception of autonomy is a far cry from the functional version that would grant reproductive access to women of limited means.[26] The Supreme Court has rejected any suggestion that the abortion right entitles a poor woman to the resources she would need to actually "avail herself" of those ostensibly "protected choices."[27] The rhetoric of choice is also rife with undercurrents of consumerism and pleasure-seeking. Autonomy talk carries with it this partisan baggage that's come to define abortion politics. And its association with abortion jurisprudence elides important differences with the interests at stake in reproductive conflicts that don't involve unwanted pregnancy and parenthood.

At any rate, the greatest value of family planning has less to do with choices than consequences. More important than reproductive autonomy is how making these decisions helps a person live well. Procreation matters most for its practical impact on the person's health, education, employment, social standing, intimate relationships, and other critical features of well-being. The U.S. Centers for Disease Control and Prevention ranks family planning among the "ten great public health achievements" in the twentieth century.[28] For men too, whether a person has children or not lays critical identities, experiences, and opportunities on the line. Few other decisions or undertakings so shape who a man is, how he spends his days, and how he wants to be remembered. Contraception and genetic testing isn't just about a person's lifestyle—it's about his life. And that's not all.

Reproductive negligence implicates more than health and happiness. Social equality also looms large. Gendered expectations of pregnancy and parenthood trade on caretaker stereotypes of women as self-denying nurturers who should assume domestic roles as wives and mothers. Disproportionate demands on women's bodies, time, and resources curtail their opportunities for school, work, and "equal citizenship stature,"[29] as Justice Ruth Bader Ginsburg has argued since before she was a justice. These traditional reproductive visions entrench "the subordinate position of women in our society and the second-class status our institutions historically have imposed upon them."[30] A 1992 plurality of the Supreme Court in *Planned Parenthood v. Casey* affirmed that a woman's say over her pregnancy helps her "to participate equally in the economic and social life of the Nation."[31] Faulty birth control and fetal misdiagnoses can erode equality between the sexes as surely as limiting access to those services and procedures in the first place.

Meanwhile, higher-tech mishaps like lost embryos and switched donors fall hardest on those who need help to form families. Surrogacy and in vitro fertilization (IVF) promote new forms of equality for people who can't conceive or gestate due to age, health, sexual orientation, the trauma of past pregnancy, or the risk of transmitting disease. People who can't reproduce suffer similar "grief, humiliation, shame, loss, depression, social alienation, [and] loss of identity and damage to relationships," regardless the "cause of involuntary childlessness, whether biomedical or social factors."[32] In much of the United States, having children imparts "marital and sexual success, personal maturity, and normality."[33] These marks of "community stature" and "cultural recognition" aren't limited to straight couples.[34] They also matter to gay, lesbian, and other Americans "whose coming-outs provoked mourning for the descendants who would never be."[35]

B. Three Branches

Modern reproductive equality recalls its origins in *Skinner v. Oklahoma*. When the Supreme Court issued that decision back in 1942, there was just one way to make a baby—it wasn't possible to conceive a child apart from sexual intercourse, or to pick and choose certain aspects of offspring makeup before birth. Today, developments in medicine and technology separate sex from conception; biology from brute luck; and genetics from gestation or childrearing.[36] Birth control, surrogacy, sperm banking, egg freezing, and embryo selection don't just enhance control over whether, when, and how to reproduce. They reveal distinct interests in choosing *pregnancy* (gestating a fetus), *parenthood* (raising a child), and *particulars* (selecting offspring traits).[37]

These interests in pregnancy, parenthood, and particulars rise and fall together when different-sex couples conceive, screen, and carry offspring without incident. At least for the woman here, she has all three interests in choosing gestation, fetal testing, and childrearing. But reproductive negligence also cleaves those interests apart. A few examples: A fertility clinic deprives only pregnancy (and not parenthood) when it implants one patient's embryos into another. An OB/GYN imposes just parenthood (and not pregnancy) when he botches an abortion operation. A sperm bank confounds particulars alone when it uses samples from the wrong donor. And a medical center deprives parenthood, nothing more, when it misreports a paternity test in a way that keeps a man from raising the genetic child he wanted.[38]

Women gestate and give birth. Men don't. If they're not transgender, they can't. Men may be involved in their partner's experience. But pregnancy predominantly affects women—it does so profoundly, and for far longer than however many months they carry a fetus (or even nurse a baby). In the United States today, where the average couple wants two children, the typical woman spends five years either being or getting pregnant—and another thirty trying not to.[39] Decisions about pregnancy implicate a woman's values, goals, lifestyle, partner stability, support networks, and financial security. They also call forth her understandings about what it would be like to carry a child, and what's expected of her during pregnancy and after it ends—in abortion, miscarriage, stillbirth, adoption, or motherhood.[40]

The "litany of physical, emotional, economic, and social consequences" that one federal court noted pregnancy brings a may be cause for elation, apprehension, or ambivalence.[41] A woman might long to bond with her future child or be inducted into "the sisterhood of women who have experienced pregnancy."[42] "I crave that experience," is how one woman born without a uterus explained why she wanted a transplant instead of adopting or hiring a surrogate. "I want the morning sickness, the backaches, the feet swelling. I want to feel the baby move. That is something I've wanted for as long as I can remember."[43] Pregnancy's power to "reshape and redirect" life in "the minutest detail" goes beyond fetal bonding or physical burdens like trouble sleeping and regulating mood.[44] Growing a new person can shore up a woman's social, romantic, and professional life, or tear it down. A friend-of-the-court brief filed in Roe v. Wade observed that the demands of labor and delivery are "arduous, tiring, and obstructive of other work."[45] Unwanted pregnancy also keeps a woman from carrying a child at a time, or in a way, that she *does* want—whether after she graduates, or gets her doctor's go-ahead that it's safe, or when she finds herself in a stable relationship, or in one with a partner with whom she'd want to raise a child.

In a 1988 opinion decriminalizing abortion in Canada, Supreme Court Justice Bertha Wilson observed even subtler ways in which pregnancy makes "the woman think about herself" differently, and about "her relationship to others and to society at large."[46] Changes in self-identity reflect "the woman's knowledge that she is pregnant, even when the pregnancy has not produced any substantial . . . physical effects." Professor Khiara Bridges describes how disorienting it can be to appreciate one's transformation "from 'woman' to 'pregnant woman.'"[47] Suddenly, she has another human life growing inside of her—before, she didn't. Justice Wilson's second point concerns a pregnant woman's place in her community. Sooner or later, her pregnancy emerges into full view as a public status with profound meaning. American society sees pregnancy as "the apotheosis of womanhood," Bridges observes, even as it "disadvantages women by th[at] very" role.[48] Social reactions to a pregnant woman are a mixed bag. Some people she encounters may treat her with love and respect, as when a stranger gives up his seat on a crowded bus. Others may "abuse her as a burden, scorn her as unwed, or judge her as unfit for employment."[49] A 2015 U.S. Supreme Court judgment made it easier for pregnant women to sue for pregnancy discrimination, while letting employers deny them even modest accommodations, like a temporary transfer from heavy lifting on a doctor's orders—so long as nonpregnant workers are treated the same.[50]

The second reproductive interest isn't just for women—it extends to men too. This is the interest in choosing whether or not to have children. Social psychologists suggest that modern attitudes about offspring aren't so much an evolutionary byproduct of sex drives, biological urges, and nurturance instincts as much as adaptations to cultural context and changed circumstances.[51] When people make plans for family life, their reasons may range from the mundane to the existential. But they rarely reflect altruistic concern for the community, environment, or future offspring.[52] What usually steers people toward parenthood, or away from it, is whether they think it will make their own lives better. Self-interested considerations include personal fulfillment, a sense of purpose, or hoped-for support in old age. Joe Saul, the woefully childless protagonist of John Steinbeck's Burning Bright sensed a "trust imposed to hand my line over to another," a duty that meant he couldn't "scrap his bloodline" and "snip the thread of his immortality."[53] Some people are expected to provide grandchildren or siblings, or to free a partner from the responsibilities of childrearing. Others leave reproductive outcomes to divine intervention, resigned to the cosmic fate that "it was meant to be" or that "God had something else in mind."[54] Underprivileged people who don't seek refuge in their faith can also experience (in)fertility as just one more setback in a life full of limitations and disappointments.[55]

The work of raising a child isn't quite like any other activity or relationship. Being a mother or father differs meaningfully from other social commitments that people undertake. Parents aren't free to part ways with offspring like they are friends or companions. They can't abandon their baby, at least until she grows old enough to care for herself. Nurturing a child is also unlike looking after an elderly parent, a sick spouse, or a disabled sibling. None of these adults exude the spontaneous and unqualified affection that a child does for her parents. A dog or cat may love as easily, but only a child shares her deepest fears and joys—and without the restraint that her parents typically exercise in return, on touchy matters like financial anxiety or sex.[56]

Most people who decide to have children are hoping for intimate relationships that reward, challenge, and fulfill them.[57] They may long to love unconditionally, to share in a child's sense of wonder, and to play again for the sheer fun of it. Those who opt against parenthood may be thinking of the lost sleep, added stress, and potential opportunity costs. The United Kingdom's highest court observes that parents must "provide or make acceptable and safe arrangements for the child's care and supervision for 24 hours a day, 7 days a week, all year round."[58] A 2018 study of American parents shows that this work continues to fall more heavily on women than men.[59] It's not just these more practical measures of flourishing that hang in the balance when unwanted parenthood is imposed, or wanted parenthood deprived.

Being able to decide whether or not to have a child is also crucial to understanding and expressing oneself. The Iowa Supreme Court captured this idea in a case that involved exes fighting over whether to use or destroy the embryos they'd created and kept frozen.

> When chosen voluntarily, becoming a parent can be an important act of self-definition. Compelled parenthood, by contrast, imposes an unwanted identity on the individual, forcing her to redefine herself, her place in the world, and the legacy she will leave after she dies.[60]

This sentiment may also help explain why many Americans attach great meaning to genetic reproduction, even when it's separated from actually raising a child. More than a dozen U.S. courts have decided cases like the Iowa one, in which one former partner makes claims on another's sex cells or shared embryos after they separate. The other partner—almost always a man—wouldn't be required to support the child, yet that biological connection might still carry perceived meaning or obligations.[61] One man objected to his ex-wife implanting their IVF embryos on the ground that he'd feel duty-bound to care for any resulting offspring:

> [I]f my DNA does bring a child into this world, I would want to be a father in every sense of the word, as [in] financial, emotional, spiritual, soccer, little league, [and] every[thing] in between.[62]

Professor Niko Kolodny says a person has good "reason to feel certain things about [] genetic children" even if he's never met them, and to take on responsibilities short of childrearing, like "agreeing to meet . . . and answer potentially intimate and painful questions."[63] The man in a different one of these embryo disposition cases resisted the "psychological and emotional burden" of wondering about "his genetic offspring."[64] Another rued the possibility that a child he regards as his own "walks the earth without his love and guidance."[65] I don't mean to diminish the claims of women in these disputes who are seeking to have a biological child. My point is simply that the very ascription of parenthood can make claims beyond its formal requirements.

Some aspiring parents care about more than just whether they have *any* child—having one of a particular type also matters to them. Choosing among these genetic traits marks the least familiar of the three core reproductive interests. That's because parents used to have no say in offspring characteristics beyond their choice of mate. But parents no longer need leave a child's genetics exclusively to random recombination. Many couples undertake some kind of screening before they conceive, or fetal testing during pregnancy. People who employ IVF—nearly 2 percent of U.S. births today—can pay extra to biopsy their three-day-old embryo for certain medical conditions before deciding whether to implant this one, or another.[66] Oncologist Siddhartha Mukherjee explains how this works in *The Gene*:

> Astonishingly, if you remove a few cells from that embryo, the remaining cells divide and fill in the gap of missing cells, and the embryo

continues to grow normally as if nothing had happened. For a moment in our history, we are actually quite like salamanders, or, rather, like salamanders' tails—capable of complete regeneration even after being cut by a fourth.[67]

gross underestimate

This technique is called preimplantation genetic diagnosis, or PGD. Professor Hank Greely predicted in 2016 that within twenty to forty years, advances in genomic science and stem cell research will make safer, cheaper, and easier versions of PGD the most common way of making babies in developed countries like the United States. His book is called *The End of Sex*. But for now, just 5 percent of IVF embryos are screened using PGD.[68] Most PGD users are trying to screen out disease or disability. But a few choose embryos *in favor* of deafness, dwarfism, or Down syndrome—usually when it's shared by prospective parents or siblings.[69] Some fertility clinics also offer PGD for nonmedical traits like "whether a future baby's eyes are blue or brown."[70] Others even claim to provide "intelligence screening."[71]

Sex selection is relatively common. A recent survey found that 73 percent of U.S. IVF clinics let patients select embryos based on sex, and that almost all of those offer gender selection to couples without any fertility problems or special health risks associated with having a boy or girl.[72] Prospective parents can even *create* embryos to be male or female. A preconception process called Microsort uses a centrifuge to separate heavier XX sperm that would produce girls from lighter XY sperm that would produce boys.[73] Sperm banks and egg vendors in turn offer choices among a staggering array of advertised donor characteristics. These range from eye, hair, and skin color to height, facial features, and celebrity likeness. Would-be parents can also select a donor for race, ethnicity, and religion, and browse profiles for SAT scores, medical histories, and handwriting samples.[74] The United Kingdom's largest sperm bank developed "a Tinder-esque mobile app that lets women filter potential sperm donors based on traits like ethnicity, occupation, personality type, eye color, and more."[75] Donor selection reaches just half of a child's biology, but a popular New York facility promises to reveal much more information to parents before they make their decision. It combines DNA from potential donors and parents to simulate thousands of "virtual embryos" and screen them for the probability and presence of a great number of "genetic conditions in hypothetical offspring."[76] *gene peeks*

Most fertility patients are looking for the qualities they think would make raising a child more meaningful or gratifying. Professor John Robertson explains that they "seek or avoid reproduction" with an eye to "the types of experiences, situations, and responsibilities that [parenting] will entail, unknown and vague as they may be at the time of choice."[77] Prenatal testing for most traits is rife with uncertainty about genetic variants of unknown significance. Some traits are more heritable; others less so. Only a few—sex, eye color, and certain single-gene diseases—can be reliably predicted before birth. For these, prenatal selection makes it possible for parents to seek out desired qualities in a child, or avoid conditions that would require a level of care they feel unprepared to take on.[78] But many of the behaviors, personalities, and other traits that prospective parents care about are shrouded in too much mystery to infer from a fetus or embryo, let alone donor or gamete, whether or how those characteristics might show up in a child. The most famous nature-nurture inquiry compared hundreds of identical twins, some raised together, others apart. This Minnesota Twin Family Study found that biology has an ample impact on interests and attitudes. But "the genome exerts [this] influence" only in "indirect and modifiable ways" through a host of circumstances and experiences during childhood, and manifests most prominently only after children leave home.[79]

Beyond the scope and efficacy of choosing offspring particulars are questions about its purpose: Why do parents exercise this reproductive interest? Whose benefit is it *for*? Parents might think they're trying to pick out traits to help their child-to-be. Selecting for a donor or embryo to be, say, free of disease, doesn't really serve the resulting child, though, just as letting her be born sick isn't necessarily bad for her, at least not accordingly to the usual way that we think about benefits and harms as events that make a specific individual better or worse off. The best-interests argument works in switched-baby controversies in which hospitals confuse whose newborn is whose. Here, parents argue that their child is less secure or less well-adjusted than she would have been if the nursery had sent her home with the right family.[80] But reproductive negligence complicates this before-and-after comparison. Mixing up *this* donor or misdiagnosing *that* embryo brings one biologically distinct child into the world, as opposed to some other. The resulting child who inherits a disability couldn't herself have been born without the condition that she has, not while remaining the same individual she is. Any able-bodied child who might have existed in her place—having come from some other donor or embryo—would be a different person altogether. The only alternative for the disabled child was never to have been born at all. This is the "non-identity problem" first posed by philosopher Derek Parfit.[81]

Prenatal misconduct can be claimed to harm a resulting child only if it impairs the genetically individuated life he began as before birth. For example, some babies are born with brain damage after an obstetrician fails to respond to signs of fetal distress.[82] And with developments in genetic engineering, embryologists might edit out the wrong splices of DNA—in vitro scientists have already edited genes in human embryos, before they're used to initiate pregnancy, to fix a mutation that causes a heart condition that can lead to sudden death later in life.[83] When prenatal misconduct does harm to a developing fetus or embryo that gets implanted, there's an identifiable offspring who comes to be born. The only exception in these cases is where "those changes have such a profound effect on the character, values, priorities, and relationships of that future child that it becomes intelligible for us to think in terms of that embryo [or fetus] as having been replaced rather than repaired."[84] Setting aside these metaphysics of existence and identity, however, the main point is that parents have their own interests in choosing offspring particulars, independent of any interests their child has. Vindicating these parental interests may well provide children with more flourishing environments or experiences. But not necessarily.

A child's interests can't be reduced to those of his parents. Each has individual interests, and these can clash: What would be good for the parent might be bad for the child. Absent evidence of abuse or neglect, however, parents are presumed to know what's best for their child. Prenatal selection is different, in that it involves adults who aren't already parents—and children who don't yet exist. But a society like the United States prizes family pluralism and the cultivation of close, stable caregiver relationships from an early age. Interests in choosing offspring particulars are of a piece with the latitude that American constitutional and family law affords parents over "the care, custody, and control of their children."[85] Even if a future child's interests take priority over a would-be parent's ones, strong social interests can still supersede the child's. In the custody context, the U.S. Supreme Court has rejected the home placement that it thought better for a child's sake, so as not to buoy racial prejudice.[86] These themes about children's interests and public policy call for greater elaboration through the lens of thwarted offspring selection for sex, race, and disability. That comes in Chapter 10.

Before turning to existing legal protections against reproductive negligence, let me say a few words about why I have concentrated on interests in pregnancy, parenthood, and particulars, without mentioning labor and delivery. Bearing a child is an integral element of procreation. Professional misconduct has left some women to endure pain-relief injections without consent, and led others to have cesarean surgery against their will.[87] But these incidents involve a distinct kind of violation that's the focus of more than one book—with good reason.[88] Unauthorized C-sections and slipshod epidurals are unwelcome touchings. Besides whatever intangible interests they implicate, they also bring physical discomfort and painful complications like infection, blood loss, and clots.[89] These bodily injuries and side effects provide the legal hook that qualifies these medical errors for ordinary malpractice claims and associated damages for pain and suffering, including psychological ones incurred during the birthing process. Most courts let a woman sue for infliction of emotional distress if she was in the "zone of danger" surrounding the incident, or if she sustained an "independent injury."[90]

crazy!

Some courts have compensated for negligently caused miscarriage or stillbirth on the ground that mistreatment was "performed upon the body of an expectant mother."[91] Others see "an injury to the fetus . . . as supporting a direct parental claim for emotional distress" because "a mother and her fetus are so interconnected that they may be considered as one."[92] The California Court of Appeals made clear in a 1981 decision that a woman "forms a sufficiently close relationship with her fetus during pregnancy [] that its stillbirth will foreseeably cause her severe emotional distress." When misconduct rather than "natural and unavoidable causes" leads a child to be born dead, that loss "is compensable as part of the mother's cause of action for malpractice to herself."[93] It's not that birthing women have an easy time obtaining legal relief for unintentional mistreatment—especially if they leave the hospital with a baby in hand. Many jurors will look at the child, especially if healthy, and doubt that a mother has reason to complain. But childbearing losses find greater vindication in the law than injuries elsewhere in the reproductive process. Existing legal claims privilege the unconsented contact and physical harm that typifies negligence in labor and delivery. These more tangible kinds of harms are precisely what's missing when specialists frustrate interests in pregnancy, parenthood, and particulars.

2

Missing Protections

You might complain, but you would get nothing for your pains but a
ruined evening; while, as for going to law about it, you might as well
go to heaven at once.

—Upton Sinclair, *The Jungle* (1906)

Legislatures and agencies are best suited to protect reproductive interests.
Elected officials have greater democratic legitimacy than one-off juries. And
governing bodies can implement measures that discourage professionals
from depriving or imposing procreation in the first place. Statutes aren't
limited to any one case or controversy, or to events that have already
happened. They look ahead and balance the interests of all those potentially
affected by a growing social problem. These institutions can weigh in on
such conflicts with the benefit of investigations and hearings to find facts
about the relative merits of incremental precautions.[1] But the peculiarly
divided character of reproductive politics in the United States gives public
regulation an outside chance.

A. Don't States Regulate?

Calls to regulate assisted reproduction has come in fits and bursts, following
sensationalized firsts over the last forty years—from "test-tube" babies and
"baby-selling" to "three-parent" and "designer" babies. Each pejorative has
come with renewed appeals to ban the emerging technology or legal development that it caricatured: in vitro fertilization in 1978, commercial surrogacy disputes in 1987, mitochondrial replacement therapy in 2016—and,
most recently, germline editing in human embryos. A technique known as
CRISPR/Cas9 can now make changes to a person's DNA that get inherited
by his offspring and any future generations.[2] In November 2018, announce-
ment of the world's first gene-edited babies in China led its government to

Birth Rights and Wrongs. Dov Fox.
© Dov Fox 2019. Published 2019 by Oxford University Press.

declare a moratorium on the research as potentially dangerous human ex-perimentation.[3] No one knows what side effects this reproductive technique could have for resulting offspring and their descendants. An international summit of leading geneticists immediately condemned the breakthrough as "deeply disturbing."[4]

Similar clamor broke out in the United States a decade earlier, after reports that Nadya Suleman, a single mother of six, gave birth to eight at-risk children at once after her doctor implanted a dozen embryos to initiate a single pregnancy. "Octomom" sparked a national debate over IVF-fueled high-order births, while commentators decried the "Wild West of pro-creative possibilities."[5] That portrayal overstates the lax state of affairs. Professional barriers to entry make assisted reproduction less of a cowboy venture than a fragmented cartel of mostly mom-and-pop shops.[6] The re-productive endocrinologists who perform IVF have to complete a three-year specialized fellowship following a four-year OB/GYN residency and another four of medical school. And private organizations like the College of American Pathologists visit most fertility clinics every couple of years to checklist them for optional industry accreditation.

But no governmental agency or authority seriously polices reproduc-tive negligence in the United States. At the federal level, the only direc-tive that comes close is the Fertility Clinic Success Rate and Certification Act that Congress enacted in 1992.[7] That law arose from congres-sional hearings in the late 1980s to address the overblown success rates advertised by many IVF providers.[8] The Act does two things: First, it asks fertility clinics to inform the Centers for Disease Control (CDC) how often their patients get pregnant. But there's no carrot for disclosing these results, or any stick for refusing or lying. The 12 percent of all clinics that don't comply keep operating without penalty. Any market pressure to comply isn't enough to make them self-report. Of all pregnancies initiated at fertility clinics in the United States, an estimated 3.3–7.4 per-cent of outcomes were omitted from the data that the CDC collects.[9] Second, the Act directs the Food and Drug Administration (FDA)—the federal agency responsible for protecting and promoting public health—to screen human donors and tissues for infectious disease.[10] Sounds promising—but the fertility industry convinced Congress to add a carve-out forbidding the agency from "establish[ing] any standard, regulation, or requirement, which has the effect of exercising supervision or con-trol over the practice of medicine in assisted reproductive technology programs."[11] So the FDA has no say over which procreation procedures are used or how they're carried out.[12]

For example, the FDA declines to regulate the non-invasive blood-test screening for chromosomal abnormalities—available as early as seven to ten weeks in pregnancy. Analysis of fetal DNA in a pregnant woman's blood sample has become a routine part of prenatal care since tests burst onto the American market in 2011. Manufacturers competing for this $3.5 billion industry promise no more large needles, miscarriage risks, or waiting months to learn whether your fetus is healthy. The FDA failure to intervene overlooks misleading claims of "simple, clear results" that are "99% accurate" and "near-diagnostic."[13] These findings are probabilistic, nowhere near reliable enough to tell whether or not a fetus actually has a particular disorder. But aggressive promotion often buries that fact in the fine print. These screens detect greater or lesser needs for yes-no diagnosis via invasive means like amniocentesis. Unconfirmed mistakes have led many women to keep pregnancies they would have ended, and even more to end ones they would have kept.[14]

At the state level, laws are mostly limited to embryonic stem cell research, insurance coverage for infertility treatment, and surrogacy rules that govern gestational agreements and carrier compensation.[15] Just three states wade any further into assisted reproduction. In 2018, Arizona passed a law that says, when estranged couples disagree about what do with the frozen embryos they created, the partner who wants to use them to reproduce wins out, even if they'd previously agreed to have them destroyed.[16] A 2015 Utah law gives donor-conceived children who are eighteen and older access to the medical histories of their biological parents—even if those donors had only agreed to provide reproductive material under conditions of anonymity.[17] And Louisiana has since 1986 required fertility doctors to "possess specialized training and skill," without elaboration on what kind of knowledge or advances that entails.[18] That's it—no other state has adopted measures to keep an eye on reproductive facilities or hold them or the specialists they employ accountable.[19]

State medical boards don't even revoke the license of repeat offenders. Dr. Rifaat Salem is medical director of the Pacific Reproductive Center in Torrance, California. Dr. Salem has been sued for medical malpractice ten times, including three times in the last four years—claims against him include false promises, untrained staff, and botched IVF.[20] Most recently, he was accused of performing an abortion without a patient's consent, as a way to cover up his having accidentally implanted another couple's embryos inside of her.[21] Dr. Salem is among the 1 percent of U.S. doctors in any medical field across the country with four or more malpractice payouts since 1990. But he's settled out of court each time, keeping complaints under the radar of California's medical board. He continues to practice there in good standing.[22]

The buck stops nowhere. Only professional organizations like the American Society for Reproductive Medicine (ASRM) set forth any industry standards or best practices—and even then, just for the fertility clinics and sperm banks that opt into its Laboratory Accreditation Program.[23] These recommendations are completely voluntary and routinely ignored.[24] ASRM lacks the authority to sanction members that violate its guidelines, or auditing power required to detect such violations. This hands-off approach frees providers to innovate "new, experimental infertility options," but opens "a gaping hole for a booming, unregulated market fraught with fraud and abuse."[25]

Not only are rules lacking to prevent or mitigate reproductive negligence—there isn't even any reliable or comprehensive system to track it. A crowd-sourcing platform called FertilityIQ has begun to fill this reporting gap. A recent poll of its patient members found that nearly 30 percent experienced clerical or clinical errors from switched or contaminated samples to misdiagnosed or misinterpreted tests.[26] But patient surveys like this often struggle with unrepresentative samples and the risk of misleading evaluations. The stigmatized character of reproductive care leaves many reluctant to disclose their names, while anonymity exposes reviews to misuse or falsification.[27] Patients are left in the dark, to plan a family at their own risk, and steel themselves against the consequences of medicine and technology gone awry. The breakneck pace of these advances isn't the only reason that test tubes and tube ties have eluded meaningful oversight.

Four factors explain this regulatory vacuum. First is the libertarian outlook on reproductive life that's left many wary of ceding the state control on any matter involving procreation. Today, any American who can afford IVF, surrogacy, and sperm or egg donation is free to use it. Onerous rules would throw a monkey wrench into market competition, imperiling the lower costs and larger freedoms that this laissez-faire regime enables. Red tape wouldn't just raise prices on valuable services, making it harder for poor people to pay for them. It's most often young, immigrant, and other vulnerable women who "bear the brunt of regulation . . . in the battle over reproductive decision-making."[28] Negligence protections could open the door to restrictions on who gets to form families and how. Potential regulators might worry that even limited controls could lead the United States down a more repressive path like those adopted by France, parts of Australia, and other places that forbid gays and unmarried people from accessing the technologies required to beget offspring.[29] But fear of over-reach isn't the main reason that professional negligence goes unregulated.

A stronger explanation has to do with the political economy of repro-ductive technology in the United States. The free-market origins of infer-tility treatment insulate it from the surveillance that government usually conducts over doctors and scientists. Most medical fields are supported by tax dollars that come with public investments in quality control. The provision of federal money is what authorizes agencies like the National Institutes of Health and the U.S. Department of Health and Human Services to enforce clinical safety measures. But Congress has called off administra-tive watchdogs, citing anxiety about complicity in the destruction of human embryos. IVF typically involves making more embryos than get implanted all at once—creating these spares lets female patients undergo a second or third attempt at pregnancy without the painful injections and risky surgeries to stimulate and extract eggs each time. Embryos that end up un-used usually get discarded or dissected for scientific research, an outcome that deeply troubles Americans who believe that life begins at conception. In 1995, Republican Representatives Jay Woodson Dickey, Jr. of Arkansas and Roger Wicker of Mississippi attached a rider to a spending bill that bars federal funding of any activity that destroy embryos.[30] The Dickey-Wicker Amendment has been renewed every year since, paving the way for repro-ductive technologies to develop unimpeded by government oversight, in the private sphere of for-profit clinics that function less as medical practices than trade businesses.[31] This multibillion-dollar industry sustains powerful lobbying forces that block efforts to rein in its operations.[32]

A third factor that cuts against regulation is its murky electoral implications. Conservatives legislate abortion and contraception all the time in the name of family values and unborn life.[33] But reproductive neg-ligence raises hard new questions that go beyond traditional family values and the sanctity of unborn life: What kinds of influence can prospective parents reasonably expect over the characteristics their child is born with?[34] Does reproductive privacy lose its purchase when parents enlist donors or surrogates?[35] How much worse is losing a three-month-old fetus than losing a three-day-old embryo?[36] The answers provoke turmoil even in reliably red or blue districts, because they can drive a wedge within core voting blocks that usually see eye to eye. Fear of fracturing their political bases leads prudent officials to avoid wading into the morass.[37] On the left, for example, fetal misdiagnosis divides feminists and disability-rights advocates. Their shared promotion of equality for the disadvantaged splinters off in different directions when it comes to special safeguards for prenatal testing. Shoring up women's informed reproductive choices risks reinforcing stereotypes about people with genetic impairments. Any position a progressive lawmaker might take is likely to alienate one constituency or the other.[38] From the right, botched IVF fragments religious coalitions over whether to sanction error-prone clinics. Evangelicals won't see a problem: They celebrate the blessings of biological parenthood—"especially [for] married, heterosexual, middle class people who desperately want a child."[39] But the Catholic Church frowns on interference with "natural" reproduction, from birth control pills to the "turkey baster" insemination. Laws protecting against fertility neglence would require recognizing as legitimate the very practices that the Church condemns. Safer not to intervene.

Fourth is the limited public outcry about reproductive negligence. Civil justice transformations of America's past have required a political climate ripe for reform. The paradigm is workers' compensation, an insurance program that enables people who get hurt on the job to recoup for medical expenses and lost wages without having to prove misconduct was to blame. Employee benefits that are now standard in every state didn't even exist until the twentieth century. Before that, there was only accident litigation, whose steep cost and deep uncertainty left most injured workers unable to secure damage awards against dangerous factory conditions and rampant child labor. Workers comp came to replace these deficient protections only because labor groups and other Progressive Era crusaders across the country demanded safer and healthier workplaces.[40] The next tort overhaul—this one, partial—came in the late 1960s, when half of states enacted a no-fault system of recovery for harms arising from motor-vehicle accidents. These auto reforms were again embedded within larger movements, this time for car safety spearheaded by Ralph Nader's muckraking bestseller, *Unsafe at Any Speed*.[41] But there's no groundswell of civic agitation to replace even medical malpractice with a no-fault system like the one New Zealand and the Nordic countries administer for personal injuries by doctors and hospitals, drugs and devices.[42]

There is one exception. Two states have experimented with no-fault compensation for birthing-related harms since the late 1980s. Liability insurance premiums had skyrocketed for obstetrician-gynecologists after a wave of high-cost litigation involving newborn neurological injuries. Virginia and Florida transferred claims from civil courts to administrative schemes financed through assessments on mostly participating physicians and hospitals. These schemes replace hard-to-prove negligence claims with guaranteed reimbursement for health care and lost earnings any time a child is born with serious spinal cord or brain injuries from being deprived of oxygen during labor or delivery.[43] Insufficient funding and dwindling subsidies have jeopardized the Virginia and Florida regimes since their inception, however. The hundreds of millions of dollars they've paid out are meager relative to those available through conventional litigation.[44] And injured parties have further destabilized these insurance alternatives by sidestepping them to pursue fault-based actions with the promise of larger awards.[45] No other state has followed Virginia and Florida's lead to resolve either birth-related claims or any other medical injuries in agency offices instead of trial courts.

B. Don't Americans Sue?

One reason is that Americans are loath to surrender access to the jury's distinctive capacity to remedy grievances and deliver justice. Courtroom battles confer legal power on victims who obtain judicial redress from those who wrong them. Litigation affords injured parties (and accused injurers) the chance to tell their stories and plead their case—in public, on the record, before a jury of peers. Aggregate settlements offer a variation on personal injury claims by letting multiple injured parties bring their similar claims all together against one or few injurers. Agreed-to awards are averaged out among plaintiffs—so victims who suffered more might get too little, while those who suffered less might get too much. But anyone unable to hire his own lawyer receives at least some compensation.[46] This mass-tort approach resolves claims that hurt lots of people in similar ways, like asbestos exposure or silicone breast implants. Cancer-causing insulation and defective gel inserts cause injuries of comparable type and severity. Harms that are traceable to a particular landlord or manufacturer can be merged into a single lawsuit without too many individual plaintiffs getting far less or far more than they might have if they had sued on their own.[47]

But reproductive errors are different. These harms vary dramatically: Some victims never get the child they hoped for; others end up with one they hadn't intended; others still get a baby whose health or heredity isn't what they had good reason to expect. These injuries are too heterogeneous to lump under any one claim. Consolidation isn't clear-cut even in single-incident cases like the freezer failures that destroyed embryos preserved by scores of fertility patients. The diversity of harms for lost materials has already served as a basis to deny negligence plaintiffs access to the courts. A 2009 medical audit revealed that labeling errors at the Ochsner Fertility Clinic in Louisiana had destroyed hundreds of embryos. Two hundred forty affected patients jointly brought suit. But the court refused to certify their legal action as a class, holding that the harms they'd sustained weren't sufficiently similar.[48] These families all lost reproductive materials. Some had a few embryos left, others none. Some had used their own sperm and eggs, others needed one donor or even two. Some already had biologically related children, others didn't. Some still planned to have children—others had grown too old to do so, or they'd gotten divorced, or adopted instead. Their variable intentions and circumstances made the reproductive losses too diverse, in the court's view—victims lacked the sufficiently common injury that civil procedures require for them to sue as a class.[49]

Most complaints, whether consolidated or on their own, never make it to court. Professor David Engel observes that "more than nine out of ten injury victims" in the United States "assert no claim at all against their injurer, even in cases where it is likely that a legal duty was breached and a claim would succeed."[50] A constellation of financial, social, and legal hindrances explains why so few bring civil lawsuits. For one, litigation is expensive and slow; many plaintiff lack support to cope with their injuries while claims are pending. There's also our pull-yourself-up-by-your-bootstraps legal culture. Americans are typecast as litigation-happy scammers who sue over hot coffee.[51] And U.S. culture demonizes injured plaintiffs as unscrupulous opportunists out for an easy buck. The Hollywood embodiment of personal injury law isn't Erin Brockovich and her underdog battle against the giant corporation that was contaminating a small town's drinking water. It's Saul Goodman, who keeps a box of neck braces under his desk for his clients to embellish or fake their injuries in court.[52] But injured Americans on the whole are in fact loath to sue.

Studies of tens of thousands of patients from New York and California to Utah and Colorado have found that a small fraction—between 1.2 percent

[margin handwritten note: Not Allowed to sue as a class action suit.]

and 2.8 percent—pursue legal action when a doctor's misconduct causes them serious injury.[53] Most malpractice victims take no action at all against offending practitioners or hospitals. A few register complaints, change healthcare providers, or contact a lawyer—but never sue. State legislatures place hedges in the path of medical malpractice actions. Some restrict plaintiffs' access to court by mandating screening panels or narrowing the window of time during which they can file legal claims. Others limit liability by making it harder to prove causation or breach of informed consent. Others still curb damages by capping overall awards and denying compensation for attorney's fees.[54]

Besides, trials can be a spectacle. They force plaintiffs to declare personal matters in the public glare of open court for the uncertain chance of unspecified compensation. It's not hard to see why negligence victims might keep their reproductive injuries to themselves, against the cultural background of gendered scripts about virile men and fertile women. Patients may fear challenges to their masculinity or maternal instinct if exposed for having undergone a vasectomy or tubal ligation.[55] Based on interviews with three hundred infertile Americans, anthropologist Gay Becker found that cultural emphasis on passing down a male's genetic line makes it "easier for women to normalize the use of a donated egg than it is for men to normalize the use of donor sperm."[56] Resort to a sperm donor can discredit a husband's fatherhood, even when an egg donor wouldn't call a woman's parental status into doubt.[57] Meanwhile, a woman's decision to pursue surrogacy or abortion "disrupt[s] traditional expectations" about pregnancy in ways that risk casting her as "the archetype of the bad mother."[58] Even those who came of age during the women's liberation movement were often raised, like author Sigrid Nunez, "to believe they would not be complete and could not be thought to have succeeded in life without the experience of motherhood."[59] One unnamed American woman divulged that "finding out about my infertility problems" made her feel "completely useless. I felt like, basically, a piece of garbage."[60] Another "began to feel defective, ashamed, inadequate. I had to re-evaluate my life, my hopes, and my identity as a woman."[61]

Historian Elaine Tyler May has traced the modern "American obsession with reproduction" back to the 1950s era of postwar prosperity and social conservativism. That's when the nuclear family gained recognition as a mark of civic obligation, social respectability, and individual happiness.[62] With few medical workarounds to treat infertility, adoption agencies sought to construct "the appearance of 'normative' marital procreation" that was "not an overtly adoptive family, but a fictive genetic family in which eve-ryone 'matched' as closely as possible."[63] Having children "came to embody the hope for the future of the nation and . . . personal satisfaction for its citizens."[64] The *Leave It to Beaver* ideal of the breadwinner father, home-maker mother, and biological offspring marginalized childless Americans "as immature at best and subversive at worst."[65] As the 1950s came to a close, advances in medicine, law, and culture transferred the reins of repro-duction from chance to choice. The FDA's approval of the Pill in 1960 made it the most popular form of birth control by 1965, when the Supreme Court struck down Connecticut's conception ban; the rise of commercial sperm banking in 1972 arrived alongside the constitutionalization of abortion in 1973; and scientific development of in vitro fertilization in 1969 prefigured the first IVF baby in 1978. This procreative revolution made it acceptable for individuals to fashion their lives to include offspring or to exclude them.[66]

But any broad resignation to reproductive self-determination was short-lived, giving way to the family-values-movement of the 1980s, with its se-lective pronatalism for white, married, and middle-class parents.[67] Fear of censure and harassment forced legal abortion into the closet, while a "cult of parenthood among baby boomers" heaped scorn on the childfree, who were "treated like traitors to the American way."[68] By 1990, state law for-mally recognized the renewed stigma surrounding infertility and its treat-ment. A St. Louis husband and wife, identified as Y.G. and L.G., had told only her mom that they'd used IVF to conceive their triplets. The Gs argued that the clinic had violated their privacy by authorizing a TV station to show their unblurred faces in a story about the "medical miracle" of assisted reproduction. The revelation shattered their expressed desire—having twice declined interviews and refused to be filmed—to shield their "procreative secrets" from public view.[69] American courts had long grappled with the privacy implications of "abortion outing."[70] The Missouri case was the first dispute over disclosing a family's pursuit of treatment for infertility. The state appeals court allowed the couple's suit to proceed, explaining that the "physical problems which exist with the couple's reproductive systems" and "their ability to "perform[] sexually are matters that could embarrass a reasonable person."[71] The decades since have seen an explosion of social media and electronic court filings. Deserving victims may fear their pre-dictable public shaming would outweigh the uncertain benefits of litigating sensitive matters.[72] Online trolls don't hesitate to brand complainants with a digital scarlet letter. And courts usually deny requests to use initials or pseudonyms out of concern for keeping judicial proceedings open.[73] Most states narrowly limit party anonymity to cases involving minors or abuse, unless litigants can prove their exceptional need to go unidentified.[74] So suing for reproductive negligence generally requires victims to use their real name on the record for all to see they have fertility problems or got sterilized.

Cultural attitudes about infertility, prenatal testing, and abortion will continue to evolve with shifting constructions of family, parenthood, and citizenship. But newfound powers to mediate the processes of procreation has made unexpected outcomes only less tolerable. "The more options that appear possible and legitimate," the historian May observes, "the less willing [Americans] are to accept a reality that differs from their desires."[75] Negligence victims who want to keep their sex lives and family plans private may suffer in silence rather than file a public lawsuit. In few other areas of medical practice do patients hesitate to report even egregious errors for fear of divulging that they needed such treatment in the first place. Reproductive medicine throws up its own barriers.[76] Steep costs and selective treatment coverage leaves many patients unable to fund a legal challenge if things go wrong. Fifty-three percent of abortion patients pay $500 to $2,000 out of pocket, atop travel and lodging for the millions of women who live far from the closest provider.[77] And a single round of IVF costs 57 percent of the average American's annual income in 2018—the multiple cycles that it usually takes to get a baby costs upward of $100,000.[78] Patients who rack up debt or borrow against retirement savings to procure these procedures don't have enough left over for lawyers' fees if negligence thwarts their efforts.[79]

These financial strains wouldn't be as great if more than just fifteen states made insurers cover fertility services.[80] And even these often limit coverage mandates to married couples unable to conceive, thereby denying equal benefits to nontraditional families.[81] Insurance access is spotty for abortion, prenatal screening, and long-term contraception too. The content of coverage is a battleground for conflict over which health-related costs should be collectively funded, and which "individuals must shoulder the burden of financing" or else go without "if they cannot afford it on their own."[82] Fertility treatment remains sufficiently controversial in the United States that it's hard to imagine lawmakers enacting a policy that remotely resembles Israel's guarantee of state-subsidized IVF for women up to age forty-five.[83] The only American court that's referred to assisted procreation as "essential" or "necessary" was summarily vacated and reversed.[84] By contrast, Australia's High Court's 2010 portrayed reproductive technology as "a legitimate medical treatment for a legitimate medical condition," one that's "necessary to enable people to live dignified and productive lives, unencumbered by the effects of disease or impairment."[85]

3

Litigation's Limits

The fairy land buys not the child of me.
—William Shakespeare, *A Midsummer Night's Dream* act 2, sc. 1

Even negligence victims who can afford the legal fees often don't think that suing is worth the risk, given what any good lawyer will tell them is a slim chance of recovery. Reproductive plaintiffs have had little success trying to shoehorn their complaints into a grab bag of ill-suited actions under available theories of civil liability. Some of these are cramped, like deeming lost embryos "property" or "persons." Others are jarring, as when they call a child's birth or life "wrongful." Courthouse claims for medical malpractice and emotional distress require showing some physical or economic harm that procreation plaintiffs can't point to when their test results get switched or sperm samples go missing. These misadventures fall through the cracks of a legal regime that's reluctant to recognize reproductive losses as real or serious. This chapter explains.

A. Contract Breach

Reproductive patients and providers always reach some sort of agreement about the performance of medical services. It's tempting to think courts could resolve disputes between them as a matter of broken promises.[1] But a legal action for breach of contract requires the formal assurance "to effect a specific result or cure."[2] Doctors must have expressly certified the outcome their care falls short of—like in the "Hairy Hand" case of *Paper Chase* lore. A surgeon gave his word that tissue replacement would give a boy whose palm had been scarred a "hundred per cent good hand." But when the surgeon grafted tissue from the boy's chest to his hand, the procedure left that palm only less functional than before—and now it had hair on it. The boy sued and won: The surgeon breached the contract that his guarantee was held to constitute. The court awarded damages for the boy's defeated expectations of how much better off he would have been with the perfect hand that "the defendant promised him."[3]

But doctors rarely make explicit promises like this. Reproductive specialists are savvy enough not to assure their patients they'll get pregnant or avoid parenthood. Professionals are careful to decline promising any result beyond the safety of patients directly under their care. So there's seldom any agreed-upon clause for courts to enforce against badly behaving defendants. It might not matter, even if there was. Courts typically excuse a breaching party if that failure to perform caused little material harm. The classic case is *Jacob & Youngs v. Kent*. A property holder refused to pay the builders he contracted with to build an upscale house because they'd accidentally used a different brand of pipes (Reading) than the one specified in their agreement (Cohoes). The builders sued to get paid for their work and won. The court reasoned that the substituted Cohoes were the same wrought-iron quality as Reading anyway, concluding that contract law didn't protect against the "transgressor whose default is unintentional and trivial."[4]

Compare this case with those in which healthcare professionals fertilize or implant the wrong reproductive materials. Of course children aren't pipes. But courts might nonetheless borrow the logic of *Jacob & Youngs* to limit recovery for using a stranger's specimens instead of a spouse's, or an embryo with some genetic anomaly instead of an unaffected one. Parents would have to prove that a baby differed in ways that weren't just incidental to the agreement, like the generic brand of pipes. They would have to show that the mix-up materially breaches the contract they signed with their fertility clinic or sperm bank. But these facilities don't assure anything more than efforts to give would-be parents a baby, *any* baby call their own—which they still got. Courts might accordingly wave away even significant departures from parents' clearly expressed expectations about the health or heredity of their offspring.

Most reproductive professionals also insist that those who enlist their services agree to shield them from liability, whether express or implied. This standard practice dates back at least as far as 1995, when a *New York Times* editorial about the first IVF lawsuit noted that fertility patients "are required to sign waivers acknowledging that embryos often do not survive, generally because they get stuck in a petri dish, dry up, degenerate or are destroyed in lab accidents."[5] The standard contract that's used by the country's leading sperm bank illustrates the typical indemnification clause.[6] California Cryobank requires anyone who wants to use one of its donors to start a family to "indemnify, defend and hold harmless Cryobank . . . against any claims, losses, damages, liabilities, demands, offsets, causes of action and expenses" resulting from "any possible loss, degradation, spoilage, contamination or the like of any portion or all of the semen for any reason, including but without limitation, as a result of Cryobank's negligence."[7] Nor do egg vendors, embryologists, obstetricians, pharmacists, fertility clinics, or surrogacy agents guarantee the viability of specimens they store, or the success of any services they provide or procedures they perform.

Reproductive specialists practice in a bustling U.S. market of roughly 100 sperm banks, about 470 fertility centers, and over 1,700 reproductive endocrinologists. These facilities vie in part to lower costs that might well rise if substantial damages were allowed. But this is also fragmented industry of mostly regional competition, which enables clinics and physicians to resist pressure to offer patients greater security or more favorable terms. The harder question is why courts are willing to enforce liability waivers for reproductive injuries when they reject negligence disclaimers in other areas of medicine. The California Supreme Court made clear in 1963 that a patient "does not really acquiesce voluntarily in the contractual shifting of the risk" because medical services are a "crucial necessity" that the patient "is in no [real] position to reject" or negotiate.[8] Any deal she strikes doesn't carry the voluntary force that contract law ordinarily requires to justify enforcement.[9] Yet courts routinely dismiss negligence claims for prenatal misdiagnosis, for example, if patients signed a clause that says providers "do not assume responsibility for the physical and mental characteristics of hereditary tendencies of any child born as a result of these procedures."[10]

One reason that courts enforce these liability waivers might be that they ascribe greater levels of wealth and education to plaintiffs who pursued assisted procreation. Maybe judges assume that fertility patients have resources sufficient to reduce the usual informational and power disparities, thereby making any agreement they reach with doctors less one-sided. But the appearance of "sophisticated consumers" belies their inexpertise and vulnerabilities.[11] Professor Jody Madeira's study of reproductive patients reveal how "women in particular may face loneliness and stigma in the shadows of disempowering popular stereotypes of the 'desperate' or 'demanding' woman battling infertility," while those who "turn to fertility professionals for emotional support as well as medical care" often appear much more knowledgeable and "in control" than they really are, and certainly far less so than the specialists they enlist to help them.[12] Liability waivers may indeed lower the prices providers set with the knowledge that revenues won't have to offset the costs of lawsuit payouts. These clauses may also encourage reproductive patients to acquire valuable information to bargain for lower-cost services. But that data's either absent or closely guarded, leaving reproductive patients ill-informed about the risks of negligent misconduct. And too many are likely to give up their right to sue anyway, based on dubious hopes of freeriding on the deterrence they assume they'd enjoy if enough others who buy into the same standardized care don't opt out.[13]

Liability waivers shouldn't be enforced. These disclaimers make it too easy for sperm banks, fertility clinics, embryologists, or obstetricians to contract around basic duties of reproductive care. Reproductive professionals should be expected to provide competent procedures and services, whether or not they manage to convince patients to sign away their right to sue. When qualified specialists agree to help someone have a baby or avoid one, they assume practice-specific duties to treat patients in ways that aren't negligent. Yet courts authorize them to negotiate around or abandon these commitments, as if they do no more than fill in contractual gaps or modify ambiguous terms in the name of good faith or fair dealing.[14] But standards of care obligate those who hold themselves out as reproductive professionals in ways they can't undo simply by having patients sign off on terms that would allow them to.

B. Wrongful Birth

At first blush, it looks like run-of-the-mill malpractice when fertility doctors, lab technicians, and pharmacists upend the lives of their patients. Malpractice law holds lawyers, brokers, accountants, engineers, and other professionals liable for not adhering to the relevant standard of care. This standard imposes a legal duty on any member of the profession to acquire knowledge and apply skills that comprise competent conduct. When deviations result in injury, that's malpractice.[15] For medical malpractice, the standard of care has long been tied to physician customs under similar circumstances. Under this framework, healthcare providers aren't liable for errors, however risky or unjustified, so long as they acted within their discipline's standard operating procedures. Some states let doctors and nurses off the hook even if a "respectable minority" has adopted similar practices. One physician who botched a vasectomy escaped liability for declining to run any postoperative tests. He convinced the court that among OB/GYNs in his locality, "some doctors do and some don't."[16] Another example: Most obstetricians recommend cesarean surgery for difficult vaginal deliveries—but enough still use forceps or vacuum extraction that any injuries to mothers and children escape charges of malpractice on the basis of "custom."[17]

The modern American trend rejects this approach. An increasing number of state courts hold that adherence to inadequate or substandard care is unreasonable when "customary medical practice fail[s] to keep pace with developments and advances in medical science." The alternative that's gaining favor today looks to the healthcare advances that patients have good reason to count on. This standard requires that practitioners conform their conduct to what's "reasonable to expect of a professional given the state of medical knowledge at the time of the treatment in issue."[18] Take genetic testing of IVF embryos. Custom long recommended discarding embryos that contained abnormal cells—it was assumed that pregnancies wouldn't keep, or that surviving offspring would have serious abnormalities. In 2015, high-resolution sequencing revealed that about one in five contain normal cells too, and that at least some of these "mosaic" embryos would actually develop normally.[19] Embryologists point out that "misdiagnosis does not necessarily equate to negligence."[20] Well sure. But all kinds of easily preventable mistakes can, from obsolete training to unsterilized labs: Probes and pipettes that aren't cleaned properly between uses can cross-contaminate genetic material.[21] Pen-and-paper labeling of samples remains common among sperm banks and egg vendors, even though identification procedures like bar-coding or number-tagging are much sounder.[22] And many fertility clinics screen embryos using techniques that look at just a handful of chromosomes, despite the fact that comprehensive testing for abnormalities on all forty-six is far less susceptible to false negatives.[23]

What's reasonable to expect can also depend on the patient-specific facts and circumstances that a physician is aware of, or should be. It can also matter what type and "amount of knowledge" a patient "needs in order to make an informed choice," as a Pennsylvania appeals court explained. But these finer points shouldn't diminish the main one: Any specialist "operating for the sole purpose of . . . creating a child" or preventing one's existence, and who "reaps handsome profits from that endeavor, must be held accountable for the foreseeable risks" of reproductive injury that his misconduct incurs to the patients whose interests it's his professional duty to serve.[24]

It's not as if reproductive professionals are forced to treat people they don't want to. A 2019 survey found that one in four U.S. obstetricians and gynecologists refused to perform abortions, a third of them citing "personal, religious or moral reasons."[25] State and federal laws protect practitioners from being sued, fired, or disbarred for saying no to any treatment it would defy their conscience to provide. The only exception is that they can't turn away a patient on racial or other grounds that antidiscrimination law singles out. California is one of the few states that forbids physicians from declining to provide medical treatment based on sexual orientation.[26] In other states, doctors are free to reject most any patient because of who she is, how she lives, or what she looks like. They face no sanctions for denying in vitro fertilization treatment to single people or unmarried couples, for example, or for declining to sterilize younger women without children.[27] Medical professionals may not have to provide any service, or perform any procedure, if they don't want to. But they have to care for the reproductive interests of whichever patients they do treat.[28]

Even so, malpractice law doesn't impose even this voluntarily assumed duty on every procreation specialist. One Florida couple was barred from bringing a malpractice action against the ultrasound technician who negligently misadvised them during pregnancy. After agreeing to review the woman's sonogram, he assured her and her husband that "their fetus had ten fingers and ten toes." Their daughter was born a few months later missing an arm, which a trained eye should have seen clearly in utero. Yet the 2009 court dismissed the couple's malpractice claim, holding that a medical sonographer doesn't qualify as the kind of "healthcare provider" who can be sued for malpractice in the state of Florida.[29] That unsatisfying conclusion brings to mind a Rhode Island court's plea a decade earlier: "If there are no legal consequences for slipshod, even misleading, genetic counseling, what legal duty is there for counselors to meet any standard of professional care?"[30] These exasperating gaps in available recourse apply only when the reproductive injuries are intangible.

Medical malpractice still provides a ready claim for the fertility patient who acquires hepatitis C after her doctor failed to screen her sperm donor for the liver-damaging virus. The malpractice tort affords recovery when deficient care leads a patient to suffer "physical injury, illness, disease, [or] impairment of bodily functions."[31] The patient could sue for malpractice in this case because the negligently caused infection leads to symptoms like jaundice, nausea, fever, fatigue, and muscle aches.[32] These bodily harms can also generate economic setbacks like medical costs and lost wages. This more tangible kind of injury is precisely what's missing when negligence defeats people's reproductive plans. The closest things to procreation malpractice are the embattled claims for "wrongful birth" and "wrongful life." They enable injured parties to bring suit against medical specialists who fail to offer carrier screenings or prenatal diagnoses in the face of increased risks like advanced maternal age (for Down syndrome) or Eastern European Jewish descent (for Tay-Sachs disease). Other wrongful birth cases involve mistakes interpreting or communicating the results of those tests. The difference between these two actions has to do with who claims the injury. For "wrongful birth," it's parents, whereas the child himself argues he's been harmed by his own "wrongful life."[33]

"Wrongful birth" and "wrongful life" gained traction after the U.S. Supreme Court legalized abortion in 1973.[34] These actions tie harm to the lost chance to abort, or be aborted, so they require proof that a woman would or should have prevented or ended her pregnancy had she not been misinformed about it. Both peg damages to the costs of raising offspring or being alive—that invites the "unseemly spectacle of parents disparaging the 'value' of their children or the degree of their affection for them in open court."[35] Statutes bar wrongful birth suits in a dozen states, while courts in another dozen reject them by common law—all of these prohibitions have survived constitutional challenge.[36] "Wrongful life" actions, meanwhile, are forbidden in every state except California, Maine, New Jersey, and Washington. Even in these four, damage awards are limited to medical expenses to treat congenital impairment.[37] In the other forty-six, legislatures or courts prohibit children from suing for wrongful life on the ground that nobody's existence can be an injury to himself.[38] But that's not really what these plaintiffs are trying to say. They're looking for recognition of real suffering they face in connection with professional wrongdoing. Still, this non-identity problem, introduced in Chapter 1, raises a vexing challenge for the wrongful life cause of action.[39] Wrongful birth claims face no such difficulty, though. So why do half of all states immunize medical professionals who fail to inform pregnant women, or give them bad advice about fetal development and prognosis?

There's a straightforward reason that even wrongful birth actions attract such fierce opposition in the United States, making them far rarer there than in most other developed countries like Canada, Australia, the Netherlands, and the United Kingdom.[40] The reason may seem too obvious to need explaining. But only one U.S. court has ever said it out loud, in an unpublished 1999 decision that can't even be cited as precedent. That Rhode Island case involved a negligent doctor's carrier screening error that led a couple to have a child with Tay-Sachs disease. The physician and hospital he worked at moved to dismiss the parents' wrongful birth complaint for "lack of injury to a foreseeable plaintiff, or lack of proximate cause, or the novelty of the claim." Judge Richard Israel denied the motion, explaining: "These cases are not about birth, or wrongfulness, or negligence, or common law. They are about abortion. . . . For those who cannot accept [that abortion is legal], no one should ever be compensated . . . just because th[at] choice [] has been thwarted."[41] Antiabortion arguments rose to prominence on the 1980 Republican Party platform as a call to preserve traditional family values and the gender roles that sustain them, albeit couched in terms of protecting fetuses or women.[42] And many conservatives are still loath to "reward[] the loss of control over disrupted [reproductive] plans when the plan was to terminate a pregnancy."[43]

The Court has sanctioned multiple interests that a state may legitimately serve in limiting women's access to abortion consistent with the constitutional right to privacy. These interests range from saving fetuses to expressing respect for the unborn; from maintaining medical standards to protecting women's own health, safety, and even their risk of coming to regret ending "the infant life they once created and sustained," as the Court insisted in its 2007 decision in *Gonzales v. Carhart*.[44] Many of these interests raise empirical questions that rely on science as much as morality or politics. Some of these scientific appeals ring truer than others, like unsubstantiated claims about fetal pain and cancer risks.[45] In *Roe v. Wade*, the Court parsed maternal mortality data to conclude that first-trimester abortions pose no greater risk of death than childbirth.[46] In *Carhart*, by contrast, the majority relied on specious findings that abortion increases the incidence of suicide, and that so-called "partial birth abortion" isn't medically necessary for women whose doctors designate it as the safest option.[47] Pseudoscientific justifications risk papering over constitutionally illicit purposes like "placing a substantial obstacle in the path of a woman seeking an abortion."[48]

A more recent example of pretextual regulation comes from the handful of states that make it a crime for doctors to terminate a pregnancy for certain specific reasons. Eight states prohibit abortion that targets fetal sex; Arizona bans it on racial grounds; North Dakota does so in cases of genetic anomaly.[49] None of these states limit parents' ability to select for those very same traits in any other way, like screening embryos or donors on any basis at all. It's just fetuses those states are concerned with, even though there's no good evidence to suggest that American women are terminating pregnancies to choose offspring for sex or race. Selective abortion bans are more plausibly designed to impede abortion access generally, or to restrict the reproductive lives of citizens the state regards as less desirable parents.[50] Lawmakers also fail to see that prenatal testing isn't always about abortion.

Most prospective parents who screen their fetus are indeed looking to reserve the option of terminating a pregnancy for a child they think they wouldn't be in a position to raise. But some instead want the chance to prepare their home or heart for a baby affected by genetic disabilities, or for the likelihood of fetal or neonatal demise. And others hope to enable timely medical or surgical treatment of a condition immediately after birth, or even before it. Surgeons have already operated in utero on dozens of fetuses to repair spinal columns that don't close right in the 1,500 to 2,000 children born with spina bifida each year in the United States.[51] In the typical procedure, surgeons have opened a pregnant woman's lower abdomen,

> eased the uterus out of her body and inserted the fetoscope, and then, through another slit, surgical tools. The doctors drained out the amniotic fluid and pumped in carbon dioxide to keep the uterus expanded, giving them room to work and allowing them to see better and cauterize when needed. They gave the fetus an anesthetic injection and then, guided by images on the video screens, began to operate on him, tugging skin and membranes over the naked spinal cord and sewing them tightly shut with five stitches.[52]

So prenatal testing isn't always or only about deciding whether to bring a pregnancy to term or end it. But abortion, and moral opposition to it, is what explains why so few wrongful birth claims make it to trial—and why the rare plaintiffs who sue and win still face crushing social condemnation in the court of public opinion.

In 2012, a Portland jury awarded nearly $3 million to a couple whose daughter was born with Down syndrome after a botched fetal test indicated that she wouldn't have the condition. Deborah Levy and her husband, Ariel, had two boys when she became pregnant at thirty-four. Mrs. Levy was concerned about the risk of genetic anomalies associated with her age, so she underwent a prenatal test called chorionic villus sampling. The procedure involves removing fetal tissue from a woman's womb—analysis revealed no chromosomal abnormalities. But the doctor had taken tissue only from Mrs. Levy and not the fetus, so the test missed the extra fetal copy of chromosome 21 that causes Down syndrome. The Levys sued for wrongful birth, a legal claim that Oregon allows, and received death threats throughout the trial.[53]

Online commentators vilified the couple: "[H]ow can any parent[s] claim to 'love' their child, yet also wish that they had aborted them? . . . [T]heir little girl had the audacity to be born with an extra chromosome, and now, they have to be paid off in order to deal with the burden of raising her."[54] Journalist Jonathan Last admonishes the Levys for voicing the "most horrible affirmation possible for a parent: *We wish you had never been born.*" Last articulates a reaction shared by many conservatives that these claims reflect a troubling egocentrizing of reproductive attitudes. He laments that a role Americans once understood after World War II as a noble duty to family and nation has now become a means of fulfilling personal values and goals. "Once parents view procreation through the lens of self," he chides, "it becomes shockingly easy for them to complain about this or that outcome. When you are the center of the universe, it's easy to interpret misfortune as grievance: You have not suffered an accident of fate; you are a victim of wrongful birth."[55]

One mother offers a more chastening perspective. When Jen Gann was pregnant, a prenatal diagnosis for cystic fibrosis never made it to her. A lab technician scribbled the test results wrong, and her doctor never followed up, so Gann didn't find out until her baby was born with the debilitating condition. She struggles with the implications of having sued medical staff for the very misconduct, without which she wouldn't have had the child she loves. "What does it mean to fight for someone when what you're fighting for is a missed chance at that person's not existing?"

[M]y family's life is now shaped around a disease I would never willingly bring into the world. . . . Having to put this kind of pain into words is, to me, the hardest part of wrongful birth. To have to specify what would make me terminate a pregnancy, to imagine my life today without a toddler. There's no escape from knowing that the opportunity for mercy quietly slipped by and that something as idiotic as a clerical error is responsible.[56]

For all the challenges occasioned by her son's presence in their family, Gann doesn't wish that the boy he is today "had never been born." She isn't saying he's undesirable or undesired. Her complaint is that the wrongful defeat of procreative will mark a tectonic shift in how she spends her days and thinks about who she is. Professional negligence has redirected the course of life plans for family and transformed her sense of self. Malpractice-type torts fail to capture this deeper harm that reproductive negligence can inflict to a victim's well-being and identity.[57] The wrongful birth tort requires patients to prove that misconduct invaded their legally protected interests. But courts think twice before crediting reproductive harms as injuries under the law. And they rarely compensate psychological or dignitary harms, standing alone, for otherwise-deserving victims of professional negligence.[58]

C. Wrongful Death

When frozen sperm, eggs, or embryos go missing or get damaged, plaintiffs have sued for "wrongful destruction" or "wrongful death," comparing reproductive materials to property or persons. Neither strategy has found much success in courts—but that hasn't stopped victims from asserting them. Wendy and Rick Penniman brought a "wrongful death" claim against the Cleveland fertility clinic whose 2018 freezer failure destroyed their last three IVF embryos.[59] In a 1986 Supreme Court case, Justice Byron White rightly described an embryo (or fetus) as "an entity that bears in its cells all the genetic information that . . . distinguishes an individual member of this species from all others."[60] But the Court has long maintained that even a late-stage fetus lacks any constitutional rights of its own that could override a woman's decision to end her pregnancy.[61] Just because a gestating fetus doesn't count as a person for purposes of abortion rights and regulations doesn't necessarily mean that a frozen embryo can't be thought of as a person in the distinct context of negligence actions involving the unborn's destruction by others. Letting grief-stricken couples like the Pennimans sue for "wrongful death" needn't afford embryos any rights under the U.S. Constitution. But that doesn't justify these lawsuits, or make them a good idea.

The peculiar history of the wrongful death tort explains how claims involving the unborn can hang together with constitutional rights to abortion. Legislatures enacted wrongful death statutes to fill an untenable gap in the early common law. Negligence liability for serious injuries attached only if a plaintiff survived—if he died, the defendant went scot-free.[62] Wrongful death suits were designed to deter misconduct and compensate the victim's survivors. Originally, recovery was allowed only for economic losses like funeral expenses and a loved one's lost wages. Most jurisdictions now let wrongful-death plaintiffs recover for emotional distress and other nonpecuniary losses of companionship and peace of mind. This allowed parents to recover for the wrongful death of relatives and other dependents whose death doesn't set them back financially, including children whose injuries had been inflicted before they were born.[63] But this expansion to infant deaths resulting from harms incurred during pregnancy invited yet another dilemma. Wrongful death now afforded relief to new parents whose fetuses survived until birth, but not those whose fetus was hurt so bad that it died before it was born. Remedies were slighter for a graver harm.

To address this paradox, the majority of states expanded the action once more, this time to cover fetuses capable of surviving on their own. Since wrongful death statutes limit its application to the death of a "person," this move required defining fetuses as persons—but just for the narrowly circumscribed purpose of allowing would-have-been parents to recover. Their claim for the wrongful death of a viable fetus speaks to the devastating loss that just-about-parents endure when negligence ends their wanted pregnancy. In this limited context, judicial recognition of "fetal personhood" doesn't entitle a fetus to any rights of its own, so it doesn't implicate the fetus's entitlement to make claims on others, including a woman's right to abortion.[64] Claims for wrongful prenatal death are allowed only for fetal deaths incurred during the final trimester—not any earlier in pregnancy. Every court that's considered the wrongful death of IVF embryos has rejected that claim on the ground that the term "person" or "human being" doesn't apply to frozen embryos under the meaning of state law.[65] But courts needn't declare lost embryos "people" to recognize that plaintiffs like the Pennimans have suffered a profound loss, or that apologies and refunds alone aren't enough to redress the negligent destruction of their reproductive cells.

The reason that states can ban abortion later in pregnancy isn't that viable fetuses have rights of their own. The Court held in *Roe v. Wade* that it's because the state has an "important and legitimate" interest in "potential life," an interest whose strength grows as a fetus does, and becomes compelling once it develops the capacity for "meaningful life outside the mother's womb."[66] The interest is the state's, not the fetus's. Thinking about the fetus as the kind of entity subject to "wrongful death" isn't so out of sync with government interests in preserving fetal life. Courts entitle not-yet-implanted embryos to far lesser deference, albeit still "special respect," on account of their "*potential* to become a person."[67] This intermediate status—"greater than that accorded to human tissues" like blood or hair, but less than a person—is what the Tennessee Supreme Court assigned to embryos in a 1992 divorce action between Mary Sue and Junior Davis. They agreed on all terms of the dissolution except what to do with the seven embryos that they had cryopreserved while they were married. She wanted to use them to get pregnant; he wanted them donated to a childless couple.[68] Tennessee's designation of "special respect" has been widely adopted to resolve embryo disposition disputes in other states.[69]

To declare embryos deserving of more than in one legal context, like tort remedies, isn't to require affording them that higher status in another, like "custody" battles, let alone abortion restrictions. But treating embryos as persons under any discrete part of the law does risk that politically charged implication of embryonic personhood everywhere. Calling embryos "persons"—even for the sole purpose of wrongful-death recovery—could bolster the cause of those who would restrict practices like IVF and stem cell research that involve foreseeable damage to embryos.[70] Today, IVF patients in every state except Louisiana can do what they want with any embryos they created and don't ultimately use.[71] Recognition of wrongful death for lost embryos could provide support for legislative proposals to limit embryo creation, mandate "adoption" of unused IVF embryos, and force female patients who don't get pregnant after the first cycle to undergo additional rounds of painful egg retrieval. At any rate, no American court has ever defined lost embryos as "persons" under the meaning of statutes authorizing plaintiffs to sue for wrongful death.

Judges have been more open to think of reproductive materials as something closer to property. This willingness has been halfhearted, however, and mostly limited to disputes over what to do with frozen sperm, eggs, and embryos that aren't lost at all, but caught in a tug of war.[72] One California case involved a posthumous battle over frozen sperm. Before Bill Kane committed suicide, he willed twelve vials of frozen sperm to his girlfriend, Deborah Hecht, so that she could have his child after he died. His grown children wanted the sperm removed from his estate and destroyed. A state appellate court ruled for Hecht. It was up to Kane who got his sperm, which the court called a "unique type of 'property.'" The California Supreme Court denied review, letting that verdict stand to resolve Hecht's quarrel with Kane's children. But it also decertified the judgment as precedent that would have any legal authority in future cases.[73] A Virginia decision accorded similar property interests to the progenitors of frozen embryos. That case pitted fertility patients Steven York and Risa Adler-York against the Jones Institute for Reproductive Medicine, which refused to transfer the couple's embryos to another clinic after multiple efforts at the Jones Institute had failed. The court held that the embryos had to be returned in the same way a valet service or parking garage has to give back people's cars. But that was only because the Institute had "consistently refer[red] to" the embryos "as the 'property' of the Yorks in the Cryopreservation Agreement" between them.[74]

Courts resist the implications of propertyzing embryos in another kind of dispute—between former spouses over what to do with the frozen embryos they had created together at a happier time in their relationship. "Equating [embryos] with washing machines and jewelry borders on the absurd," courts insist. They have reluctantly classified embryos as "marital property," in the limited sense of nonperson entities acquired during the marriage. But that doesn't mean that embryos can be sold on the open market. Judges use "property" here as a legal term of art that designates control over how something can be used. Any "interest in the nature of ownership" over frozen embryos is limited to "decision-making authority concerning the[ir] disposition." Courts explain that recognizing these narrow property interests in embryos is consistent with affording them the "special respect" they deserve by virtue of "their potential for human life" and "symbolic meaning for many people."[75] There's nonetheless an undeniable "awkwardness" to treating embryos as "personal property."[76]

This body of law faces other problems in trying to resolve negligently mishandled embryos. One is that property disputes involve contested ownership claims. This might work for reproductive disputes between (ex-) husband and wife, clinic and patients, or the decedent's girlfriend and his children, with each party vying for control over existing entities whose where-abouts are known. But for professional negligence, when frozen tissues de-compose or go unaccounted for, no competing party claims them as his own. Lost sex cells are just that—lost. Rules for misappropriated property could still be adapted to missing or destroyed eggs or embryos, but remedies are constrained. It isn't just that compensation levels would be too low. The vocab-ulary of property law can't articulate the meaning of these losses, or compute a suitable remedy for their defeat.[77]

The challenge of determining damages came to the fore in the first-ever IVF lawsuit in the United States, in which three couples sued for the loss of their total of nine embryos. The state court in *Frisina v. Women and Infants Hospital of Rhode Island* allowed the families to recover for the missing embryos "based on the loss of irreplaceable property."[78] It had a hard time pinpointing the basis for awards. There's no market for frozen embryos, so they lack commercial value—but so do lots of other unique forms of per-sonal property like family heirlooms or custom-made suits.[79] "Replacement cost" is one option—but age, health, or other factors may make it too late for progenitors to replace lost reproductive materials. What about the price of creating them? That would be small change for sperm, a few thousand dollars for eggs, a couple more for procedures to create embryos and store them, plus time and resources expended. This is the kind of tallying that courts have applied to assess damages for the wrongful destruction of re-search materials.[80]

But embryo loss has far greater significance and meaning for people who had sought to reproduce rather than experiment with them. Courts like *Frisina* struggle mightily to translate defeated life plans under the auspices of property law. The closest analogy that court could find was a basement flooding that caused the "discomforts and annoyance" of being denied the use of one's home.[81] Being robbed of one's prospects for procreation is a weightier kind of injury, one whose repercussions reach further than inconveniences or sentimentalities. Casting that loss as tantamount to the nuisance of damaged property distorts and devalues the kinds of harm that reproductive negligence characteristically inflicts. Property law misses the real losses sustained and corresponding damages owed. Courts resist treating frozen gametes or embryos as the kinds of entities that people can own or put a price tag on. And they get stuck trying to appraise thwarted family plans in terms of damaged possessions. Neither the cost of procedures to extract eggs nor the symbolic value of embryos created can capture their worth.

PART II

THE PRICE OF ACCIDENTS

Distinctive features of reproductive loss make them hard to define, confirm, and appraise. This part asks how courts should address the intangible and open-ended nature of these harms within the contours of American civil justice. Chapter 4 mines the history of personality torts for common-law analogs in products liability and privacy rights. Chapter 5 asks whether procreation rights are monolithic or multiple, who those rights should protect, what their remedies are for, and which parts of our legal system are best equipped to deliver them. Chapter 6 spells out two components to assess damage awards. First is the relative severity of reproductive harm, in terms of its practical consequences for patients and their partners. Second is the extent to which misconduct (as opposed to some other factor) is responsible for having caused those injuries.

4

Elusive Injuries

[T]hese silent, intangible rebukes, were galling in the extreme—
the more so, because they were intangible, and he could bring no
counteracting force against them.
> —Emerson Bennett, *Rosalie Du Pont* (1851)

Constitutional guarantees of reproductive privacy didn't emerge out of thin
air.[1] The seeds of *Roe* and its progeny were planted in a branch of law called
torts.[2] Tort law redresses civil wrongs that don't rise to the level of crimes.
The torts system lets injured parties sue individuals or institutions—whether
governments or nonstate actors—for violating duties of care in ways that
cause foreseeable harm. The rights to abortion and birth control draw inspi-
ration from "personality torts" that safeguard less concrete human interests
like hurt feelings and mental anguish.

A. Past Is Prologue

For most of American history, courthouses weren't the place to work
out intangible harms to emotional tranquility or reputation. Up until
the twentieth century, judicial redress was limited to physical injury or
property damage. The only exceptions were torts for assault (threatened
touching) and false imprisonment (restraint without consent or justification). And these were explicitly grounded in battery or detention,
whose bodily interferences were imminent or already manifested. All
other losses were consigned to the rough and tumble of quotidian social affairs—people just took those less tangible harms on the chin, unless they responded through verbal retaliation or physical dueling.[3]
Informal mechanisms might have worked in small towns, where people
knew each other and shared core values—but not in the big cities where
rural workers flocked en masse in search of commercial jobs. Urban

Birth Rights and Wrongs. Dov Fox.
© Dov Fox 2019. Published 2019 by Oxford University Press.

dislocation between 1880 and 1910 obscured the forces responsible for wounding one's sense of self or worth, making it difficult if not impossible to defend one's honor "with the sword."[4]

Courts came to hold greater promise for resolving these disputes as they began grappling with the injuries born of modern work and social life. Technological advances from Thomas Edison's light bulb to Henry Ford's assembly line produced flash burns and broken bones on a larger scale than ever before. The U.S. Supreme Court observed that "[t]he industrial revolution multiplied the number of workmen exposed to injury from increasingly powerful and complex mechanisms," while "[t]raffic of velocities, volumes and varieties unheard of" suddenly "subject[ed] the wayfarer to intolerable casualty risks."[5] Consumer goods from soft drinks to power tools let dangerous defects loose on unsuspecting patrons. Lawmakers couldn't be expected to foresee every harm these innovations might generate. And the slow churn of the legislative process took too long to erect effective guardrails before those injuries happened. But after-the-fact victims could still find relief in court.[6]

In 1910, Donald MacPherson was badly injured when the wood-spoked wheels fell off his Model 10 Runabout while he was driving it in upstate New York. The hitch corkscrewed his car off the road, where it ricocheted off a telephone pole, and tumbled end over end into a three-foot ditch. MacPherson sued the manufacturer for his broken wrist, cracked ribs, and battered face. Buick executives contended that the motor company hadn't made MacPherson any promises. He hadn't bought the automobile from them, after all, but from a go-between retailer that made no specific representations about the car's quality either.[7] Judge Benjamin Cardozo rejected Buick's argument that liability claims couldn't extend past the sales vendor. He was adamant that the brave new world of increasingly remote transactions demanded more of the law than cramped enforcement of face-to-face agreements. Just because merchants didn't do business directly with consumers couldn't justify immunizing those firms from liability for whatever injuries their products unleashed on them. Basic principles of fair dealing and reasonable care required that courts let injured parties sue companies they never shook hands with. Cardozo concluded:

> We have put aside the notion that the duty to safeguard life and limb, when the consequences of negligence may be foreseen, grows out of contract

and nothing else. We have put the source of the obligation where it ought to be. We have put its source in the law.[8]

"The law" in which Cardozo placed this legal duty is torts, which he celebrated for its doctrinal agility and moral imagination.[9] Negligence liability enables injured parties to obtain recourse from the faraway firms that create the products that harmed them. This tort doctrine isn't limited to physical injuries like MacPherson's, which can be traced to faulty parts from distant factories. It also protects against the dignitary harms that mudslingers and peeping Toms do to self-image and reputation. That's where "personality torts" come in—libel, slander, defamation, intentional infliction of emotional distress.[10]

The most famous such tort is the right to privacy. This is the right that former wrestler Hulk Hogan famously asserted in 2016 to win a $140 million judgment that bankrupted Gawker after the media giant posted his sex tapes online.[11] Established as that right is today, American law shut its eyes to such unconsented exposure of secrets until the late 1800s, when advances in picture-taking made natural bedfellows with professional muckraking. News outlets used to be an exclusive enterprise, with the handful of major papers focused on economics, politics, and art.[12] Photography was at that time an unwieldy and time-consuming undertaking in which willing participants had their portraits taken in a formal studio.[13] Cheaper and quicker printing techniques ushered in a competitive tabloid industry that used salacious reporting to sell papers.[14] Yellow journalism got a major boost from the invention of handheld cameras that let amateur shutterbugs pry into the personal spaces of other people and memorialize their guarded moments for the whole world to see.[15]

Privacy incursions by this penny press found no redress in the law of contract, defamation, copyright, or otherwise. In 1888, Thomas Cooley, former Chief Justice of the Michigan Supreme Court, proposed that the legal system do something. The second edition of his famed treatise on torts set forth a novel right "to be let alone."[16] Two years later, law school classmates Samuel Warren and Louis Brandeis filled in the details of that right in the pathbreaking article they published in the *Harvard Law Review*. (Brandeis, like Cardozo, would ascend to a seat on the U.S. Supreme Court.) Warren and Brandeis argued that individuals should be entitled to control the extent to which their depictions, "sentiments, and emotions shall be communicated to others." Fearing that "what is whispered in the closet shall be proclaimed from the house-tops," they proposed a civil action to sue for the public disclosure of private facts.

> The press is overstepping in every direction the obvious bounds of pro-priety and of decency. . . . To satisfy a prurient taste[,] the details of sexual relations are [] broadcast in . . . the daily papers. To occupy the indolent, column upon column is filled with idle gossip, which can only be procured by intrusion upon the domestic circle.[17]

Highbrow dailies piled on this indignation against voyeuristic snapshots in news and advertising. The *Los Angeles Times* decried the state of affairs in which ordinary individuals, who "in no way put themselves before the public," found themselves "dragged into notoriety by any adventurer who thinks he can fill his pockets by exploiting them." The *New York Times* took these mercenary "kodakers" to task for "outrages" that led even the most "thick-skinned" celebrities—hardly "shrinking violet[s]"—to "revolt from the continuous ordeal of the camera."[18]

Judges initially rejected appeals to Warren and Brandeis's privacy action for straying too far from existing precedents in the common law. The very "phrase 'right of privacy,'" they complained, originated with that "clever ar-ticle in the *Harvard Law Review*." In 1902, New York's high court protested that even the "[m]ention of such a right is not to be found in Blackstone, Kent or any other of the great commentators upon the law."[19] But just three years later, Georgia became the first state to recognize the privacy right when its supreme court ordered an insurer to pay the man whose image the company had used in its advertisements without his consent. "One who desires to live a life of partial seclusion," that court affirmed, "has a right to choose the times, places, and manner in which and at which he will submit himself to the public gaze."[20] By 1941, most states recognized the now-familiar tort of privacy.[21]

A similar story can be told about reproductive negligence today. Just as click-camera incursions placed privacy interests in sharp relief, switched donors and lost embryos bring to fuller expression the meaning and sig-nificance of the interests people have in matters of procreation. Tort law is equally equipped to accommodate reproductive injuries that don't involve any unwanted touching, broken agreement, or damaged belongings. Or so I suggested in a 2017 article in the *Columbia Law Review*.[22] Some scholars resisted the analogy I drew to privacy's origin story. The strongest critique came from distinguished torts theorist Gregory Keating, the William T. Dalessi Professor of Law and Philosophy at the University of Southern California Gould School of Law. His commentary in *Columbia*'s pages later that year began: "The invocation of this glorious past tugs at the heartstrings of any torts scholar. But it moves my mind less than my heart."[23]

Professor Keating argues in his response that "the common law of torts is poorly positioned to respond to this particular kind of wrongful harm" because the ways in which "reproductive negligence interferes with its victims' pursuit of their [life] projects differs from the interferences with which tort law is characteristically concerned." The tort system "protects people's lives and possessions as they are," he explains, rather than "as they might be." This domain of law presumes that existing value "makes a greater claim on us than value that has yet to be created."[24] Torts remedy the wrongful deprivation of health, wealth, or other goods that plaintiffs have already come to enjoy—not the mere absence of goods they wish they had. Professor John Gardner makes a similar point in his 2018 book, *From Personal Life to Private Law*, when he writes that tort law redresses harms to "the life one already has before one, with its current trajectory." Gardner makes clear that torts are just for damage to "the house that the potential plaintiff already lives in," or the "work she already does," or the "peace and quiet she has already found." This body of law doesn't also guard against injuries to the bigger house or better work or sounder peace that she dreams of.[25] By these lights, tort protections are limited to preserving what the plaintiff had at the time she got injured—torts don't protect anything else that she might have gotten after that point.

This priority of existing losses over potential ones reflects the widely held view that behavioral economists call the endowment effect. This is the sense that it's worse to have something taken away, if it was already yours, than it is to be denied that very same thing, if you don't have it yet. Cognitive psychology principles like "loss aversion" and "prospect theory" try to explain why people care more about losing what's theirs at the moment, than they do missing out on equivalent gains just around the corner.[26] We usually think of harms and benefits in these temporal terms that measure a person's present state of affairs up against her past (harm) or future (benefit). Harms worsen a person's position in the here and now, as compared with the position that she found herself in before that event or circumstance. Benefits, by contrast, upgrade her current position by looking ahead to how she can reasonably expect it to improve. It's like the difference between being infected with a disease and being denied the vaccine during an outbreak. The infection harms you presently, by impairing your existing medical condition, relative to what it was previously, whereas going unvaccinated leaves you at risk of the illness moving forward. That loss doesn't cause you harm, in Keating's terms—it withholds a benefit. So too with reproductive negligence, he argues.

When professional misconduct strips your chances of parenthood, what you miss out on is the future experience and relationship that would almost certainly have brought your life great meaning or satisfaction. Yet that unrealized benefit isn't as bad as a harm to the same good you'd enjoyed before, Keating says. His argument doesn't apply to the childfree existence that people had already come to value when defective birth control imposed procreation on them. Nor does it work for parental lives that didn't used to involve caring for debilitating disease before prenatal misdiagnosis confounded their plans for offspring health. But at least for cases in which procreation is deprived, Keating's critique is a formidable one: These transgressions don't inflict the more serious kind of setback that he refers to as harms—they simply deny benefits. It's this fundamental asymmetry, he argues, that makes tort law "inhospitable to the recognition of [those] reproductive wrongs."[27]

Prenatal losses don't harm fertility patients, in the sense of worsening their post-negligence family life, as compared with what it was before. Dropped embryos and negligently caused miscarriages frustrate the parental future that plaintiffs hoped for, but not any present or past existence they'd already laid claim to. And the tort system responds only to harms, on Keating's account—it was never supposed to remedy the unfulfilled benefits that people had so far just set their sights on. That's why he says that tort law can't vindicate reproductive interests in pursuing pregnancy and parenthood. Keating doesn't mention that in other contexts, the U.S. Supreme Court has taken a decidedly dimmer view of the distinction between harms and benefits. For example, the Court has expressly rejected a harms/benefits-based dividing line for government takings when it distinguishes compensable intrusions on private property from takings that the state doesn't have to pay property owners for. Justice Antonin Scalia, writing for the majority in *Lucas v. South Carolina Coastal Council*, explained that "the distinction between 'harm-preventing' and 'benefit-conferring' regulation is often in the eye of the beholder," depending on nothing less subjective than "the observer's evaluation of the relative importance" of the underlying activity.[28] Whether some regulation gets designated as a "harm" or "denied benefit" to the people it affects may, in other words, be a function of implicit judgments about the (in)significance or (un)worthiness of the activity it targets.

These points aren't lost on Professor Keating. He doesn't scoff at reproductive negligence. And he appreciates that harms and benefits are just "pluses and minuses" on either end of "the same scale," with one logically identical to the other, except that harms are bad and benefits good. His argument is that tort law is right to draw a sharp line between these twin concepts because "[h]arms and benefits stand in very different relations to autonomy." Here, Keating echoes an idea that Professor Arthur Ripstein articulated in his 1999 book on *Equality, Responsibility, and the Law*, namely, that "certain security interests are protected" because of "their importance to leading an autonomous life."[29] These core interests are the ones Ripstein says we need in order to exercise our moral capacity for meaningful choice about the direction our lives take. Professor Seana Shiffin expounded in an article she published that same year in the journal of *Legal Theory*. What distinguishes harms like pain and property loss, she wrote, is that they "impose experiential conditions that are affirmatively contrary to one's will" or "seriously interfere[] with the exercise of agency."[30] Keating picks up where Ripstein and Shiffrin left off, singling out intrusions on "our bodies and [] our possessions" for how acutely they "impair the principal means at our disposal for . . . exert[ing] our wills upon the world." This impairment of present abilities and tools strikes a greater blow to autonomy than being denied future goods, especially when those future setbacks are also less concrete, Keating says: Suppressing intangible aspirations rarely "rob[s] us of our normal and foundational powers of agency."[31]

But blocked benefits aren't really so different in this respect from harms to what's already mine. Unrealized benefits can keep me from quarterbacking my life no differently than harms do. What matters is how reasonable I was to have expected the good or goal in the first place, and how not getting it foreseeably affects me. Say I've arranged my life around building a house, or getting a job, or having a child when a wrongful injury spoils everything just before the last coat of paint, or round of interviews, or stage of pregnancy. That loss isn't singularly less devastating just because I wasn't quite a homeowner, employee, or parent. My life can be upended even if I haven't yet moved in, or gotten a paycheck, or held the baby in my arms.[32] All it takes to see this is replacing an historical comparison between my present and past state of affairs, with a counterfactual one between my present and an alternate universe in which things went how they were supposed to. The distinction between historical and counterfactual comparisons comes from philosopher Joel Feinberg. He recognized that something can still be bad for me even if I'm no worse off than I was before. If a surgeon leaves a small blunt medical instrument in my body, I'm actually better off than before the life-saving operation, albeit not nearly as healthy or happy as I would have been if she'd taken the object out.[33] Procreation deprived is similar: It leaves my life just as bereft of children as it was before, but my reproductive options are worse for me than if my infertility had been treated in a way that wasn't negligent.

Professor Keating has a point when he talks down benefits on the grounds that their putative good for me might not in fact be "congruent with [my] will." He explains that to "thrust an unsought benefit upon [me] and de-mand compensation . . . for the value conferred" would conscript me in a project that I haven't chosen. Getting a house or job or child I didn't con-sent to risks depriving me of the very autonomy that Keating says tort law is designed to preserve. But the benefits I hope to derive from IVF or sperm donation aren't unsolicited. Patients seek out these services with the express purpose of having a child. When specialists frustrate that purpose, it foists a lifetime of childlessness on patients who made clear their preference to grow their family. These injuries disorder their lives no less than "broken bones, crippling pain, [or] significant disability."[34] Reproductive negligence erodes personal agency and self-determination too. More practical reasons than individual autonomy do a better job of explaining why tort law tends to privilege existing harms over future benefits.

Benefits are harder to prove and calculate. That they haven't yet happened clouds what might have been realized, and obscures the value of goods that never were. Suppose two reckless drivers each crash their car into another one around the corner from a hospital's labor and delivery wing. One of those other vehicles was on its way home after childbirth, the other on its way there for the same. The post-birth collision claims the life of a newborn. The pre-birth one causes the would-be mother to miscarry. Why should tort law distinguish so conspicuously between the two cases, allowing full recovery in the first, and forbidding it altogether in the second? The clearest difference between them has nothing to do with reproductive autonomy. It's that a newborn assumes an instant vividness in her parents' world, whereas a fetus can't be heard or held. The parents in the post-birth case can close their eyes and imagine the sound of their baby's cry or the touch of her hand wrapping around their finger. But when those sensations are just conceptual possibilities, as in the pre-birth case, visualizing them requires the more demanding task of peering into one's mind's eye.[35] Out of sight, out of mind.

The Supreme Court of California hummed a few more bars about the opacity of prenatal loss in a 1977 wrongful death case involving negligent hospital midwives:

> The parents of a stillborn fetus have never known more than a mysterious presence dimly sensed by random movements in the womb [whereas] the mother and father of a child born alive have seen, touched, and heard their baby, have witnessed his developing personality, and have started the lifelong process of communicating and interacting with him. These are the rich experiences upon which a meaningful parent-child relationship is built, and they do not begin until the moment of birth.[36]

And yet certain features of the long-awaited place of potential offspring aren't all that hard for prospective parents to conjure up. The expected child occupies an overriding role in their life that no other person could. Uncertain though that loss will necessarily be in its more precise contours and consequences, it can still be projected clearly and confidently enough to sustain a remedy in tort. That's why most courts treat the two car accidents similarly. They compensate for a baby's wrongful death, whether before and after her first breath. The amount might vary, but if a court awards damages when a child "dies immediately after birth," it also does for "a stillborn child."[37]

For Professor Keating, tort law should approach these cases differently. Only after a wanted child arrives do parents enjoy goods associated with her tangible place in their life, such that her loss would substantially impair their ability to plan it. Before her birth, these parental goods aren't yet theirs to lose. Acquiring those benefits might "enlarge the reach" of their will, he grants, but not getting them doesn't impair it.[38] Keating makes too much of this harm/benefit asymmetry and its ostensible connection to autonomy. It doesn't matter so markedly whether reproductive losses already materialized, provided that a victim had sound reason to expect that they would, and to plan her life accordingly. Tort law is capacious enough to remedy unfulfilled benefits. Indeed, sometimes it does.

Courts allow medical malpractice grievances for future risk and disrupted expectations. Damage awards are available for the lost chance to achieve some more favorable outcome like the lost "opportunity to obtain a better degree of recovery." In one case, an obstetrician's bungled surgery left a woman with fine health for now, but higher odds of bowel obstruction down the road. The court approved compensation for that 8–16 percent chance of an ailment she didn't yet face and might not in the future either.[39] It's not just doctors. Accountants have been held liable for bad investments that lose a client potential revenue. And drunk drivers are forced to pay for the income that a dead victim might have earned, even if the deceased is a child who never had a job to give up in the first place.[40] So tort law already responds to more than just existing harms. It also redresses certain blocked benefits that injured parties didn't yet have—investment returns, employment earnings, the chance for improved health—so long as those plaintiffs were reasonable to count on getting them if they hadn't been mistreated.

B. Emotional Distress

The personality torts were radical because civil recovery for wrongful injury usually requires harm to the victim's person or possessions. Even today, the U.S. Supreme Court maintains that emotional harm alone doesn't qualify for compensation under circumstances in which modest bodily injuries would. The modern precedent comes from 1997. A train track pipefitter named Michael Buckley was among the "snowmen of Grand Central," so called because the end of each workday saw them covered with white insulation dust. It was asbestos. Buckley's employer, Metro-North Railroad, conceded that it was wrong to have used the known carcinogen. Wracked by anxiety that his prolonged exposure to the known carcinogen would inflict a slow and painful death, Buckley sued the company for negligent infliction of emotional distress. Medical checkups didn't point to any signs that he had asbestos-related diseases. Then again, it can take years before a person who's inhaled the toxic fibers develops mesothelioma, asbestosis, or lung cancer. And symptoms of these often-fatal diseases may not manifest until down the road.[41] But the Court held that Buckley couldn't recover for his present fear, because mental angst couldn't be readily discerned. The majority worried that claims of emotional harm alone are too easy to fake and too hard to disprove. Plaintiffs or their attorneys could cook up any heartache and lay it on thick through poignant accounts that defendants would be hard-pressed to dispute. To "distinguish between reliable and serious claims" of emotional anguish from "unreliable and relatively trivial" ones, the Court refused to remedy Buckley's injury without proof that he'd suffered physical or economic harm too.[42]

Lower courts pile on concerns that run deeper than problems with evidence and risk of fraud. They add that "mental distress of a trivial and transient nature is part and parcel of everyday life." The ubiquity of fleeting anxieties leaves judges wary of catering to oversensitive victims or "curry[ing] to neurotic patterns in the population."[43] These considerations help to explain the barriers that American tort law puts up in the way of recovery for freestanding emotional harm. Plaintiffs are required to show that intangible loss was accompanied by bodily injury or physical impact from within a "zone of danger."[44] Where courts entertain claims for emotional distress at all, they set the bar high, demanding proof of grave and lasting damage. A bystander who witnesses a horrific accident can't recover, however grave his panic or manifest his shock, unless he's "closely related" to the victim, "present at the scene of the [physical] injury," and "aware" of it in real time.[45] Courts reject claims for missing embryos, switched donors, and failed birth control on the ground that victims don't experience "present and demonstrable physical injury" and didn't witness "the occurrence which caused" their emotional distress. Nor do any resulting children, back when embryos or sex cells, count as the kind of "victims" to which their future parents might claim relation or proximity at the scene.[46]

Even recovery for intentional infliction of emotional distress requires that the defendant's misconduct be "outrageous."[47] Deliberate reproductive malfeasance isn't just the stuff of sci-fi dramas, contemporary comedies, and *Law & Order* reruns.[48] Just-for-fun DNA kits like 23andMe and Ancestry.com have exposed four doctors who inseminated patients decades ago using their own sperm.[49] Clinics in New York and Texas stole eggs and embryos from their patients.[50] And in the mid-1990s, Pulitzer-winning investigation by the *Orange County Register* exposed a web of cover-ups, employee intimidation, and hush money payments at UC Irvine's Center for Reproductive Health. Fertility specialist Ricardo Asch and his medical partners took eggs from patients without their consent, mixed and matched them with sperm from others, and implanted the resulting embryos into different people.[51] Especially for intentional wrongs like these, but also for reproductive negligence, concerns about opening the floodgates to disingenuous claims don't justify restricting remedies for emotional distress. Would-be cheats face too many hoops to jump through—they'd have to stage costly or invasive procedures gone awry, or at least produce reliable, contemporaneous evidence sufficient to substantiate their asserted reproductive plans. To weed out smoke and mirrors, courts need only ask for hard-to-fake medical records, corroborating witnesses, and long-term preparations. Even if the absence of physical harm did invite "greater opportunity for fraud," the California Supreme Court has explained, that threat would "not warrant courts of law in closing the door to all cases of that class."[52]

Yet tort law generally refuses to compensate freestanding emotional distress. Outside of the reproductive context, courts have made three exceptions: First are cases in which doctors or other medical specialists misdiagnose a potentially fatal disease, like telling a patient he has cancer or AIDS when he doesn't.[53] In the second class of complaints, military or law enforcement professionals inform family members that their loved ones died when they haven't.[54] The last exception is the most common among these today. It involves the mishandling of corpses, such as cremating a body intended for burial. When plaintiffs win in negligent-infliction cases like these, courts rely on the collective judgment of juries to come up with damages for standalone emotional harm. Recent courts have approved awards of between $200,000 and $450,000 for the negligent loss or destruction of a relative's corpse.[55] Courts have singled out three features of these dead-body cases that justify special recovery. First is that the social practice at stake is valued deeply across our moral culture—honoring loved ones by disposing of their remains in accordance with religious rituals, family traditions, or parting wishes. Second is the considerable degree of faith that vulnerable victims, such as grief-stricken mourners, place in the hands of professionals, like undertakers, morticians, coroners, embalmers, and funeral directors. Third is the lack of alternate measures to deter misconduct. The departed themselves can't bring a claim if their survivors aren't allowed to.[56]

Reproductive losses register close parallels along all three dimensions. First, efforts to have or avoid children occupy a central place in people's lives. Bringing a new member into one's family can be as emotionally charged and fraught as sending off an old one. Indeed, a 2008 Connecticut court expressly analogized the "dignity interest" in "preserving the potential for human reproduction" to giving the deceased a "comfortable and dignified resting place."[57] Second is all-out reliance on specialists in matters of procreation, just as in matters of death. A 2018 federal court in Idaho explained that the "position of trust" assumed by reproductive healthcare professionals gives them special "access to, and power over, areas of life that are unusually intimate and sacred."[58] Finally, no better-suited plaintiff emerges to help discipline the mishandling of human materials at the beginning of life, like at its end. Potential children have no more standing to sue than the deceased. Yet courts haven't carved out a similar emotional-distress exception for reproductive negligence. The Connecticut court recognized the lopsided result: Remedies are available to mourning parents whose "deceased child was cremated despite their instructions to the mortician to embalm the child for an open casket wake"—but the law affords no relief to heartbroken couples whose "only hope for having a child together was discarded by their medical provider."[59]

Signs of change can be gleaned in the *American Restatement of Torts*, a widely cited legal treatise that summarizes general principles of tort law. The most recent edition of the *Restatement* from 2012 would forgo the physical manifestation requirement for negligently inflicted injuries sustained in the course of activities "fraught with the risk of emotional harm." That *Restatement* didn't specify any relevant factors—a professional relationship or contractual obligation, for example—that might qualify for exemption from the general bar on recovery for internal distress that isn't outwardly apparent. It left judges to identify contexts in which plaintiffs need show only "credible evidence" of "serious" harms that they weren't idiosyncratic or unreasonable to experience.[60] But courts have so far applied this relaxed standard sparingly, limiting it to legal malpractice in child custody or criminal defense cases that lead clients to lose visitation rights or be wrongfully incarcerated.[61] So the "parents of a child [born] with a serious disease [still] cannot recover for emotional injury" related to bungled prenatal test results any more than they can for "distress arising from having a child who is not [their] biological offspring."[62]

Physical and economic setbacks alone can't capture the dislocation of life plans and cherished relationships. These conventional harms miss real and serious losses to people who end up with a child they can't care for, or without the one they'd give anything to have.[63] Not that letting victims recover for mental harm would be a panacea. Looking only to their subjective anguish can't sort out more deserving reproductive claims from less worthy ones, or objectively legitimate claims from those without merit: a misfilled birth control prescription that doesn't result in pregnancy; dropped embryos that leave enough left over to have children; switched donors that differ in trivial ways. But these are exceptions. Anxiety, disappointment, and sorrow are part of any reproductive injury—they're not the whole of it, though, or even most. The loss of prenatal misdiagnosis goes beyond the "shock of discovering" that parenthood will take a radically different shape, after an ultrasonographer failed to report a ravaging disorder.[64] And the lasting consequences of an embryo mix-up reach further than any "psychological trauma" associated with "the possibility that the child that [an IVF couple] wanted so desperately" could, because their embryos were misimplanted into another patient, "be born to someone else and that they might never know his or her fate."[65] The "shock" and "trauma" that these courts reduced this harm to don't speak to the frayed marriages or haunting loneliness that reproductive negligence predictably incurs to lived experiences and personal identities.

C. Too Hard to Define

Critics decry recovery for reproductive losses as too arbitrary and prone to abuse: They say there's no sound way to translate such unfamiliar and imprecise harms into hard-and-fast dollar amounts; there's no objective test to appraise the severity of injuries that depend so heavily on subjective testimony; there's no clear mechanism to channel legislative or judicial deliberations about corresponding damage awards; there's no market value available to set principled limits within some ceiling or floor.[66] Nor can courts pretend to "weigh the value of life" against "the utter void of nonexistence."[67] The Supreme Court of South Carolina opined that even "a jury collectively imbued with the wisdom of Solomon" would be powerless "to weigh the fact of being born with a defective condition against the fact of not being born at all. . . . It is simply beyond the human experience."[68]

But just because reproductive injuries can be nebulous doesn't mean they're not "concrete," at least not in the "usual meaning" the U.S. Supreme Court has ascribed to that term, namely, "'real,' and not 'abstract.'" Not getting the baby you wanted, or getting one you didn't, is a harm in fact, not just in theory. "Although tangible injuries are perhaps easier to recognize," the Court said in a 2016 case, "intangible injuries can nevertheless be concrete."[69] That's why as far back as 1931, the Court let a paper company recover for intangible injuries arising from a competitor's antitrust violation.

Its decision in *Story Parchment Co. v. Paterson Parchment Paper Co.* authorized damage awards as "a matter of just and reasonable inference," even though no harm "could be measured and expressed in figures not based on speculation and conjecture."

> Where the tort itself is of such a nature as to preclude the ascertainment of the amount of damages with certainty, it would be a perversion of fundamental principles of justice to deny all relief to the injured person, and thereby relieve the wrongdoer from making any amend for his acts.[70]

The Court also affirmed the principle that "the risk of the uncertainty [in measuring damages] should be thrown upon the wrongdoer instead of upon the injured party."[71] A Michigan court sharpened the point in a wrongful death case thirty years later. "[I]t is not the privilege of him whose wrongful act caused the loss to hide behind the uncertainties inherent in the very situation his wrong has created."[72]

Indeterminacy and incommensurability complicate remedies for reproductive harms, but not uniquely or prohibitively so. It's just as hard to come up with suitable dollar awards for successful claims of nuisance, trespass, libel, or slander—let alone for established torts like wrongful death, wrongful conviction, and wrongful imprisonment. Yet courts do it all the time. The difficulty in assessing subtle losses of life, liberty, and dignity in these contexts doesn't justify refusing compensation outright. The same goes for the humiliation of the privacy intrusion, the betrayal of fiduciary breach, and the lost choice of uninformed consent. Judges even entertain suits for the quintessentially ethereal harm of "wrongful living" when medical providers resuscitate someone whose healthcare directives clearly said not to.[73] Courts should redirect their attention in these cases from collateral distress to the frustration of underlying interests that are more readily perceptible and to the point—not any generic interests that victims have in maximizing utility or being happy, but specific ones in freedom, seclusion, fair dealing, truth in advertising, or individual agency over one's medical treatment or end of life.[74] For reproductive negligence, that means looking to thwarted interests in choosing for or against pregnancy, parenthood, and offspring particulars. Courts shouldn't throw up their hands just because these losses require care to enumerate, appraise, and falsify.

A 1982 case illustrates. Joseph and Trudy Burger's Eastern European ancestry left them at risk of passing along Tay-Sachs if both carried the genetic disease. When they went to get tested early in pregnancy, the couple was told "there was no need to test Mrs. Burger unless Mr. Burger tested positive." So the hospital "withdrew blood from Mr. Burger alone" and placed it "in two tubes labeled only with a number." The tubes were marked with no other information that identified the samples as his. "[T]est results showed Mr. Burger was not a Tay-Sachs carrier. Satisfied with the report, Mrs. Burger 'went ahead and had' her baby." The girl was born with that "fatal disease of the brain and spinal cord" that causes "blindness, deafness, paralysis, seizures, and mental retardation" before an early demise within "two to four years." Mr. Burger's blood sample had been switched with a noncarrier's.[75] Virginia's supreme court let the Burgers recover for whatever "reasonable and proximate consequences" could be reasonably "foreseen or anticipated" from "the breach of the duty owed them," exempting the prenatal screening error from the "general rule [that] such damages are not recoverable unless they result directly from tortiously caused physical injury."[76] To deny the couple compensation for their intangible losses, the Court held, would "constitute a perversion of fundamental principles of justice." It let the Burgers recover for whatever "reasonable and proximate consequences" could be reasonably "foreseen or anticipated" from "the breach of the duty owed them." The state justices approved a $178,674 jury award for harms that included the "emotional stress and mental anguish [they] suffered as a result of the child's worsening condition."[77] The court could have done better still by pinpointing the defeated interest in selecting for offspring free of devastating disease, estimating its disvalue by reference to more established intangible interests, and then gauging the degree and intensity of its impairment for the Burgers—perhaps using expert opinions or representative surveys of revealed preferences by similar populations.[78]

This interest-based approach doesn't secure watertight compensation levels. But it approximates losses better than emotional harm can. At the same time, it's likely to jack up dollar totals beyond whatever medical expenses or psychological anguish victims incur. And exorbitant damage could reduce access to reproductive care, even if they're not unfair to badly behaving professionals. Eye-popping awards could drive specialists out of the field altogether, or chill their delivery of higher-risk procedures that represent some patient's only hope to treat their fertility or infertility. This concern would be mitigated if effective forms of insurance were available to cover the costs of reproductive negligence—clinicians and facilities could pool their resources to protect against steep payouts. That's how it works in most fields of medicine, where hospitals and doctors carry deep coverage for adverse outcomes. But insurance carriers are wary of liability exposure to the prohibitive costs and moral hazard that typify reproductive care. Insurers call it a "triple risk activity" because it can harm not just the patient, but her partner and offspring too, any of whom might be able to "pursu[e] a lawsuit against the physician, nurse, and/or hospital for bad outcomes."[79] Then again, service providers probably won't absorb legal expenditures.

These charges will more likely get handed along to future patients in the form of higher-priced care that may become too steep for some to afford. These pass-through costs were the reason that the California Supreme Court gave in another context for denying nine children the $100,000 that each requested in 1977 for their mother's lost "tutelage and affection" after she was seriously injured by a lighting fixture that fell on her from an airport ceiling. The nearly million-dollar payout would ostensibly rest with "the 'negligent' defendant or his insurer." But the court reasoned that it would ultimately "be borne by the public generally in increased insurance premiums or in the enhanced danger that accrues from the greater number of people who may choose to go without insurance."[80] Still, reproductive specialists wouldn't be held to any higher standard of care. Authorizing claims against them just wouldn't exempt their misconduct from ordinary professional duties by virtue of its connection to family planning. And liability would at least spread these costs across all patients, instead of concentrating their full force on the luckless victims who have procreation deprived, imposed, or confounded.

5

Courthouse Claims

These times are too progressive. Everything has changed too fast.
Railroads and telegraphs and kerosene and coal stoves—they're
good to have but the trouble is, folks get to depend on 'em.
— Laura Ingalls Wilder, *The Long Winter* (1953)

Existing legal claims have a hard time trying to remedy reproductive
wrongs. But procreation patients and their committed partners should be
able to seek meaningful recovery for professional negligence that thwarts
their legitimate family plans. I distinguish three kinds of unwanted reproductive outcomes: (1) no baby, where victims had sought one; (2) any
baby, where the goal was none at all; and (3) a particular type of baby,
where parents undertook efforts to have one with different traits. Our legal
system should recognize each of these complaints—that's what this chapter
recommends. The first tort action that I propose is for negligently frustrated
attempts to pursue pregnancy or parenthood. The second concerns dashed
efforts to avoid those activities and roles. The third is for offspring selection gone amiss. I call these the rights of *procreation deprived, procreation
imposed,* and *procreation confounded.*

A. Lump or Split

Should protections against reproductive negligence take form in one right
or many? Negligence suits could bundle reproductive interests into some
one, overarching cause of action—or they could carve up those interests into
multiple, distinct actions. A unitary claim for all of family planning would
furnish the convenience of a single place for citizens to locate a remedy in
the law when they sense that someone's infringed on their interests in pregnancy, parenthood, or particulars. This centralized core would also stream-
line the sources of authority for lawyers and judges tasked with resolving

Birth Rights and Wrongs. Dov Fox.
© Dov Fox 2019. Published 2019 by Oxford University Press.

such disputes. Most crucially, an all-encompassing appeal to procreation writ large makes it easier for law to adapt to changing conditions in a rapidly evolving field of medicine and technology.[1] On the other hand, a uniform right would flatten out finer-grained distinctions among reproductive facts, norms, and consequences. And an underspecified procreation right risks dissolving into disarray if its protections are too nebulous to implement in practice. A more conceptually rigorous approach would differentiate among reproductive harms and corresponding remedies.

The privacy tort has aged well by breaking off into constituent pieces.[2] Courts divided the privacy right into what Dean William Prosser recognized as four discrete claims: (1) public disclosure of private facts; (2) publicity in a false light; (3) intrusion of solicitude; and (4) appropriation of name or likeness.[3] Each works out differently on the ground. The public disclosure tort concerns the broadcasting of offensive or embarrassing personal details. Examples include the publication of photographs like plastic-surgery before-and-afters, a loved one's death scene, and undergarments exposed by a gust of wind.[4] This first claim balances an individual's dignitary interests in keeping those details secret against the political or cultural value of making such factual information known. The false light action, by contrast, protects nonpublic figures from being humiliated or embarrassed by the reckless communication of misleading representations about them. Under this second tort, a tabloid had to pay the ninety-seven-year-old Arkansas woman it portrayed as pregnant,[5] and a biographer couldn't knowingly lie about a subject's military decoration.[6] The third claim has nothing to do with the content, veracity, newsworthiness, or use of personal information. The intrusion tort concerns the inherently discomforting way in which facts are acquired. It includes stealing looks into another person's home, for example, or tracking his words or movement, or snooping around his personal effects. Finally, the appropriation tort—for using a celebrity's voice or image in an advertisement—protects commercial interests more than anything that could fairly be designated as a right to be let alone.[7]

These four actions implicate discrete defenses and forms of damages that might get run together if courts framed privacy as a monolithic right. Reproductive negligence is like this too. Not all transgressions are created equal. The fertility clinic that loses a cancer survivor's sperm, or the genetic counselor who says that continuing a pregnancy would be dangerous when it wouldn't—these wrongs leave the affected families painfully incomplete. Compare the pharmacist who fills a prescription for birth control with something else, or the OB/GYN who botches an abortion procedure—in both cases, a woman is left to carry or raise a child she was in no position to care for. Finally, there's the doctor who swaps her patient's reproductive materials, or the embryologist who misses a terrible disorder—trespasses like this can change the experience of raising a child, and make it harder to achieve the parenting goals that people value.[8] Each of these three pairs of examples represent a distinctive interference with reproductive interests. The first *deprives* people of their wanted ability to gestate or raise a child. The second *imposes* pregnancy or parenthood on individuals seeking to steer clear of these roles. The third *confounds* efforts to have not just any child, but one of a particular type. Practical differences among these injuries can't be captured by any single cause of action. Three separate rights should protect against the wrongful defeat of reproductive avoidance, pursuit, and selection.

Procreation deprived impairs interests in pursuing pregnancy or parent-hood. These are errors that deny aspiring parents the chance to have off-spring. Pleading this tort requires plaintiffs to produce credible evidence like healthcare receipts and clinical visits that substantiate their efforts to get pregnant and/or become parents. They'd also have to show that negli-gent misconduct substantially contributed to those efforts being defeated—that some other outside factor wouldn't have left them childless even if they'd received perfectly good reproductive care. The level of compensa-tion due for successful claims would depend on the demonstrated reasons why plaintiffs had wanted to be parents, and the consequences of their not getting to be. It might also matter whether they already have kids, or even how many, and whether they might still be able to. Defendants could deflect liability on the ground that preexisting infertility, a natural disaster, or any other cause that defendants aren't responsible for, gave the plaintiffs little if any chance at reproducing regardless. Defendants might also resuscitate Professor Keating's defense from the last chapter that distinguishes between harms—which tort law remedies—and denied benefits, which it doesn't. Any lost chance to reproduce doesn't *harm* plaintiffs, in the sense of making them worse off than they were before. It just denies them the benefit of the potential pregnancy and parenthood they pined for, but didn't have already. These goods weren't really theirs to lose, at least not in the way that our tort system requires of the wrongful losses it compensates for. That's what defendants could try to argue, anyway, when plaintiffs sue them for procre-ation deprived. The other reproductive wrongs are different.

Procreation imposed thwarts interests in avoiding unwanted gestation or childrearing. These offenses block concerted efforts not to reproduce. A prima facie claim for procreation imposed requires proving that plaintiffs adopted specific measures to evade parenthood, as by precluding or terminating pregnancy. Those who bring suit under this cause of action must again demonstrate that a defendant's wrongdoing was to blame. But this time, it's for the plaintiffs' *getting* pregnant or giving birth, and potential alternative explanations include user error (e.g., the failure to use birth control as directed) or bad luck (e.g., the tiny fraction of cases in which it just doesn't work to prevent conception). Where defendants are found liable for imposing procreation, damage awards would depend on why plaintiffs had sought to abstain from having offspring, and what followed from having parenthood foisted upon them. Among the defenses unique to this tort is that, despite any wrongdoing, pregnancy or live birth didn't ultimately ensue. When it does, defendants might try to argue that plaintiffs weren't harmed anyway, because even an unplanned child is a blessing not a burden. Or they could make the case that the plaintiffs could still have avoided that outcome they didn't want by opting for abortion or adoption. Not that either of these defenses should win the day—but defendants could plausibly raise them in trying to fend off complaints that they wrongfully imposed procreation.

Procreation confounded deals instead with frustrated efforts to have kids of a particular type. Professional misconduct that leads to the birth of sick baby rather than the healthy one parents tried for poses distinct issues of liability and damages associated with inexact genetic testing, nebulous disease manifestations, controversial ordering among more and less "serious" conditions, and counterfactual speculation about the experience of raising a child who's born one way rather than another. Defendants could say it's impossible to know how any given reproductive mix-up will turn out for the plaintiffs—their lives might actually be made better, not worse—or point out that parents will end up loving whatever child they end up with at any rate. Confounded procreation also raises distinct policy concerns. It's one thing for parents to choose offspring born with or without particular genetic qualities in the first place—that's just families acting in their own private capacity. It's another thing for a court of law to pronounce, in the voice of the community, that selection against children with certain traits—like sex, race, or disability—deserves special protection, or that thwarted efforts to choose for this or that characteristic—a boy instead of a girl, or white child instead of a black one—counts as a legal injury.

B. Lovers Who Lie

Claims for deprived, imposed, and confounded reflect the responsibilities that certain individuals or institutions owe to preserve the reproductive interests of others. Formal obligations in matters of pregnancy and parenthood is what sets professional negligence apart from otherwise similar transgressions at the hand of intimate partners. Fertility doctors and other healthcare practitioners assume practice-specific duties of care that nonspecialists do not. More on this distinction shortly. For now, it bears mention that people who mislead sexual partners into having or avoiding offspring aren't just careless or reckless—they're intentional. What this kind of duplicity has in common with negligently botched procedures and services is that both can deprive, impose, or confound procreation just the same—also that in neither context are offenses designated as crimes against society at large. The only exception is domestic abuse and sexual violence that forces a woman to start an unwanted pregnancy, or end a wanted one. The U.S. Supreme Court recognized these reproductive dimensions of marital rape and assault in the 1992 case of *Planned Parenthood v. Casey*, when it struck down a spousal notification requirement for abortion. The Court explained that "[f]or the great many women who are victims of abuse inflicted by their husbands," that mandate "enables the husband to wield an effective veto" over his wife's constitutionally protected decision whether to keep her pregnancy. That's why it forbid the state from compelling a woman to tell her spouse that she's carrying his genetic offspring before she's allowed to get an abortion.[9]

Partners may also deprive, impose, or confound procreation in less violent ways. The case law recounts all kinds of scams through which people have compelled pregnancy or parenthood on their partners. Some deceive lovers into thinking that conception isn't likely to result from sex. Women have sued men for putting holes in condoms, for example, and for falsely claiming to be sterile or to have had a vasectomy.[10] Men, in turn, have accused women of lying about being on the Pill and furtively removing an intrauterine device.[11] Intimates have even imposed procreation without vaginal intercourse by smuggling sperm from a used condom or otherwise.

Richard Phillips told his former girlfriend, Sharon Irons, that he didn't want to father a child outside of marriage, and insisted they engage only in oral sex acts that the appellate court said "no reasonable person would expect could result in pregnancy." Yet Irons had a baby girl whom DNA tests linked to Phillips. He claims that shortly before he broke off the relationship, she saved his semen in her mouth, and put it to the "unorthodox, unanticipated" use of inseminating herself, in the court's words.[12] Phillips didn't learn of the pregnancy or birth until years later, when Irons sued him for child support. The court ordered Phillips to pay $800 a month, while dismissing his counterclaim of fraud. Phillips "may not recover on allegations of physical and emotional distress," the court held, because "the tort of fraudulent misrepresentation historically has been limited to cases involving business or financial transactions."[13]

People have also *deprived* pregnancy by tricking their partners into thinking that conception is possible when they know it's not. Most cases involve concealing knowledge of one's sterility or sterilization.[14] But schemers also deny parenthood in other ways. One man duped his mistress into having an unwanted abortion in reliance on a false promise that he would impregnate her again after leaving his wife.[15] Others have drugged a pregnant partner with abortion pills that induce miscarriage, either by spiking their drinks or switching out prescription medications.[16] Meanwhile, spouses have long *confounded* procreation by failing to disclose some medical condition that offspring would be likely to inherit. In 1933, Bernice Leventhal sued the father and sister of her ex-husband Abraham Liberman for making false promises that induced her to marry him. Her in-laws had assured her that Liberman he "had never been sick, was a well boy, and that he had no bad habits known to them." In truth, they knew full well that he suffered from tuberculosis susceptibility and addictive personality traits whose adverse effects he risked passing along to any child they might have together.[17]

Judges rarely award damages to people whose intimate partners manipulate them in ways that deprive, impose, or confound procreation. The legal system doesn't even recognize claims for wrongful deception or offensive touching against the wrong of "stealthing." That's when, during intercourse, a man removes his condom without consent or goes back on his promise to withdraw before ejaculating.[18] Why do courts tolerate these efforts to distort or manipulate reproductive goals, risking pregnancy for partners who seek to avoid it, or childlessness for those who make clear they want to be parents? Some judges say that lovers assume the risk. As one defendant argued: "Every schoolboy over the age of twelve knows that sex can be a risky business."[19] Never mind that pregnancy is magnitudes more likely if intercourse is unwittingly unprotected.[20] Or that courts don't hesitate to impose liability on people who fail to disclose known risks of sexually transmitting diseases like herpes or genital warts.[21] The idea is that people should realize that unwanted outcomes are possible when they engage in sexual relations. These things happen—they're not cause for legal action.

Other courts give egalitarian-sounding reasons for rejecting more intimate claims of reproductive wrongdoing. These courts hold that, in the absence of special power imbalances between partners, each is equally capable of affirming his or her own reproductive interests. Judges scoff at the genetic father who resists paying child support after his partner said she was on birth control even though she wasn't. Her lie, they insist, "in no way limited" his own ability to have used a condom.[22] But this rationale doesn't make for a very satisfying justification to condone "the promises made between two consenting adults as to the circumstances of their private sexual conduct."[23] Neither does the he-said-she-said problem that available evidence may not bear out one partner's word over another's. Nor the worry that reproductive transparency invites fraud or smothers spontaneity.

The best reason not to enforce bedroom vows is this: Intimate partners don't owe each other a formal kind of obligation of the kind that medical specialists do to those they serve. A partner's deceit, however dreadful, doesn't breach any duty of reproductive care—at least not in the absence of a contract like the one that gestational surrogacy agree to in exchange for money and expenses. By contrast, sperm bank operators, fertility doctors, and OB/GYNs all assume just this sort of obligation toward their patients. In this professional context, patients may not even be the only ones entitled to sue specialists for reproductive negligence against them.

Abortion case law about spousal consent and notification requirements supports the idea that protections should extend to partners who share in the patient's reproductive plans. In the 1976 case of *Planned Parenthood v. Danforth*, decided just three years after *Roe*, the U.S. Supreme Court affirmed a woman's right to have an abortion over her partner's objection, explaining that, as the one "who physically bears the child," she "is the more directly and immediately affected by the pregnancy." Abortion regulations "have a far greater impact on the mother's liberty than on the father's" because they touch "upon the very bodily integrity of the pregnant woman."[24]

The reason the majority gave for striking the balance of interests in her favor isn't that an expectant mother's interest is presumptively stronger, or that her parental role is more natural or more important to the family unit than a father's is. A plurality of justices reaffirmed, in their 1992 *Casey* opinion, that what prioritizes her decision over her partner's opposition is that a woman alone "bears the child." That's why, "when the wife and the husband disagree" about having an abortion, she gets the final word.[25]

Her constitutional right-of-way in abortion conflicts means that he is legally powerless to decide whether she keeps a pregnancy. But *Danforth* and *Casey* made clear that this conclusion doesn't negate his "deep and proper concern and interest . . . in his wife's pregnancy and in the growth and development of the fetus she is carrying."[26] The Court explained that men have important reproductive interests too—those interests simply lose out to a woman's when abortion is involved. Men's interests regain functional significance whenever the tiebreaker of gestation isn't front and center. This helps to explain why the right to birth control isn't limited to women. The Constitution entitles men to contraceptive access as well. The Supreme Court cast that fundamental liberty in gender-neutral terms, as a right belonging not to women alone, but to any "individual, married or single," to make "decisions whether to accomplish or to prevent conception."[27] No law may stop a man from buying or using condoms, even though he wouldn't carry a child who results from unprotected sex. The man's claim to birth control vindicates more than just his female partner's reproductive interests in choosing for or against pregnancy and parenthood. It also recognizes his own interests in choosing whether to become a father.[28]

Many reproductive patients and their partners are spouses, different-sex or same-sex. Those who aren't married may nevertheless be committed to common family plans when they decide to enlist medicine or technology to help them have a child or prevent one. The rights for procreation deprived, imposed, and confounded should extend to any reproductive partner who shares the same "deep and proper concern and interest" in a patient's treatment as a husband has in his wife's pregnancy. That's how the Texas Court of Appeals reasoned when a reckless driver struck Dori Anna Dean's car while she was thirty-six weeks pregnant. The collision led her to deliver a stillborn child the next day, after nine hours of labor. The question on appeal was whether Mrs. Dean was the only one who could sue for corresponding emotional distress, or if her husband John could too. The court could come up with no compelling state interest in a gender-based denial of a father's right to recover damages for his own mental anguish from the negligently caused loss of his viable fetus, a denial which "perpetuates the myth that only a woman grieves and suffers the mental anguish caused by the loss of a baby in the womb."[29]

The Sixth Circuit reached a similar conclusion when a surrogacy broker failed to counsel the gestational carrier about the risks that intercourse with her unscreened husband around the same time as the procedure could cause health problems in any resulting child. The court held that the broker had breached its duties not only to the surrogate and intended parents, but also to the surrogate's husband—at least under circumstances in which the husband had signed the surrogacy contract, participated in his wife's medical care during pregnancy, and ultimately parented the child whose severe neuromuscular disorder left that child unable to walk or eat without a tube.[30]

What matters for the partner's own entitlement to sue under the procreation actions is how actively he participated in treatment for fertility or infertility, and the level of commitment he sustained to the negligently thwarted project. A 2018 federal district court explained that while the partner isn't a patient "in the traditional sense of the word," he can still resemble one in that a reproductive professional may agree "to help *them* with *their* infertility." The partner is "not merely a third-party family member in this case; rather, he was an integral part of the procedure."[31] The question is whether that involvement triggers a medical duty to the partner like the one that courts have, under rare circumstances, imputed to certain nonpatients in other contexts. For example, when a doctor fails to notify transfusion patients that they received blood contaminated with HIV or some other disease, courts have held the doctor liable to the sexual partners or offspring who patients foreseeably transmit that diseases to, even many years later.[32] Courts have also held a psychiatrist liable to the parents of a suicidal minor, when the parents had "participated in group therapy" with the patient (their child), "received information concerning [his] treatment and status," and "intended to personally benefit" from their immersion in his care.[33]

The partners of reproductive negligence victims are rarely permitted to sue, let alone recover, whether procreation is imposed or deprived. In a 2005 Maryland case, the partner was a woman faced with unwanted pregnancy after her husband's doctor failed to provide a post-vasectomy referral to confirm the procedure's success. The court held that the physician owed no duty to the patient's wife.[34] A California case two years earlier involved a fertility doctor who prescribed the wrong drug to a male patient, leaving him unable to provide sperm for IVF. That court likewise refused to recognize any duty of care to the patient's wife, who was thereby prevented "from becoming pregnant" with the couple's child.[35] The healthcare specialists in these cases agree to treat only the patients, not their partners. So they don't owe those partners any professional duties that would entitle them to sue for reproductive negligence on their own behalf.

Only in an unpublished 2014 opinion did a Connecticut court allow a husband to sue a doctor for negligence after a false positive for "serious chromosomal defects" led the man's wife to end the pregnancy they'd wanted to keep and "would have [made him] the father of the child, if born."[36] Michael Distassio and his wife, Anne Meleney-Distassio, had long awaited the future child she was carrying. After a prenatal visit, however, her OB/GYN's office told them the fetus had ambiguous genitalia, which also carries risks of hormonal abnormalities and organ dysfunction. After much agony, they opted for abortion. But a fetal autopsy revealed that the prenatal test results had been wrong. A secretary had accidentally typed "XY" instead of "XX" in the field for fetal sex, a mistake that the lab, hospital, doctors, and genetic counselors all missed. The female fetus actually had normal genitalia, and there was no reason to think their girl-to-be would have experienced any of the complications the misdiagnosis had indicated.[37]

Judge David Tobin held that the doctor breached a duty of care not only to Anne, but to Michael as well, given their "binary relationship in the realm of procreation." If Anne could sue for professional wrongdoing, he concluded, then so could Michael. "[T]here is no sound reason why a spouse (father) cannot assert what amounts to a particularized form of derivative injury, one that is no less real and no less significant than" long-recognized losses for companionship when a bad actor's to blame for disabling or killing a plaintiff's spouse.[38] Judge Tobin dispensed with various arguments the defendants advanced for why the patient's husband shouldn't be allowed to sue. Authorizing "one and only one, clearly identifiable, additional claimant per incident" wasn't "likely to [drive] any appreciable increase in litigation," the judge explained. He found other objections no more persuasive:

> There can be no concern about unidentifiable claimants or unlimited scope of potential claimants; there is unlikely to be a flood of additional litigation; there is no intrusion on the physician-patient relationship; there

can be no concern about trivial claims being pursued; and the interests being invaded/harmed are substantial, having received recognition as a right with constitutional implications.[39]

Judge Tobin's logic applies generally to a broad swath of reproductive projects and relationships between medical professionals and their patients' partners. But this ruling wasn't selected for publication in the case reports, so its conclusions carry no precedential value even as persuasive authority in any future cases.

Courts have even entertained patient-adjacent recovery only for partners who have made legally recognized nuptial commitments. They give two reasons to limit potential entitlements to spouses: to privilege marriage relationships and to keep tort liability from expanding too far.[40] But procreation rights should extend to committed and involved nonspouse partners too, at least when a doctor knows that those partners share in a common project to grow, limit, or otherwise shape their family. In a botched vasectomy case, another court held that "awareness is sufficient" to hold a physician liable for injuries associated with the pregnancy imposed on the patient's female partner. The important fact wasn't that she was his wife, but that those injuries "result[ed] from [the] negligent performance of the procedures she [reasonably] relied upon, despite the lack of any direct doctor-patient relationship" between her and the surgery.[41] Committed partners should be entitled to sue along with the patients who undergo fertility or infertility treatment themselves. Extending the rights of procreation deprived, imposed, and confounded to partners recognizes the dual impact that misconduct characteristically has on the family plans they share.

C. What Payment's For

When courts set out to resolve legal controversies, their main goal is to achieve fair and just outcomes for the parties involved. But that's not all— "the law is also there to crystallize constitutive norms, to affirm social significance, or to emphasize solemnity."[42] Judicial rulings about reproductive negligence can say something important about the meaning of interests and injuries related to pregnancy, parenthood, and offspring particulars. The might let providers know how it's reasonable for them to carry out this work of caring for these interests. Or they could tell people who are planning out their families together what kind of vindication is reasonable to expect in the event that procedures or services go wrong. Whatever messages the rights of procreation impart will depend in part on how they're enforced.

The legal remedy for successful claims isn't apology or reparations. The currency to right most wrongs in the American civil justice system is cash. Tort law is no exception. Courts make tortfeasors pay the parties they injure. But it stands to ask what exactly that money is for. The point isn't to make amends or give those at fault their just desserts. Retribution may motivate criminal punishment or punitive damages for certain intentional torts. But it's rarely invoked for ordinary negligence, short of outrageous or reckless indifference to others.[43] And even the most contemptible infractions escape liability if the sheer luck of nonpregnancy or a miracle baby avoids meaningful harm. That makes moral comeuppance a weak candidate to justify remedies for procreation deprived, imposed, and confounded.

Nor is the primary objective of damage awards to discourage reproductive negligence. The specter of steep awards may lead specialists to implement precautions that are likely to reduce the incidence of injury-causing errors. But fear of massive payouts could also invite gratuitous safeguards that drive up prices for fertility patients, or make it too expensive for medical facilities to offer certain valuable procreation procedures. To improve the quality of reproductive care in ways that avoid these dangers, victims shouldn't be able to recover too much or too easily. If the goal is to deter misconduct in anything like an optimal way, then compensation levels should incentivize the adoption of protective measures that cost less than the injuries they'd prevent. If economic efficiency were the objective, juries or judges could try to guess at the required trade-offs among relevant risks, expenses, and alternatives. Fewer errors—as long as they didn't come at too great an expense to basic access of reproductive care—would certainly be a welcome byproduct of remedies for reproductive negligence. But that's not their main point.

Legal recourse for procreation deprived, imposed, and confounded is, above all, about how much and what kind of reproductive harm these wrongs inflict. Tying remuneration to loss doesn't require "making the victim whole," except in the loose sense of helping, as far as money allows, to get her life back on the track that it was before she was subjected to reproductive injury.[44] Cash awards could never pretend to fully or adequately restore the setbacks that fetal misdiagnoses or embryo mishandlings incur to plaintiffs' autonomy, equality, and well-being. As the Supreme Court affirmed in a 2003 wrongful death case, the purpose of compensation is instead "to redress the concrete loss that the plaintiff has suffered by reason of the defendant's wrongful conduct."[45] Reproductive losses aren't especially concrete. Hospital X-rays and itemized receipts do little to substantiate the injuries associated with disrupted family planning. And it's tough to detail reproductive harms or put a figure on their gravity. But remedies aren't an exact science in most areas, and precise totals almost always reflect a healthy measure of arbitrariness.

One approach would be leave damage determinations to the black box of the jury. But without any guidance or points of reference, jurors would struggle to dole out proportional or predictable awards. And jurors aren't accountable in the way that legislators are beholden to their constituents, the way that agency administrators answer to elected representatives, or that unelected judges articulate reasons for their rulings. Skeptics also worry that juries reach decisions out of emotion and ignorance more than shared understandings of what justice requires under the precepts our legal system sets forth. Critics depict the jury as a lawless threat to medical innovation and quality health care, dispensing jackpot justice and inflicting undeserved losses on unpopular healthcare professionals.[46] Empirical data paints a different picture.

Studies of trial evidence and verdicts suggest that jury awards closely track "the severity of a plaintiff's injury."[47] And post-trial surveys reveal that jurors actually tend to disfavor complainants for "fraying the social fabric that depends on a personally responsible citizenry."[48] At their best, juries operate to preserve core values while protecting against corporate or governmental abuses of power. Relative to a single judge, a representative jury of peers draws on the "collective wisdom" of "everyday life experience" to speak with "the voice of the community."[49] Lawyers and judges screen jurors to weed out any personal connections and conflicts of interest that could bind them to the political constraints of elections or outsized influence of lobbyists. A jury's "common sense" equips it to grapple with the fact-sensitive appraisal of reproductive injuries, while its independence lends these determinations a measure of impartiality.[50] This isn't to say that juries should be given free rein to set damages for intangible reproductive injuries—unbounded juries would threaten awards that are too high or too low.

The risk of erratic, arbitrary, or outrageous verdicts demands mechanisms to make remedies for reproductive negligence more reasonable and fair. It's not enough that judges tell jurors to apply prudence in evaluating the value of impaired interests in pregnancy, parenthood, and particulars. There is little evidence to suggest that such generic instructions have much effect on jury deliberations. Nor would it suffice to present jurors with a bell curve of recovery for similar injuries, adjusted to reflect the relative price index in the trial's jurisdiction. Informing jurors of award patterns or injury profiles might even entrench the unwarranted variability or extravagance of past damage totals. Besides, grounding future awards on existing ones wouldn't be much use until a sufficient number and diversity of new claims come before courts.[51]

Since 1975, thirty-five states have responded to concerns about open-ended liability in medical malpractice by capping recovery for noneconomic injuries to between $150,000 and $1.5 million. Proponents tout how upper award limits keep insurance affordable for service providers, while preserving much of the jury's discretion, since caps kick in only at the extremes. But these restrictions apply indiscriminately among all claims to which juries assign the greatest or least compensation. Maximums and minimums respond only to these absolute totals, so they do little to distinguish meritorious suits from frivolous ones, or undue awards from those that are justifiably high or low under the circumstances. Damage caps also pay no mind to overvaluation below the ceiling or undervaluation above the floor.[52]

The risk that caps will arbitrarily reduce redress for those who suffer the most serious injuries explains why seven state supreme courts have invalidated them as unconstitutional.[53] A handful of other legislatures have repealed or revised their caps to deflect similar challenges, after courts warned that prevailing award maxes could be struck down.[54] More nuanced strategies would guard against capricious or uneven awards. A compensation schedule for reproductive negligence could single out relevant factors, break them up along a principled spectrum, and convert distinct injuries to corresponding dollar figures.[55] The next chapter looks to the frameworks developed for workers' compensation, insurance claiming, and sentencing guidelines.

6

Damage Awards

> Yet the misery, for which years of happiness were to offer no com-
> pensation, received soon afterwards material relief.
> —Jane Austen, *Pride and Prejudice* (1813)

Reproductive losses might seem too vague to quantify in dollar terms for purposes of tort compensation. But these injuries aren't so different from other kinds of intangible harms that judges and juries appraise every day.[1] The calculation process isn't precise, but it's not so mysterious either. Adjudicators start with provable facts and plausible judgments about the ways in which misconduct foreseeably harms victims. Then courts ballpark these injuries in flexible terms of "emotional distress," "pain and suffering," or "loss of enjoyment of life." It's more art than science, but hardly new or enough already. Two questions should guide award determinations for procreation deprived, imposed, and confounded. First, how serious is the plaintiff's reproductive loss? The answer goes to the nature and duration of that loss's practical consequences for the plaintiff's life. The second question asks how likely any future loss is to come about, and the extent to which its cause can be traced to the defendant's misconduct, as opposed to some other factor for which the defendant isn't to blame.

A. Grading Harm

Any measure of reproductive injury begins with identifying whether and how it infringes on the interests in parenthood, pregnancy, and particulars. Anchoring more particular harms to these basic intrusions marks out salient features that influence their real-world life consequences for the individuals affected. Chapters 7 through 9 show how these determinations play out across a range of cases in which procreation was wrongfully deprived, imposed, and confounded. American law and policy offer a number of plausible models for computing reproductive harms. One candidate is the nine-point index that private insurance companies use to assess the value of malpractice claims based on stock illustrations of injury severity and duration.[2] Another possible prototype for gauging reproductive loss comes from the sentencing guidelines that prescribe parameters for criminal punishment according to offense and offender characteristics. Judges exercise a limited measure of discretion to depart upward or downward from those fixed rankings in view of more idiosyncratic facts or circumstances that seem relevant to the badness of a particular claim or conviction.[3] Most promising are the measurement standards that workers' compensation programs adopt to specify payouts for workplace injuries—without regard to employer fault.[4]

Injuries sustained in the course of employment range from carpal tunnel to herniated disks to heightened risks of lung cancer. Workers comp schedules are tailored to reflect social judgments about the relative magnitude of those injuries in context.[5] Professor Ellen Pryor gives the example of two employees who suffer the same injury that requires amputating three fingers on the left hand. These could nonetheless yield different awards based on how seriously they impede the two different workers' functioning on the job.

> [B]oth would have a significant disability in activities that made heavy use of the left hand, such as typing, sorting, or gripping. . . . If one worker had minimal education and had been employed for many years as a mail sorter, the injury might result in a significant job-related handicap. If, by contrast, the other worker were an accountant, the injury might produce little if any job-related handicap.[6]

For American workers' compensation, every state compensates for health expenses, rehabilitation costs, and professional setbacks like lost wages and expected earnings. Just some also redress harms that aren't medical or economic—like the stigma of disfigurement or the loss of sexual functioning. And very few states cover even less concrete injuries such as pain and suffering.[7]

Commentators have criticized these kinds of tables and catalogs for tending to drag down awards in a way that undercompensates victims. Lower damages might be okay in a claimant-friendly system of reliable payouts. But across-the-board discounts risk treating negligence plaintiffs unfairly. Unlike injured workers, plaintiffs bear the burden of proving a defendant's at fault. This fine-grained approach also ties the jury's hands from customizing damages based on case-specific factors.[8] Any "schedule or formula for total awards could only very roughly match payments to need," scholars explain. "a 'one size fits all' damage schedule would inevitably be unfair both to claimants having greater [] losses and defendants causing lesser [] harm."[9] A slate of reproductive injuries shouldn't straitjacket the jury by imposing specific dollar figures. But it could guide them with a range of plausible awards. The remaining leeway juries exercise wouldn't go unchecked—judges still act as a safety valve on unreasonable verdicts. A Rhode Island judge emphasized this point in dissenting from his court's decision to impose compensation limits for victims of botched sterilization: "[N]ot only can a trial ju[dge] set aside a jury-verdict damage award that he or she believes to be excessive or so disproportionate to the proven injury and damages." Higher courts of review also maintain "appellate authority to do likewise."[10]

The severity of reproductive injuries isn't subjective—it calls for objective inquiry into how a reasonable person in the plaintiff's shoes would be affected. Permanent injuries will tend to be more severe than temporary ones because they can be expected to cause greater disruption to major life activities like education, work, income, marriage, friendships, parenting, leisure, and emotional well-being. The question isn't what plaintiffs would have done if they'd known that negligence would dash their efforts—it's how much those injuries can be expected to impair their lives, from the perspective of their own (not illegitimate) ideals and circumstances. This focus on well-being bears resemblance to two species of damages that courts already award for intangible harm. The first is "loss of enjoyment of life." It concerns the lasting ways in which an injury makes a person's lived experiences less fulfilling. These enduring consequences may span across the person's valued plans, projects, roles, and relationships. His injury may make it considerably more difficult for him to complete his education, pursue his career, pay his rent, keep his home, live on his own, sustain his marriage, support his family, take pleasure in activities like bridge or basketball or piano or cooking.

A 2000 New Hampshire court found it salient that a retired car accident victim was forced to give up certain "household chores, travel, and other pursuits" that gave him satisfaction, including "wrestling with his grandchildren and coaching them in sports" as well as "mowing the lawn and assisting his children with their home improvement projects." A jury awarded him $75,000 for these losses of enjoyment that he sustained apart from physical pain or emotional suffering.[11] Fifty years earlier, the Louisiana Court of Appeals would have authorized similar damages for the deprivation of prospective parenthood. *Valence v. Louisiana Power & Light* is an obscure case, hardly ever cited since it was decided in 1951. But it articulates a profound account of compensable reproductive injuries. A reckless bus crash was linked to a pregnant passenger's delivering her child dead five months later. The court ultimately denied her redress, unconvinced that the stillbirth could be traced to trauma from the crash as much as it could the woman's own maternal diabetes. But these causation questions aside, the court endorsed loss-of-enjoyment-style damages for wrongdoing that "prevent[s] parents from having children." The court would have calculated that award as a function of sustained sorrows and related disruptions that keep victims from enjoying their life. "[W]hen parents are actually expecting the arrival of a child, and they are deprived of the fruition of that great expectation by the actionable negligence of someone else, they may recover from the tortfeasor as an item of damage for that particular loss."[12]

Frayed relationships get their own special category of damages for "loss of consortium," or what modern courts refer to as "loss of companionship." Consortium losses were customarily limited to spouses—and originally just to husbands, based on the assumption that wives were their property. But states have increasingly modernized companionship awards to account for relationships with other close family members including parents, grandparents, and dependents.[13] An example comes from the 1993 case of an Ohio mother who sued the hospital that negligently administered an antibiotics overdose to her eleven-month-old son, leaving him permanently deaf. The state supreme court let the jury's consortium award stand at $200,000, explaining that the mother "will be unable to enjoy a number of life experiences normally shared between parent and child." The court dispelled the concern that her testimony about what forms of music, communication, and other shared experiences those might entail would unduly "degrade the child or minimize the importance of the parent-child relationship in our society."[14]

The procreation context adds a couple of wrinkles. One is the metaphysical issue explored in Chapter 1 about misconduct that's simultaneously responsible for a child's very existence. Say instead of making a hearing child deaf, a doctor implants an embryo with deafness in place of the hearing embryo he was supposed to. That switch doesn't deprive a parent of any hearing-based experiences she could have had with that same child. That's because the child she has—him, as opposed to some other one, born with the ability to hear—could only ever have been born with the genetics for deafness that were already present in the embryo from which he developed. Any loss-of-consortium claim for the failure not to implant a hearing embryo couldn't, as in the Ohio case, compare what the mother could otherwise have shared with her child if it hadn't been for the negligent mix-up. The only comparison that makes sense in this case resorts to the existential: How would her relationship have been better with some altogether different child, one who would have been able to hear?

There's another distinctive feature of reproductive negligence that transpires before implantation or conception. This second point of contrast harks back to Chapter 4's discussion of harms and benefits—it's the temporal frame of reference for what's been lost. Damages for lost enjoyment or consortium look back in time to compensate victims like the Ohio mother or New Hampshire grandfather for the "impairment or destruction of the capacity to engage in activities [or relationships] formerly enjoyed by the injured plaintiff."[15] Losses associated with procreation deprived are different. These look ahead to the experience of gestating or raising an expected child that victims didn't yet have. What victims miss out on in these cases isn't some already-enjoyed past, but a future they had hoped to share with a potential child they never got to meet.[16] These losses are harder to clearly apprehend. But that doesn't necessarily make them less serious or worthy of redress. What matters is whether, if plaintiffs hadn't been hurt, their chances of acquiring that denied benefit were foreseeable or merely speculative. That's how it works with loss-of-enjoyment claims associated with frustrated plans to get some future job. Damages hang on how much progress the plaintiff can show she had made toward obtaining qualifications for the would-be promotion or intended line of work.[17] Courts don't compensate for disappointed ambitions if a plaintiff didn't do enough to make it foreseeable that she would have realized her professional goals if it hadn't been for the injury.[18]

Courts have adopted a similar alternate-universe vantage point to benchmark awards for the loss of companionship when parent-child relationships get cut short. These damages for the wrongful death of a newborn extend beyond whatever connection a parent was able to develop during the infant's fleeting life. When doctors negligently cause a stillbirth, consortium remedies aren't limited to that few moments of bonding before misconduct headed off their nascent relationship. Compensation reflects the basic attachments and activities that eager parents had good reason to expect they otherwise would have shared with their child in the years to come: caregiving and affection in infancy, play and guidance during the toddler years, socialization and interest-shaping over the course of adolescence. These are the sorts of affinities and undertakings that parents characteristically enjoy with their child. Those losses in companionship are as foreseeable close to birth as they are after it. They're not "sheer speculation," as the North Carolina Supreme Court explained, simply because we "cannot know anything about [the particular] personality and other traits relevant to what kind of companion [a stillborn child] might have been."[19]

Just a few courts haven't conditioned consortium awards for the loss of a potential child on his or her having been already born. When a reckless driver took the life of a seven-month-pregnant woman, the Iowa Supreme Court allowed her husband to recover damages for the anticipated companionship of their unborn fetus as well. That "loss does not vanish because the deprivation occurred prior to birth," the court held. "To the deprived parent the loss is real either way."[20] The unborn needn't be treated as persons with legal interests of their own for prospective parents to have "developed a relationship with them," an Arizona court clarified in assigning damages for the loss of stillborn twins. To justify consortium awards, it's enough that parents were reasonable to have "developed love for them and expectations for their future."[21] Compensation speaks to "the missed opportunity" of the burgeoning parent-child relations that "would have flourished over time" if medical errors hadn't impaired them.[22] Whether procreation is deprived, imposed, or confounded, the first step in determining damages is this objective inquiry into how that harm can be reasonably projected to impact a plaintiff's life. The more serious it is, the greater the award.

B. Tracing Blame

There's more to calculating recovery than ironing out the absolute magnitude of whatever reproductive injury plaintiffs suffer, whether that's childlessness or unwanted parenthood. The severity of reproductive injury can't be the only basis for setting awards. Courts must also account for issues of injury causation and variable expression. The first consideration is whether misconduct is entirely to blame for having caused the injury. Defendants shouldn't be held responsible for any part of the injury that can be traced to factors other than their bad behavior. Liability should be reduced by the extent to which some other influence—aside from professional negligence—is what reduced plaintiffs' chances of a more favorable outcome. Claims for confounded procreation also raise questions about whether the reproductive injury will actually transpire. Some of these injuries won't have come into view yet; others may never come to pass. For example, a genetic condition missed by prenatal testing might manifest more or less severely in different people, in ways that aren't obvious until down the road. The speculative character of this kind of loss doesn't necessarily make it any less serious. But it's unfair to make negligent providers pay the full price of reproductive harms that might not come about to the nth degree, or even at all.

The causation element of this damages inquiry asks: What are the odds that plaintiffs would have suffered the complained-of reproductive outcome if it hadn't been for the professional misconduct? After all, outside forces can also bring about these very same results in the absence of any wrongdoing. Those claiming procreation deprived may have suffered from infertility that predated their IVF embryos getting destroyed without their say-so. How likely is it that competent care that preserved their embryos still wouldn't have given them a child? Another example: When procreation is imposed, user error can compound faulty birth control. What are the chances that unwitting parents would have ended up with the child they did anyway?

The answer to all these questions can be found in "loss of chance" doctrine, which apportions awards according to the defendant's level of fault for the plaintiff's injury. Courts have adopted this probabilistic approach in "a substantial and growing majority of the [s]tates that have considered" it in medical malpractice cases. Plaintiffs must show that negligent conduct was at least as much to blame for their injuries as other factors. This affords plaintiffs with preexisting conditions an opportunity to recover for their lost "chance to survive, to be cured, or otherwise to achieve a more favorable medical outcome."[23] That patients were already disposed to illness or death means a bad outcome might have happened even if their treatment went right. At-risk patients can't prove that malpractice is what caused their injury, at least not in the traditional "but-for" sense that they wouldn't have suffered as bad a fate without it. They may still have suffered just the same.

What these patients have lost is the greater likelihood that competent treatment would've given them for a better outcome like a cure or survival. A 2013 medical malpractice case in the Minnesota Supreme Court illustrates. Proper diagnosis of a six-year-old girl's cancer "would have given the plaintiff, at a minimum, a 60% chance to survive the illness." The defendant's negligence cut those chances "down to 40%." Even if the girl survived anyway, proportional remedies would still let her recover for the resulting 33 percent "reduction in her chances to stay alive"—less by one-third compared to her life expectancy before the misdiagnosis.[24] So too if she died, but her parents couldn't prove that she wouldn't have anyway.

Courts have mostly limited this approach to medical malpractice damages. But there's no reason why judges can't or shouldn't recognize loss of chance in other applicable contexts.[25] Reproductive negligence presents similar kinds of uncertainty about how misconduct relates to an injury. Here, also, it would be unreasonable to demand that plaintiffs prove causation in the usual way. This wouldn't be any harder than in the standard case: Start with the award total that corresponds to the absolute reproductive loss in question, then reduce it by the extent to which the loss was caused by other forces. That's it. An example will help.

Imagine a couple undergoes IVF and creates six embryos they freeze and store with a fertility clinic before it negligently destroys four of them. Suppose the full-blown injury of deprived procreation is valued at $100,000—that is, if pregnancy and parenthood were rendered hopeless, after having been previously assured. Assisted reproduction doesn't guarantee a pregnancy, let alone a baby—for most who seek treatment, IVF is a high-stakes gamble. Say this couple's age and health gave them a 30 percent chance of having a child with their six initial embryos. Losing them all would have represented a loss of three-tenths that total ($30,000), while the actual loss of four (leaving the two remaining) still gave them a one-tenth shot (valued at $10,000). The resulting 66 percent loss of chance—from 30 percent down to 10 percent—translates into a $20,000 award for the loss of this particular couple's four embryos.

Similar methods can account for different possible harms, as with the more or less severe manifestations of some genetic disorder that results from procreation confounded. The condition may leave the child unable to communicate; make it difficult for him to walk; or hardly affect him at all. Or the effects of the disease may be assured, while the age of onset varies greatly, whether at age two, twenty, or fifty. These wildly disparate consequences call for far correspondingly greater or lesser levels of compensation. It won't do to average out credible outcomes equally—at least not if medical studies and early symptomology make some of these prognoses more likely than others. And a court can't just hold off to see how the child's future actually unfolds. A judge or jury has already ascribed liability, and damage awards must be determined now. Loss of chance has an answer for this kind of case too: Multiply each potential outcome (e.g., $$$ grave, $$ moderate, $ negligible) by its relative likelihood (e.g., 35 percent, 50 percent, 15 percent), and then sum up the weighted values (e.g., 0.35 x $$$ + 0.50 x $$ + 0.15 x $).[26] The chapters to come put these remedial and other principles to the test through a number of real-life cases and controversies involving procreation deprived, imposed, and confounded.

PART III

TO ERR IS TOO HUMAN

This final part puts a human face on freezer failures, birth control mix-ups, and donor switches by analyzing scores of real-life cases. And it seeks to work out remedies for reproductive negligence that won't penalize specialists unfairly or restrict access to valuable services. Chapter 7 develops the tort of procreation deprived by showing how *not* getting a child can be a real and serious harm, and how the legal doctrines of lost-chance and harm-mitigation account for complicating facts like preexisting infertility and the availability of adoption. Chapter 8 defends the action for procreation imposed against objections that people can abort if they don't want to be parents, and that they offend basic decency when they claim that the children they have are more trouble than they're worth. Chapter 9 expounds the right of procreation confounded based on reasons for choosing offspring of particular types, and on the repercussions, however speculative, of having those efforts thwarted. Chapter 10 wrestles with thwarted selection for traits like disability and sex, resemblance and race, intelligence and perfect pitch. It also fine-tunes recovery to avoid routinizing trivial practices or championing troubling ones.

7

Procreation Deprived

And can it be that in a world so full and busy, the loss of one weak
creature makes a void in any heart, so wide and deep that nothing
but the width and depth of vast eternity can fill it up!
                            —Charles Dickens, *Dombey and Son* (1848)

The ubiquity of controversies over abortion and birth control makes it easy
to forget that professional negligence can also deny pregnancies that are very
much wanted. Sometimes, the medical specialists entrusted to help people
become parents render their sex cells unusable or reproductive capacities in-
operative. Fertility clinics have lost, destroyed, and contaminated the frozen
sperm,[1] eggs,[2] or embryos[3] that patients were counting on to have children.
Others have put one patient's embryos or sperm into another.[4] Physicians
have botched procedures that leave patients unable to conceive or gestate.[5]
They've also misadvised women to end the pregnancy they wanted to keep,
lest they risk a specious danger to their own health or that of the would-
have-been child they longed for.[6] Doctors have even misprescribed abortion pills to happily pregnant women, an error that pharmacists failed to
catch too.[7]

A couple of examples give a sense of the stakes. Cindy Baker and her
husband eagerly awaited the birth of their child. She was five months pregnant when an abnormal pap smear indicated perils of proceeding into the
last trimester. Her doctor ordered a biopsy to test for malignant cells in her
cervix. When the test came back from the lab, the doctor called Baker to
break the news: "Your pap smear came back Stage III. It's on the verge of
becoming invasive cancer." He told her that the only way to treat it was to
terminate the pregnancy "as soon as possible." He made the appointment
for her that week. Only after having the abortion did she learn that she was
healthy. Her tests had never indicated a greater threat of cancer. Her doctor
simply misread the results. Baker could have kept her pregnancy and had
the child she and her husband so desperately wanted without any special

Birth Rights and Wrongs. Dov Fox.
© Dov Fox 2019. Published 2019 by Oxford University Press.

risk to her own life or the baby's. She was haunted day and night with "panic attacks" and "feelings of suffocation" at the horror that she'd "had an abortion for no reason at all."[8]

Sarah Robertson married her high school sweetheart, Aaron. The couple decided they'd start a family after completing their degrees and buying a house. They were well on their way when a stroke landed Aaron in a coma that took his life at twenty-nine. Before he died, Robertson had his sperm extracted to cryopreserve his reproductive material, while she went back to school and saved up for the home. She set her heart on carrying out the plan they had made together. But when she was ready to have their child, the clinic informed her the vials were gone. They were her only chance to have a baby who would share her husband's genetics. Robertson's lawyer figured the facility never told her because it "believed she would never come back to use that sperm," that she'd probably "find someone else in her life to move on [] and start a family with." For Robertson's part, "[i]t's been heartbreaking . . . to lose your husband then have something like this happen. I still feel like I'm in a nightmare."[9]

Tort law usually compensates for intangible losses only if they're closely connected to material ones. But plaintiffs like Baker and Robertson can't point to any bodily harm or financial setback that's tied directly to the reproductive injury they've suffered. Claims for deprived procreation almost always fail because patients don't incur any property damage (eggs and embryos aren't considered property) or physical intrusion (aside from whatever medical procedure they freely agreed to). Besides, courts point out, even if fertility treatment goes as planned, patients might not have been able to conceive or carry a pregnancy to term anyway. And they can still adopt. Judges who don't dismiss these suits outright keep a tight rein on damage awards.

A. What Might Have Been

Shattered dreams of pregnancy and parenthood find little solicitude under American law. A couple identified as Jane and John Doe managed to create three embryos after several attempts at in vitro fertilization. To store them, their clinic used a solution that had been infected with a "fatal neurological disorder" that's "the human equivalent of . . . 'Mad Cow Disease.'" The manufacturer had previously sent the clinic a "Product Withdrawal Notice" advising customers to "immediately discontinue its use." But the clinic used the solution anyway, exposing all of the reproductive materials it touched, including the Does'. Yet the couple's claims were summarily dismissed. "[T]he loss of their embryos," the court explained, resulted in "neither personal nor property injuries" that "would entitle them to relief." The invasive IVF procedure was "an elective process" that the Does "chose to undergo" prior to the contamination. The court concluded that the Does had no valid negligence action because they could "prove no actionable physical harm or property damage resulting from Defendants' actions."[10]

Another court gave Cora Creed and her husband the same reason for rejecting their complaint against the clinic that negligently transferred their embryos into somebody else. IVF had required hormone drugs—some ingested, others injected—as well as surgery. But that "intrusion into the plaintiff wife's body to extract her ova was not a cause of the subsequent improper implanting" of their embryos "into the other woman." That error itself didn't physically harm Creed.[11] Our legal system fails to recognize reproductive suffering from which a plaintiff's body and bank account emerge unscathed. This failure stymies recovery for deprived procreation even in more egregious circumstances.

Glenda Ann Robinson's doctor tied her fallopian tubes without her knowledge while she was under anesthesia for a cesarean section. A 2001 Maryland court wouldn't entertain her claims for intentional battery or informed consent, and not just because there was a chance that the mistake could have been chalked up to a simple administrative mix-up. Even if negligence were to blame, the unwitting sterilization "was not harmful because it did not cause any additional physical pain, injury or illness other than that occasioned by the C-Section procedure" that she had already agreed to. The court also suggested that Robinson, an African American mother of six, didn't need any more kids. The court didn't care that "she and her husband were planning on having a seventh child" (three "born out-of-wedlock," it went out of its way to mention). The court concluded that denying Robinson the "ability to have a seventh child after previously giving birth to six children is hardly something which would offend a reasonable sense of personal dignity."[12]

These courts miss the centrality of procreation to aspiring parents and the magnitude of its wrongful deprivation. There isn't good evidence of how reproductive negligence specifically measures up against other serious adversities that people may face in their lives. But available surveys come close. Americans rate their inability to conceive or carry a child they want as no less devastating than divorce or diagnosis with a terminal illness.[13] It can be hard to define this sense of emptiness and alienation that negligence victims face when they're denied the children they want. Professors Dan Solove and Danielle Citron capture something similar to this loss in a metaphor they used to describe a very different injury—personal data breach. Having your sensitive or identifying information leaked and vulnerable to malicious use doesn't encroach on you in physical or economic ways, or at least it hasn't yet. But it still intrudes on your life like an unseen obstacle "in the middle of a crowded room."

> We may not be able to see an invisible object, but we see how everyone is bumping into it, how they are changing where they stand because of it, how they are walking different routes to avoid it, and so on. The object is invisible to the naked eye, but it is having a significant effect.[14]

Like data-breach victims who invest time and energy to protect against identity theft, patients deprived of procreation go to great lengths to secure a child. They exhaust savings. They endure prying queries, onerous appointments, and risky medical procedures. They make professional and personal plans around the parenthood they anticipate—they pick names, prepare nurseries, scout preschools. These efforts testify to the significance and sincerity of that reproductive interest. Professional negligence denies grieving individuals and couples a calling and intimacy whose value is impossible to substitute or at least very difficult to try to replace.

A couple of outlier courts have awarded limited recovery for negligent infliction of emotional distress by exempting plaintiffs who've been deprived of procreation from the usual physical injury requirement. Carolyn Witt and her husband planned to have a family together when she was diagnosed with breast cancer. Lifesaving radiation therapy would leave her infertile. So she had a doctor at Yale New Haven Hospital remove the ovarian tissue she'd need to have children and keep it safe until they were ready. But when that time came, they learned the hospital had "unilaterally discarded it without consulting or even notifying the Witts." The mistake "foreclose[d] the potential for the plaintiffs to ever conceive a child together." Even though that loss incurred no bodily injury, the court found the hospital liable for having "creat[ed] an unreasonable risk of causing emotional distress."[15] But only mental harm—that was it.

Another case involved two infertile couples, Rogers and Fasano, who were receiving treatment at the same clinic. They'd occasionally bump into each another there. The husbands, Robert Rogers and Richard Fasano, would exchange small talk while their wives, Deborah Rogers and Donna Fasano, were being treated for ovarian stimulation and egg retrieval. The women were scheduled for implantation on the same morning, but only Mrs. Fasano got pregnant. She ended up giving birth to two baby boys. One looked like the Fasanos, who are white; the other like the Rogerses, who are black. The Rogerses were awarded custody of their biological child, and sued the doctor. He had implanted one of their embryos in Mrs. Fasano, and another of theirs in some other patient the clinic couldn't identify.[16] The court awarded the Rogerses narrow damages for the "emotional harm caused by their having been deprived of the opportunity of experiencing pregnancy, prenatal bonding and the birth of their child," and for the fear "that the child that they wanted so desperately . . . might be born to someone else and that they might never know his or her fate." But the court took pains to restrict compensation to claims substantiated by medical affidavits about psychological treatment to address the toll the mix-up took on them.[17]

Victims should be entitled to recover for more than emotional distress. Facts and context can help distinguish more serious expressions of harm from lesser ones. An embryo switch that denies just pregnancy but not parenthood isn't as bad as an otherwise similar error that denies parenthood too. Shannon and Paul Morell's twin daughters were two and a half when the couple decided they wanted to give them a little brother or sister. They'd used IVF to conceive their twins, and had six embryos already in storage to have another child. But when they returned to the fertility clinic, the embryos were nowhere to be found. "We were totally powerless," Mrs. Morell said.[18] Not just that—the clinic had transferred them into another patient, Carolyn Savage. She and her husband, Sean, were devout Catholics who'd been trying to have a baby themselves. They decided not to abort or sue for custody after Mrs. Savage gave birth to the boy they called "Little Man." The Morells were beyond grateful to receive their biological child. But still, Mrs. Morell noted that "[a]ll the emotions a woman has during pregnancy to bond with her child I haven't had. I never felt the baby kick—none of that."[19] Carolyn's act of kindness left her with post-traumatic stress disorder. "That absent child is always with you, a loss you feel some days as yearning and other days in a gasp of pain."[20]

Permanent deprivations are likely to cause more acute harms than temporary reproductive setbacks. And psychology studies on the impact of infertility suggest that the inability to have a first child tends to cause greater heartache than missing out on an additional one.[21] It's not so different when professional negligence is to blame. In another context—disputes between former spouses about whether to use their frozen embryos—courts have already gauged the relative strength of reproductive interests based on whether the parties already have offspring or might yet be able to. In a 2012 Pennsylvania case, the former wife sought access to implant their cryopreserved embryos over the man's objection. The ex-couple hadn't reached any prior agreement about what should happen to the embryos in the event of divorce. So the court balanced their reproductive interests, concluding that hers—in favor of procreation—were more compelling under the circumstances. Not only was she childless. Her age (forty-four), health (cancer survivor), and marital status (single) meant that the embryos were "likely her only chance at genetic parenthood and her most reasonable chance for parenthood at all," given that adoption agencies prefer married couples.[22] In a similar 2017 Connecticut case, the one-time husband and wife again hadn't entered into any contract over how to dispose of the IVF embryo they'd created. This time, it was the woman who wanted the embryos destroyed, while the man wanted them implanted, in a surrogate. The court awarded the woman control over the embryos, in deference to the "life-long emotional and psychological repercussions" of having genetic parenthood foisted upon her. It reasoned that the man's existing biological children and potential to reproduce made his interest in the embryos weaker by comparison.[23] He "is already a father and is able to become a father to additional children, whether through natural procreation or further in vitro fertilization."[24]

Being deprived of procreation can also devastate people who have children already, or might still in the future. Hewing compensation levels too closely to family size undervalues the significance of parenthood for any child beyond the first. And it risks sanctioning injuries that disproportionately affect African Americans and Latinos, who are twice as likely as Caucasians or Asians to have four-plus children.[25] Courts also err when they deny damage awards for a negligently caused miscarriage, just because the couple conceived again, or are young and healthy enough that they still could.[26] A Louisiana judge explained that later-born offspring can't "take the place" of the stillborn child and may not diminish the enormity of that loss.[27] Medical accidents like these aren't as malicious as the eugenic programs of compulsory sterilization that states across the country had long maintained to keep unpopular groups from reproducing their kind. But it's not just that government misconduct is worse than private offenses, or that intentional wrongs are worse than negligent ones.

B. Preexisting Infertility

There's another glaring difference between losing an infertile couple's in vitro embryos and forcibly sterilizing a healthy twenty-something like Jack Skinner. He's the chicken-thief who challenged Oklahoma's mandate in the 1942 Supreme Court case described in Chapter 1.[28] Skinner's attorney noted that his client was a "red-blooded, virile young man." Skinner himself testified during trial that he hoped to "become an honest citizen, and marry and settle down and raise possibly a child or maybe two."[29] The vasectomy would have kept a man of his youth and vigor from having the offspring he was capable of having. But procreation is far from a sure thing for most fertility patients. Disease, accidents, cancer treatment, prenatal history, and passing years leave one in eight American couples today unable to conceive or gestate without the help of reproductive technology.[30] Those who struggle with fertility have modest prospects to get pregnant and carry a child to term even in the absence of professional misconduct. The severity of harm that's attributable to the defendant's negligence in these cases depends in part on the plaintiff's pre-injury chances of gestation or live birth, in the event that their treatment had gone just right.[31]

Reproductive health varies from couple to couple, person to person. Age and sex are the most salient factors. Male and female fertility diminish at different rates. Women's biological clocks tick faster. Their fixed number of eggs grow more fragile over time, increasing the risk of miscarriages or genetic anomalies for women who hold off on procreation until they're older, whether to focus on career, find a partner, or any other number of reasons.[32] In 2016, the Centers for Disease Control and Prevention reported that, for the first time, American women ages thirty to thirty-four gave birth at higher rates than women in their late twenties.[33] The take-home-baby rate for female fertility patients under thirty-three hovers around 30–40 percent.[34] At thirty-five or so, many "women confront a 'fertility cliff,' when the chances of becoming pregnant decline sharply as the[ir] eggs decrease in number and quality."[35] The average forty-year-old woman has a 5 percent chance of getting pregnant. By forty-five, her chances drop to one in a hundred.[36] A lost embryo or pregnancy might be that woman's last chance to conceive. Men typically have more time.

Male fertility doesn't decline as dramatically with age. Men replenish sperm throughout their lives, enabling biological offspring until later. Billy Joel, George Lucas, Steve Martin, and Robert De Niro all had kids in their sixties. The man in a different-sex relationship usually has a larger fertility window. That reproductive leeway won't make much difference to straight couples who are committed to conceiving with half of the genetic material from each partner, or else not at all. But a man's longer time horizon might temper the loss of deprived procreation for different-sex couples who are open to using donor eggs. Same with single or gay men for whom reproductive negligence denies the chance for a child in a one-off or potentially temporary way—not the destruction of a cancer patient's only pre-chemo sperm; rather, the loss of embryos that can be replaced, or the unsuccessful pregnancy that a surrogate can try again.[37] But for most victims of procreation deprived, it's not like taking a baby home was a safe bet. Their chances of reproducing were iffy, even before professional negligence rendered their materials or capacities unusable.

Badly behaving specialists shouldn't be liable for the infertility that patients already suffered from, or other reproductive complications they would have anyway, no matter what quality medical care they received. Probabilistic recovery offers a principled way to compute damages for the wrongful destruction of gametes or embryos under these circumstances. Suppose a couple's age and health gave them a 30 percent chance of live birth if the clinic hadn't dropped the tray containing their embryos; the error reduced that probability to 3 percent. Courts should start by coming up with some dollar figure that roughly captures the denial of all-but-guaranteed procreation—that is, if the couple had been young and virile like Jack Skinner when they created the embryos, but now couldn't make any more. To calculate awards for their actual, lower odds of pregnancy and parenthood before the embryo loss, discount that larger number by the three-in-ten chance that competent care would have given them to reproduce with their frozen embryos intact. Finally, take 90 percent of that discounted amount, since negligence still left them one-tenth of that chance they'd had either to conceive on their own or possibly to create another embryo with which to initiate a successful pregnancy. Say a jury valued the assurance of parenthood at $100,000. Thirty percent of that absolute loss would be $30,000, and nine-tenths of that then amounts to a final remedy of $27,000. That award would just be for the reproductive injury of procreation deprived. It wouldn't replace but add to whatever separate compensation may be due for out-of-pocket costs related to the failed procedure, the price of replacing it, or any associated medical or work expenses.

Plaintiffs in a case like this would need to show that the lost chance was not insignificant—that competent treatment would have given them a reasonable chance to reproduce. For some people—women over forty-four, or men of any age who have no working sperm count—their potential for biological children was already so low that even the most egregious mistake wouldn't make procreation much less likely than it was before.[38] In one of the cancer survivor cases from the last section, the court noted that Carolyn Witt and her husband would "not be entitled to recover" if her lost ovarian tissue had given them "no chance of success" anyway, at least assuming this should have been "known and understood by the plaintiffs."[39] That's the conclusion a Louisiana court reached in a 2011 case of shoddy obstetric treatment. Zsa Zsa Dunjee was a thirty-six-year-old diabetic woman with fibroid problems. Board-certified experts agreed that her doctor "deviated below the standard of care" by failing to postpone her fertility treatment until her diabetes was under control and her fallopian tubes were no longer infected. But the court found "no record facts to support the conjecture that . . . Ms. Dunjee would have been able to conceive" in her health at that age, even if her doctor hadn't forged ahead, and provided otherwise high-quality care. Since Dunjee "had no real chance of becoming pregnant" anyway, the court didn't hold the negligent doctor liable for that negligible and "speculative loss."[40]

That's not to say that her doctor shouldn't have lowered Dunjee's expectations by advising her that procreation was next to impossible. Feeding patients' unrealistic expectations about their reproductive outcomes isn't unusual. The former director of a leading fertility clinic recently divulged that many IVF programs "massag[e] the data" to feign "extraordinarily high rates of pregnancy even in women over 40."[41] Public outrage over inflated fertility clinic success rates brought federal and state regulation in the early 1990s. But it wasn't enforced. And by 1996, an American Medical Association report found that "deceptive advertising and insufficient informed consent" were rampant in assisted reproduction.[42] The report said that misrepresenting the likelihood of success violates moral obligations of informed consent—before proceeding with any procedure, a doctor must obtain the patient's go-ahead after disclosing the relevant side effects and alternatives. False promises of IVF success often omit pertinent facts about proposed care. But it's hard for patients to prove that they would have refused treatment if they'd been made aware of those facts.[43] And reproductive specialists are given a pass on informed consent by offering patients a cursory overview of forms to read rather than anything like a meaningful exchange.[44]

Some fertility patients get creative in their quest for legal relief after being misled. After seven failed IVF cycles, Jayne Karlin of New York sued her clinic for misrepresenting success rates and health risks under the state's laws against deceptive business practices and false advertising. She won, but only after an investigative report by the TV program *20/20* exposed the wildly exaggerated claims splashed across the clinic's promotional materials, broadcast advertisements, and seminar presentations.[45] And the damage awards for these consumer protection claims are trifling—the penalty is usually a small fine at most. Besides, claims for breach of informed consent requires proof of bodily injury from hidden side effects or foregone alternatives. That's why courts reject such suits where the harm from "undisclosed risks" relates "to the condition of pregnancy itself," as opposed to "the patient's physical integrity."[46] The action for deprived procreation remedies precisely that reproductive thwarting—for its own sake, independent of any more tangible loss.

C. The Adoption Option

There are more than 100,000 boys and girls in American foster care who want for families they can call theirs forever. This need raises hard questions about the right to recover for procreation deprived: Can't negligence victims who want a child just adopt one instead? Does this alternative path to parenthood diminish the injury of lost sperm, thawed embryos, or misdirected abortions? And if it does take the edge off of that reproductive injury, by how much? This section provides multilayered answers. In short: The availability of adoption doesn't negate this reproductive loss or the need for our laws to redress it. It's true that genetics and gestation don't make someone a parent in the full or most meaningful sense of what that role entails—love and support do. The U.S. Supreme Court has long adhered to an "understanding of 'family' [that] implies biological relationships, and most decisions treating the relation between parent and child have stressed this element."[47] But more recently, the Court has recognized that prenatal contributions in conception or pregnancy aren't necessarily enough to establish legal parentage if someone doesn't actually care for a child, or intend to, after birth.[48] That's why lower courts deny parental rights to men who help to conceive a child, but don't carry out the functional work of raising him.[49]

A parent is the adult with ultimate and enduring responsibility for ensuring a child is cared for. Most children in the United States today are still raised by the people who conceived (and gestated) them. Professor Charles Fried portrays parenthood as "a physical continuity which is also bound up with spiritual and moral continuity through our influence on our children."[50] This social role can also be performed just as well without any "physical continuity," and often is. Adults needn't beget or bear a biological relationship to sustain and promote a child's welfare and development. Philosopher Jean-Jacques Rousseau described children as both in-the-moment and on-the-way-up. This dual nature obligates parents, Rousseau said, to indulge childhood's "games, its pleasures, its amiable instinct," and at the same time to steer their child toward a fuller picture of what they consider a good life for him.[51] Nourishing the child's body and character in this way doesn't require shared DNA. Assuming that a couple cares for both of the kids they have, they aren't any "less" parents to the child they adopt than the one they conceive. That's not to say there aren't real differences between adoption and reproduction, with or without technological assistance.

Neither is open to everyone. Adoption is expensive, especially through private agencies. Some people are too poor to afford it. For others, their health, lifestyle, or impairment is disqualifying. There's a stubborn pattern of discrimination based on the age, class, disability, and marital status of aspiring parents. And even in straightforward cases, they may have to wait years to gain custody.[52] Then there's the "probing, intrusive, and humiliating" questions that people hoping to adopt must answer about their "sex life, contentment in marriage, and feelings for [their] parents."[53] For same-sex couples who have a child using IVF, surrogacy, or donor gametes, many states still require the nonbiological partner to navigate the adoption process in order to be named a legal parent—even though he's already parenting the child in every practical way, just as the couple had intended before the child was conceived. A 2016 federal court in Indiana observed that this requirement forces the partner "to undergo fingerprinting and a criminal background check," to "submit[] her driving record [and] financial profile" and to "write an autobiography and . . . parenting philosophy."[54] The invasive screening and crushing paperwork required to adopt doesn't merely reflect society's vested interest in the welfare of already existing children, as opposed to potential offspring who haven't been born yet. These bottlenecks also presume adoption's "inferiority to the biologic family," according to Professor Elizabeth Bartholet, and "proclaim the dangers allegedly inherent in raising children apart from their birth families."[55]

Parenting surveys and practices reveal that American adults strongly prefer having genetically related children to adoptive ones—indeed, this preference is so strong that many prospective parents say that adoption isn't even worth trying, or that it would be only if every other path to parenthood has been categorically exhausted.[56] Some evidence of that preference for assisted reproduction over adoption comes from research by Professors Glenn Cohen and Daniel Chen. Cohen and Chen looked at before-and-after rates of adoption in states that mandated insurance coverage for fertility treatment. If adoption were seen as an equally attractive way to form a family, we'd probably expect to see a trade-off with increased use of in vitro fertilization as IVF became less expensive, while adoption costs remained the same. The subsidies did attract more IVF in those jurisdictions, but no fewer adoptions. The researchers draw the implication that adoption never competed against IVF in the first place. They conclude that "[m]ore empirical work is needed to answer the question" of why those who wanted to be parents, but couldn't afford IVF before it was insured, didn't consider adoption an adequate substitute.[57] One reason might be that adoption doesn't give women who want it the adventure of carrying a child. One court has remarked that "being pregnant" facilitates an intimate "bond" between woman and fetus that makes procreation "a distinct experience from adoption."[58] That only assisted reproduction offers this experience of pregnancy doesn't chiefly explain why so many Americans prefer it to adoption, however. The allure of genetic affinity—and the social norms and expectations surrounding it—matters far more.

The most comprehensive study of U.S. attitudes about adoption revealed that a bare majority believes "adoptive parents receive the same amount of satisfaction from raising an adoptive child as from raising a biological child." Fully a quarter of respondents think that adoptive parents don't "love their children as much as they would have loved their biological children."[59] Some may think that adoptive parents "lack the presumed naturalness that characterizes the love felt by a 'real' parent for a child."[60] Whatever their reasons, many Americans perceive adoption as "not quite as good as having one's own" children.[61] Part of what many parents want in a child is the genetic connection that adoption can't provide.[62] The reason may be as mundane as yearning to witness similarities in their child's appearance or temperament.[63]

> Perhaps everybody who comes home from the hospital with a newborn looks for traits that show the child's pedigree. Certainly every grandparent who visits the next week clucks over some claimed resemblance, no matter how difficult it is for others to see.[64]

But the attraction of genetic ties goes beyond whatever satisfaction some family members get from being able to make out perceived likenesses in a new arrival—or even the control that parents or close relatives perceive over a child's inherited traits, or the pride they take in offspring qualities to which DNA is thought to contribute.

Biology assumes a much larger significance in American family life and law. Our legal system has long treated it as a presumptive basis (rivaled only by marriage) for determining inheritance, guardianship, and child support. Courts privileged "blood relations" over "adoptive ones" well into the twentieth century. That rendered adoption "a custody device more than a total transfer of family membership."[65] Shared genetics, gestation, and birth are still widely accepted to "legitimize the child as part of the family" and "construct the child's identity within" it.[66] The reasons people give for wanting genetic offspring include strengthening their "real" or "natural" connection to a future child.[67] This idea that shared biology naturalizes families builds on widely held conceptions of parenthood that prize common DNA over the social commitment, emotional connection, and the functional activities required to parent a child.[68]

Many religious and cultural communities credit genetic affinity as a social or psychological anchor from one generation to the next. Eastern European Jews are one. That sense of belonging explains the "drive to procreate" that consumed William Stern of the "Baby M" case. He was the father in that first American surrogacy dispute, which reached the New Jersey Supreme Court in 1988. Stern's wife, Elizabeth, suffered from multiple sclerosis that made pregnancy too risky. The couple passed on adoption in favor of a surrogate they found in a newspaper ad. Mary Beth Whitehead accepted $10,000 to be inseminated with Mr. Stern's sperm, carry the child to term, and relin-quish the child to the Sterns after she was born.[69] When she couldn't bring herself to part with the baby, the ensuing custody battle set off a national firestorm over the ethics and law of surrogacy. Mr. Stern's ancestral tie to the girl represented a cherished legacy for him, as the last Holocaust survivor in his family. "[M]aintaining the genetic line" would enable him "to ward off existential loneliness."[70] Stern's not the only one. A 2018 *New York Times* ar-ticle profiled childless Americans who can't "shake the feeling of being last one to turn the lights out."[71] Anthropologist Kaja Finkler explains: For those who believe that "DNA binds a person's past and future into a single family narrative," becoming a step- or adoptive parent can't satisfy a felt lineage, rooted in flesh and blood, that "reinforce[s] continuity" with one's forebear and "act[s] as a repository of memory for an individual's past, which may have been otherwise forgotten."[72]

Persisting disfavor of infertility may also help to explain part of the pref-erence for assisted reproduction over adoption. Infertility stigma may drive some different-sex couples to prefer IVF over donor services, or, if using a sperm or egg donor, to prefer one who shares a partner's coloring or build.[73] These couples may seek to improve the chances that their family will be able to "pass" as nuclear—"the child *as-if-begotten*, the parent[s] *as-if-genealogical.*" They may "not want the world—or the child—to know they used a sperm bank to conceive."[74] Same-sex couples aren't actually so different in this respect. It's true that gays and lesbians don't face the same expectations to reproduce or pressures to conceal fertility challenges. And whereas 90 percent of heterosexual men and women report "a strong de-sire for biological children," that compares with 40 percent of lesbians and 34 percent of gay men. Same-sex couples are also nearly three times as likely to raise an adopted or foster child.[75] But same-sex couples still prefer to share DNA with their children to the extent possible, opting for surro-gacy or donor insemination by wide margins over adoption.[76] To one les-bian couple, the choice was clear: "[W]e could have at least one of us in our children," or neither.[77] Many same-sex couples also choose a donor or sur-rogate who looks like the nongenetic parent, in hopes of enriching parent-child bonds or departing less from traditional norms of family formation. The presence and appearance of genetic affinity appeals to many same-sex couples too.[78]

8

Procreation Imposed

[W]e were alarmed with the fatal Signs of her being pregnant;
I purchased and gave her such Drugs as could cause Abortion, but in
vain, and she grew big.

—Penelope Aubin, *Lady Lucy* (1728)

Millions of Americans use reproductive medicine and technology to steer clear of gestation or childrearing. In *Roe v. Wade*, the U.S. Supreme Court justified a woman's right to terminate her pregnancy by reference to the far-reaching consequences "of bringing a child into a family already unable, psychologically and otherwise, to care for it."[1] Women or men may have any number of reasons for deciding that they can't, or don't want to, carry or raise a child—now or ever. A negligently failed abortion, birth control, or sterilization foists on them the very roles that they enlisted professional assistance to avoid. Tort law mislabels these medical mistakes under the actions for "wrongful birth" or "wrongful pregnancy." It's not the child or the fetus that's in any sense "wrongful," but rather the misconduct that's disrupted people's plans to rein in the size of their family. Frank judges admit that this existing taxonomy of procreation torts "more often serves to obscure the issues than to elucidate them."[2]

These cases are better divided in terms of *post-conception* errors that prevent people from ending an unwanted pregnancy, and *pre-conception* ones that force them into a pregnancy to begin with. Post-conception transgressions include unsuccessful abortions—through surgery or pills— and failures to diagnose the fact of an unwanted pregnancy until it is too late to safely or legally terminate it.[3] Pre-conception negligence involves botched sterilization and birth control: mistied tubes, misprescribed pills, misinserted rings, misinjected shots, and misapplied patches.[4] Imposed procreation is rarely as madcap as TV rom-com *Jane the Virgin*, in which the devout protagonist is accidentally inseminated, during a routine pap

Birth Rights and Wrongs. Dov Fox.
© Dov Fox 2019. Published 2019 by Oxford University Press.

smear, with the cryopreserved sperm of her cancer-surviving former crush.[5] But it can be.

There are several reported cases in which fertility clinics never asked or informed a man before implanting the frozen embryos that he and an estranged partner had created.[6] In a 2015 case, Joseph Pressil wasn't even told that his semen was used to make embryos in the first place. The Texas Court of Appeals explained that his former girlfriend Anetria Burnette had "surreptitiously collected samples of his sperm" from the condoms he had used to prevent conception while the two had been dating. Burnette told a local fertility clinic "that she was Pressil's wife and that the couple needed help conceiving a child. The clinic successfully inseminated Burnette, and Burnette eventually gave birth to healthy twin boys." Pressil sued the clinic for "failing to investigate and obtain [his] consent."[7] The question wasn't whether Burnette's interests in reproducing outweighed Pressil's against procreation. It's whether the clinic was liable for making Pressil an unwitting father, twice over. The court let the clinic off the hook, for the same reason that judges wave away most complaints that procreation's been imposed. It's not just that plaintiffs can't point to the requisite physical injury: "[N]o medical procedure was performed on Pressil," the court pointed out, while "Burnette['s] was apparently a rousing success." What's more, judges insist, is that someone like Pressil isn't really harmed at all by getting the very off-spring he'd sought to avoid. To the contrary, he should be grateful for the gift of life and good fortune of parenthood. Never mind that he didn't ask for or want it. The court held that Pressil "cannot recover damages" associated with any "healthy child born as a result of the medical provider's negligence . . . because the intangible benefits of parenthood far outweigh" the "burdens involved."[8]

A. Babies Are Blessings

Judicial decrees that every child "is presumed to be a blessing" date back to the Great Depression.[9] A 1934 Minnesota court was the first to dismiss a man's complaint about a failed vasectomy on the ground that he and his wife should greet their surprise arrival as a "blessed" event.[10] A Pennsylvania judge followed suit in 1957, in another botched vasectomy case. For the patient to designate "the normal birth of a normal child" as a legal harm, the judge reasoned, would be "foreign to the universal public sentiment of the people."[11] A slew of courts have since joined in their "unwillingness to hold that the birth of a normal healthy child can be judged to be an injury to the parents."[12] Even if being pregnant or giving birth endangers a woman's health, or if having a baby to raise keeps her from getting an education, pursuing a career, or supporting the children she already has—pregnancy and parenthood simply can't be bad for her life, these courts stand firm, not all things considered. The very suggestion, they maintain, "offends fundamental values attached to human life."[13]

Other courts try to shroud this article of faith in less moralistic objections. It's too hard to define the harm of an unplanned child, or to determine offsetting benefits, or to measure the corresponding dollar damages. Judges throw up their hands that it's simply too hard to predict the future or pin down such speculative losses. "Who can place a price tag on a child's smile," or "strike a pecuniary balance between the triumphs, the failures, the ambitions, the disappointments, the joys, the sorrows, the pride, the shame" that comes from raising a child who may "turn out to be loving, obedient and attentive, or hostile, unruly and callous"?[14] These grumbles call to mind judicial complaints from Chapter 4 that a convincing calculation of reproductive injuries would elude even "a jury collectively imbued with the wisdom of Solomon." And no one's saying it's easy to get a handle on such uncertain and incommensurable trade-offs. But these challenges aren't all that different from similar ones that courts manage to figure out and move on from all the time when they award damages for tentative losses like future income, or amorphous ones like pain and suffering. Yet courts routinely pander and defer to them in the context of procreation. District Judge Solomon Blatt, Jr. of South Carolina exposed these what-are-we-to-dos for what they really are. In a little-known 1981 ruling on deficient prenatal counseling, he called this coterie of gripes about the "ascertainment of damages" mere cover for the "thinly-disguised policy argument that the birth of a child [is] a 'blessed event,' the benefits of which would as a matter of law outweigh its burdens."[15]

That blessed assumption makes recovery for procreation imposed seem doubly unfair. First, it's unfair to defendants, who get punished for benefiting the plaintiffs. It's also unfair to those plaintiffs, who get rewarded with an undeserved windfall. If unplanned babies are boons, then compensating parents makes them "twice-blessed": They get to "tousle the hair of a well-loved child with one hand while [] cash[ing] support checks from the doctor with the other."[16] But these judicial dogmas about imposed procreation repudiate the plaintiff's moral agency to decide what's good for her own life. People have all sorts of reasons not to procreate. For some women, getting or staying pregnant would risk medical dangers or genetic disorders. For men and women alike, the prospect of having a child might stir up fears of recreating their own traumatic childhoods. Those who have kids already may lack the energy, resources, or desire to care for any more. Other people don't feel suited to take on the major, lifelong role of parent. Or they want to drive their career, lifestyle, or relationships in a direction that being responsible for kids would encroach on.[17]

It's specious and patronizing to think that any and every unsuspecting parent will come to be glad that professional misconduct rode roughshod over her decision to be sterilized or have an abortion.[18] Even if a negligence victim who had recoiled from motherhood now finds meaning or happiness in that role, this doesn't imply that her efforts to avoid procreation were misguided, or that her life wouldn't be better yet for her today, if the measures she adopted had worked how they should have to prevent or end pregnancy.[19] The distinction that Professor Carol Sanger draws between loss and regret helps to explain why a person's enjoyment of parenthood is nevertheless consistent with its negligent imposition having harmed her.

> Regret implies that one would have made a different decision at the time
> if only one had known (something). In contrast, loss rues not the decision
> but one or another aspect of its consequences. One experiences loss when
> one focuses specifically on the costs of a decision, costs that have been
> weighed against benefits or against the avoidance of even greater costs.
> Even if one thinks the decision is justified—even if one has no regrets
> about the decision—the costs that it involved don't cease to be costs, and
> they may well be experienced as a form of loss.[20]

A person whose values and circumstances led her to conclude that parenthood wasn't right for her may still of course find satisfaction in the baby she'd sought not to have. She might indeed already have taken these fulfillments into account, and decided that their sacrifice was justified in view of other considerations. Just because she might be expected to have felt some loss from a child's absence—loss that she may well have fully appreciated as part of a complex decision-making process—doesn't mean that she now regrets having sought sterilization or abortion in the first place, or that her life has been improved for having had that decision effectively thwarted.

By the same token, just because many men and women welcome parenthood or pregnancy as a gift doesn't mean that everyone should think of these roles that way, especially not those who undertook measures to keep their distance. The act of using birth control or terminating a pregnancy makes plain that negligence victims didn't want to have children, at least not at this time. They shouldn't be presumed better off for having that unwanted procreation foisted upon them, not even if they may yet want offspring later on, under different circumstances. One woman described the difference that such changes can make in a letter that abortion rights advocates included in a brief they submitted to the U.S. Supreme Court in the 1986 case of *Thornburgh v. American College of Obstetricians & Gynecologists*:

> Today I am a little more than two months pregnant. My husband and I are thrilled about it. Almost exactly a decade ago, however, I learned I was pregnant, and my response was diametrically opposite. I was sick in my heart. . . . It was as if I had been told my body had been invaded with cancer.[21]

Usually reliable efforts to avoid pregnancy and/or parenthood testify loud and clear to a person's considered judgment that not being pregnant and/or a parent would be good for her. To say she got it wrong—to insist she's better off for having procreation imposed against her will—isn't so different from saying that forced intercourse isn't rape just because people often enjoy sexual intimacy. Whether sex is wanted or not is precisely what differentiates that activity as legitimate, often gratifying—or intolerably criminal.[22] The wantedness of procreation marks a similar difference between its being presumptively good or bad for the person who experiences it.[23] And just as prosecuting rape doesn't disavow the value of consensual sex, nor does negligence liability for imposed procreation negate a baby's worth, deny his parents' love, or cast doubt on the profoundly positive meaning that pregnancy and parenthood can have for those who want it.

You have to go back some decades to another obscure case—this time a 1982 controversy involving botched sterilization—to find even a single American judge willing to call out the judicial gospel that babies are blessings. In *Boone v. Mullendore*, Justice James Faulkner of the Alabama Supreme Court penned a "specially concurring" opinion cautioning his colleagues not to confuse the sanctity of life with the joys of parenthood. He chided their "[p]ublic policy arguments" that "the value of human life . . . precludes any action for wrongful pregnancy." Such objections "often serve as a smokescreen hiding the true issue," he wrote. "The ultimate issue is whether a physician is liable for negligently failing to perform an operation or for negligently misrepresenting" its breakdown.[24] To be clear: The injury of imposed procreation isn't a baby's birth or a fetus's existence. Nor is that harm the fact that only women get pregnant, or that parenthood necessarily oppresses them. The loss lies in how professional misconduct foreseeably displaces a person's plans and prospects for a life without a fetus to carry or child to raise. Setbacks to a person's experiences, opportunities, and identity are less tangible than medical complications or financial bankruptcies. But these reproductive disruptions, disappointments, and disadvantages are no less real and serious, or wrongful and worthy of remedy.

Whatever led someone to enlist medicine or technology to avoid procreation, it shouldn't disqualify her from recovering if pregnancy or parenthood is negligently imposed. And yet more reliable or permanent methods of contraception might still, under some circumstances, signal graver losses of this kind. And certain reasons that people may have could also make that injury more severe, or less—can't afford dependents, loves independence, hates kids. That this sort of context might matter seemed obvious to a 1971 Michigan court that asked: Doesn't "the unwed college student who becomes pregnant due to a pharmacist's failure to fill properly her prescription for oral contraceptives" suffer "far greater damage than the young newlywed who, although her pregnancy arose from the same sort of negligence, had planned the use of contraceptives only temporarily, say, while she and her husband took an extended honeymoon trip?"[25] But other courts have criticized purpose-based approaches to assessing the severity of reproductive harm. They say that it "encourages after-the-fact reformulations of the parents' actual intentions" and demands too much of "the jury in sorting out the parents' differing motivations."[26] This risk of ambiguous or fabricated aims is easy enough to address, though: just require that plaintiffs substantiate whatever reasons they give by clear evidence and contemporary corroboration. Other factors affecting injury severity are more readily apparent: The harm of impose procreation is less acute when compelled gestation doesn't also leave victims with a child to raise. Miscarriage, stillbirth, or abortion can cut a pregnancy or newborn life short. Those who do give birth could also opt for adoption.

Negligence victims who do end up with a child to raise should also be entitled to economic damages that respond to more than just the intangible harms associated with unwanted pregnancy and parenthood. Caring for a child incurs considerable economic expenses. Yet most states deny relief for childrearing outright, or limit such recourse to the medical expenses and lost wages related to gestation, labor, and delivery.[27] Just four state fully redress basic expenses for a child's food, clothing, health care, and education—and only one of these provides remedies for anything else.[28] Some courts try to split the difference by appeal to an eighty-year-old tort doctrine that eschews all-or-nothing awards.[29] It works by taking the compensation level for whatever harms the misconduct caused, and reducing that total by the value of any countervailing benefits. This "benefit-offset rule" mitigates damages "[w]here the defendant's tortious conduct" at the same time "conferred upon the plaintiff a special benefit."[30]

Not just any kind of simultaneous benefit will do—the claimed benefit must lift up the same sort of interest that the injury brings down. This same-interest condition keeps the benefit-offset rule from depreciating one kind of interest, such as financial security, based on benefits to a different sort of interest, like the intimate rewards of parenting. Under this rule, out-of-pocket expenses to raise a child could be balanced against his anticipated help in the family business to the extent that it reduced labor expenses. But courts err by offsetting economic costs by emotional gains: The "fun [that] parents will have in raising their child will not enable them to purchase diapers or formula," and "hospitals who provide medical care to the child will not accept the parents' pride in the child as payment."[31] Successful claims for procreation imposed would entitle plaintiffs to recover whatever costs of childcare foreseeably result from a defendant's misconduct. In most cases, those costs can be reasonably approximated using the most recent government estimates of average spending on a healthy child in the United States—the 2017 figure was $233,610.[32]

But negligently failed birth control or abortion can also result in offspring with special needs, some of which cost money for plaintiff-parents to meet, potentially a lot. Damage awards shouldn't cover those needs unless there's good reason for the defendant professional to have expected them. Olga LaPoint's doctor botched her tubal ligation. At the time of that surgery, there was no way to predict that Ms. LaPoint would give birth to a son with an umbilical hernia—an unclosed opening in the baby's abdominal muscle after his umbilical cord passes through it. The court explained that "the only foreseeable consequence" of the negligent sterilization procedure was "a subsequently induced pregnancy," not the complication leading up to childbirth.[33] Another sterilization plaintiff, Alice Williams had a son born with "congenital hyperactivity disorder," which causes learning disabilities and can require special psychological and educational care. The obstetrician who fouled up the operation knew that Mrs. Williams had previously had a child with the disorder. But Mrs. Williams never told the doctor that's why she and her husband didn't want any more kids. Nor did her medical history make it likely that a subsequent child would also have the disorder anyway. The court refused to treat its incidence as a compensably "foreseeable consequence of the defendants' negligence."[34]

In other cases of imposed procreation, foreseeability warrants redressing the full cost of caring for a child's special needs. Cynthia and Kenneth Williams informed her OB/GYN that they both carried the sickle cell trait, a fact they'd learned after their first child, a boy, had been born with that very serious blood disorder. So the couple was familiar with the pain and peril the anemia brings. This Mrs. Williams underwent a tubal ligation in order to avoid having another child who'd have to endure what their son had—and they made clear to "the doctor performing the procedure" that they were seeking permanent birth control "precisely for that reason."[35] But the surgeon left one of her fallopian tubes open, and she gave birth to a daughter afflicted by the very same condition. Here, the court allowed the parents to "assert a claim for the extraordinary costs they will incur in raising their child." It was altogether predictable that the failed operation would incur far more than standard childcare expenses. The girl's special needs for hospital stays, doctor's visits, and educational accommodations were a "foreseeable consequence of the negligently performed sterilization."[36] Dozens of similar cases have involved the negligent failure to diagnose a disease like rubella that's known to pass along from a pregnant woman to her child.[37] Judges again worry about misjudging costs that will vary wildly, this time based on unknown outcomes, available treatments, and insurance coverage. One way that courts can rein in such under- or overestimates is to establish a reversionary trust or supervised guardianship that disburses funds (only) as plaintiffs pay for applicable costs of their child's care—with anything left over returned to the defendant.[38]

Imposed procreation can also be more serious if a badly behaving professional knew that birth control was sought because a family was unable to support additional children. Varonica Jackson and her husband were working-class parents of three, already treading water when her doctor's negligence handed them another baby. He failed to replace her contraceptive intrauterine device (IUD), as he had assured her he would, after having to remove it during ovarian cyst surgery. The time, money, and attention required to raise the resulting child took a heavy toll on their marriage and ability to care for their existing brood.[39] A higher-tech version of this overload problem befell Patricia and Peter Thompson. They didn't have any kids yet, but wanted to start a family—a small one—and made it clear to their fertility doctor that they wanted just a single child. Two at most, but no more. The doctor nonetheless implanted three embryos at once. The couple didn't find out until after the procedure that left them with triplets. They love their children dearly, Mrs. Thompson explained, "but the effort of looking after three children rather than the maximum of two we had planned is absolutely exhausting and stretches our physical resources."[40]

B. Accidents Happen

Even when there's no disputing that the reproductive injury is serious, courts must also determine whether professional misconduct is what caused procreation to be imposed. Defective birth control, botched sterilizations, and extra embryo transfers can't guarantee that sperm would fertilize, that an embryo would implant, or that a fetus would develop to birth. Even vasectomies and abortions aren't foolproof.[41] Done right, however, they're highly reliable at preventing or terminating pregnancy. The half of all pregnancies that are unplanned usually don't involve contraception. Effective rates are more than 99 percent for vasectomies, IUDs, and surgical abortions, and roughly 95 percent for condoms, oral contraceptives, and medical abortion by pill. When negligence makes these measures futile, it's foreseeable that the sexually active people who rely on them will end up with a fetus or baby. For vasectomies and tubal ligations, medical records will usually give plaintiffs enough evidence to pin unplanned conception or childbirth on provable transgressions. But sometimes it's harder to determine what imposed procreation, and whether negligence was a more significant cause than anything else.

One hundred thirteen women in twenty-six states sued for unplanned pregnancies in 2015, after a birth control manufacturer disclosed packaging errors. The packages are supposed to distinguish certain-color rows of active pills that women take while they're ovulating from different-colored rows of placebos when they're not. The faulty packs switched the rows, dramatically reducing the drug's efficacy at preventing pregnancy. The pharmaceutical that makes the pills copped to its mistake in a product recall of 3.2 million mislabeled packages. Similar errors had led to previous nationwide recalls of birth control pills in 2011 and 2018.[42] It's highly plausible that the packaging defect is what caused the affected women to get pregnant. But it's also possible that they didn't take the pills as directed. And it's only fair to hold defendants liable for whatever portion of the reproductive injury their negligence caused, or the corresponding chance that their misconduct is to blame for causing it. This relative ascription of liability poses hard questions of fact and analysis that vary across particular controversies. What's clear is that courts shouldn't dismiss complaints either, provided that plaintiffs can show—as in the pill pack cases—that negligence increased the chances of unwanted procreation by a non-insignificant degree. This causation condition sets a low bar for claims of procreation imposed to proceed.

Uncertainty about the role of negligence in causing pregnancy can also matter for another dimension of this legal right that has nothing to do with the threshold for plaintiffs to file suit. That uncertainty may also affect how much defendants should pay. Consider a twist on a 1989 case, in which a Catholic hospital withheld Plan B from a rape victim. Nor did it inform her that the drug gives a smaller chance of stopping pregnancy as time passes after intercourse, and isn't expected to work beyond three days out.[43] In this variation, a woman visits a drugstore for the morning-after pill two days after having unprotected sex. A pharmacist's oversight delays her access by *another* couple of days, now putting her beyond the window during which the intervention is effective. The woman gets pregnant and gives birth. The pharmacist-caused delay made unwanted procreation more likely. But he wasn't responsible for the initial delay in making to the pharmacy in the first place. The woman didn't get there until two days after intercourse, at which point the drug already would have lost some of its efficacy. It's still possible that she might have gotten pregnant even in the absence of any wrongdoing—if she had received the drug right when she asked for it.

Numbers illustrate. Suppose competent provision of the drug would have given her a 60 percent probability of avoiding unwanted pregnancy. Negligently postponed access reduced that chance to 15 percent. The non-insignificant chance that misconduct was responsible calls for a remedy. But damages should be less than they otherwise might have been based simply on the absolute injury of impose procreation. Proportional compensation should account for two facts. First is the 60 percent chance she had to prevent pregnancy after the initial forty-eight-hour deferral, prior to any wrongdoing. Then there's the 15 percent odds of protection that the pill still afforded her even after the four days. Probabilistic recovery would reduce the award for the absolute injury of imposed procreation by that 75 percent loss of chance—from 60 percent down to 15 percent—to avoid unwanted procreation.

How serious any reproductive injury is depends on individual facts about its extent and duration under the circumstances. The few precedents that exist to give a sense of possible dollar amounts all come from outside the United States. A 2004 British case involved a failed sterilization resulting in childbirth. The physician conceded negligence. The plaintiff was a single woman who'd had her tubes tied out of concern that she couldn't care for a child without a partner. The U.K. Supreme Court ordered the doctor to pay her, but didn't detail how it arrived at the amount of £15,000 (about $18,000).[44] That figure seems awfully low, but let's go with it as a measure of reproductive harm for the sake of the Plan B hypothetical. Proportional recovery would in that case yield one-quarter of that total, or $4,500. Uncertainty about the causal role of misconduct would not, however, render imposed procreation noncompensable—not unless, that is, the pharmacist could prove that user error in taking the pills, or some other factor other than professional negligence was responsible for the woman's getting pregnant and becoming a parent against her will.

C. The Duty to Abort

There are things that negligence victims can do to keep pregnancy from resulting in birth, or to keep birth from resulting in parenthood. Courts have accordingly asked whether "parents who seek to recover for the birth of an unwanted child" must seek to "avoid[] the consequences of a negligently performed" sterilization or pregnancy diagnosis by having an abortion or putting the child up for adoption.[45] Why should a doctor or pharmacist have to pay for their patient to raise their own child, when that patient could have avoided that outcome by ending her pregnancy or giving up legal responsibility for the child after birth? Some judges reason that the "decision to forego the option of releasing the child for adoption constitutes most persuasive evidence that the parents consider the benefit of retaining the child to outweigh the economic costs of child rearing."[46] Others say that a plaintiff's "failure to avail herself" of abortion "should operate to bar her present claim for damages."[47]

The "duty to mitigate," as it's called in tort law, requires injured parties to undertake practical efforts to limit whatever damages they sustain. This mitigation duty denies victims compensation for any spin-off harms they could have avoided through reasonable post-injury measures. The question under the tort duty to mitigate is whether abortion or adoption is reasonable to expect of negligence victims before allowing them to recover for damages associated with imposed parenthood? It's up to a woman to decide whether or not she stays pregnant—setting aside, for the moment, the miscellany of legal, financial, religious, social, and practical pressures that can limit access to abortion. Some judges think that a woman's formal ability to prevent a would-be child's birth, or to relinquish responsibility for the child's care, counteracts any unwanted parenthood that reproductive negligence would otherwise exact. Courts have accordingly denied damages for imposed procreation when "adoption or abortion would clearly mitigate the expense of raising the child" after a "negligent sterilization."[48]

This application of the duty to mitigate takes a woman's power to abort or surrender for adoption all out of context. Abortion and adoption aren't just ways of avoiding parenthood. Besides their economic costs, physical intrusions, and bureaucratic inconveniences, decisions to terminate a pregnancy or parental rights impose social pressure and stigma in a gendered, pronatalist culture that prefers women to have and raise any child conceived. Even if a woman "decides against motherhood" by having an abortion or putting a child up for adoption, "she must bear the moral [and] pragmatic [] weight of making that decision" to end a relationship "to her fetus" or "to the child that it [has already] become."[49] And just because a person tried to get sterilized or use birth control to prevent pregnancy doesn't mean that she would be comfortable ending it if she nevertheless conceived. She might have special moral or religious objections to abortion, even if she doesn't toward contraception.

Carmen Martinez was a devout Catholic who regarded abortion as a sin "except under exceptional circumstances." She and her husband eagerly awaited the arrival of their fifth child. But her doctor recommended abortion. He informed her that a medication she'd been taking when the couple conceived critically risked that their "baby would be born with the congenital birth defect of microcephaly (small brain) or anencephaly (no brain)."[50]

When Martinez balked at the prospect of terminating her pregnancy, her doctor pressed:

> I don't think you realize how serious this is . . . the baby would need machines to do what the brain couldn't do, would probably need machines to breathe, that it would have to be fed intravenously, that this baby was never going to leave the hospital, that the baby would be another Karen Quinlan.[51]

Quinlan was the woman at the center of the landmark right-to-die case decided a few years prior—irreversible brain damage had left her in a persistent vegetative state.[52] Martinez decided to abort. Two days later, her the doctor learned that he'd gravely overstated the risk of fetal abnormality—by a factor of 2000. It turned out there was no reason to think that her baby wouldn't have been perfectly healthy. A fetal autopsy confirmed it. Martinez was "in a complete state of shock" for over a year after "being misinformed that her fetus was hopelessly malformed and that an abortion [had not been] necessary." According to court documents, she "couldn't function well at all" and "didn't want to go anywhere" or "enjoy doing anything anymore." The feeling that Martinez had killed her own baby racked her with guilt and "completely ruined her life."[53] The court held the doctor liable, but only for "the psychological injury directly caused by her agreeing to an act which, as the jury found, was contrary to her firmly held beliefs" and "deepseated convictions" about abortion.[54]

Any decision to end a pregnancy or give up a child is a grave one. As a Wisconsin court recognized, compelling parents to "choose between the child and the cause of action" forces a woman who's already been made unwillingly pregnant into a choice that's far from free. That choice traps her between two options, one more emotionally freighted and socially pressurized than the next.[55] As Professor Reva Siegel explains:

> Hypothetically, a woman compelled to bear a child she does not want could give it up for adoption, abandon it, or pay someone else to care for the child until maturity. In this society, however, few women are able to abandon a child born of their body. . . . Once compelled to bear a child against their wishes, most women will feel obligated to raise it.[56]

Insisting that negligence victims cut off ties with a fetus or child as a condition of recovery disrespects their interest in making reproductive decisions for themselves. Forcing their hand yet again only exacerbates that injury to such a meaningful part of their lives that specialists had previously given them legitimate reason to expect. Raising the unplanned child may be worse for them than the childless future they'd hoped for—but abortion or adoption may be worse than either of those. The mitigation duty requires only that tort plaintiffs act reasonably, not that they be forced into that Sophie's Choice to qualify for damages. Most courts agree that abortion and adoption "are so extreme as to be unreasonable" prerequisites for relief.[57] Nor do decisions to continue an unintended pregnancy, or to keep a resulting child, make imposed parenthood harmless or break its causal connection to negligence. It's unreasonable to condition recovery on the expectation that a woman extinguish the fetus inside her or relinquish care of the child she gave birth to. Plaintiffs shouldn't be denied the compensation they're entitled to just because they exercise their protected liberties to decline abortion or adoption. A 2012 Pennsylvania court gestures in the right direction.

Natalie Catlin was a mother of two who suffered from a blood-clotting disorder. Giving birth before nearly killed her—her first delivery caused dangerous levels of bleeding, and the second required a blood transfusion to save her life. Catlin's doctor recommended a postpartum tubal ligation to prevent future birthing complications. She agreed to the sterilization, but his negligence rendered it ineffective. He didn't use "the more secure and safer surgical procedure" on her left fallopian tube that had been necessary to close her right one—a less reliable technique had failed on the left one too, but without the extra precaution. When Catlin got pregnant again the following year, she opted to terminate rather than face the life-threatening risks that childbirth would have posed. The abortion alone caused her massive hemorrhaging and multiple transfusions. A total hysterectomy was ultimately required to remove her uterus, ovaries, and fallopian tubes.[58] The court didn't deny that her doctor's negligence had caused Catlin a cognizable reproductive harm just because "there was no birth." The court did well to affirm that victims "must be compensated for all that they lose and all that they suffer from the tort of another"—but not for any harm that wasn't sustained or foreseeable. "In awarding damages for past or future non-economic loss," the court instructed the jury to consider all relevant factors bearing on her frustrated interests in choosing against unwanted pregnancy.[59]

9

Procreation Confounded

The best laid plans of mice and men oft go astray.
—Robert Burns, "To a Mouse," in *Complete Poetical Works* (1897)

The third category of reproductive activity is the least familiar and most controversial. These cases involve reproductive patients who wanted a baby, and got one—except that negligence resulted in the baby's being born with traits that his or her parents had selected to be different. The prospective parents wanted a child, yes, but not just any child—they were trying for one of a particular type. Most often, infertile couples are looking for a child to be either genetically related to them, or free of some disease that they risk passing on. Some are trying to have a girl or boy; others, a child who looks like them. They carefully review donor profiles or genetic screens that let them learn certain information about potential offspring. And they use that information to decide which eggs, embryos, or fetuses to fertilize, implant, or carry to term. But professionals misdiagnose, misrepresent, or switch their reproductive cells or entities. These errors lead the patients to initiate, continue, or terminate pregnancies in ways that thwart their efforts to have a child of one kind or another. Examples of confounded procreation abound in case reporters and news headlines.[1]

Nancy and Thomas Andrews of New York were struggling to "have a child who would be biologically their own." A 2007 court described Mr. Andrews as Caucasian, and Mrs. Andrews as Dominican, with "skin coloration and facial characteristics typical of that region." The couple used IVF so they could combine his sperm with her eggs before having the resulting embryo implanted in Mrs. Andrews. The pregnancy was a success, but when their baby girl was born, the couple noticed that her skin was much darker than theirs, with "facial and hair characteristics more typical of African, or African-American descent." When Mrs. Andrews confronted the clinic about this apparent discrepancy, the doctor assured her that their baby girl

Birth Rights and Wrongs. Dov Fox.
© Dov Fox 2019. Published 2019 by Oxford University Press.

would "get lighter over time." But they were skeptical, so they had her DNA tested: no match to Mr. Andrews. The court had little trouble concluding the clinic had "negligently used someone else's sperm to fertilize [her] eggs." Mrs. Andrews insisted that "[w]hile we love [our daughter] as our own, we are reminded of this terrible mistake each and every time we look at her; it is simply impossible to ignore."[2]

The court dismissed their complaint, "unable to hold that the birth of an unwanted but otherwise healthy and normal child constitutes an injury to the child's parents." It was unwilling "to adopt a rule, the primary effect of which is to encourage, indeed reward, the parents' disparagement or outright denial of the value of their child's life." This concern that recovery implies parental rejection is what dooms most claims against negligence that frustrate efforts to select offspring traits. Judges worry that compensating parents would insult their child, and disfigure the love between them. The only harm the *Andrews* court would entertain damages for was the anxiety associated with not knowing what became of Mr. Andrews' sperm. Having disposed of the case on these race-neutral terms, the court made no mention of the couple's complaint that the clinic's negligence had "forced [them] to raise a child who is not even the same race, nationality, color."[3] This chapter sets forth the metes and bounds of the tort action for procreation confounded. The next one takes up policy objections to redressing reproductive injuries in cases like this.

A. Reasons and Results

Foiled offspring selection can yield more or less serious harms, depending on its foreseeable impact on people's lives. Injury severity is an objective inquiry that begins by asking what kind of child the plaintiffs wanted and why. Did they pursue IVF in order to continue a bloodline with special significance? Had they screened embryos to avoid a disorder they risked passing on? Was their goal to have a girl with mom's red hair or a boy who's tall like dad? Or did they hope to share a physical resemblance or cultural identity by choosing a sperm donor advertised with those same characteristics? Some offspring preferences may be inferred, even if they're not made explicit. One New York court found it "difficult to conceive that parents, concerned about whether the egg donor had freckles and with the size of her eyes and ears, would not have expected full disclosure of information regarding whether she carried" a debilitating disease.[4]

But different people may be looking for different traits in their offspring. Many want children with their own DNA, but some opt for a sperm or egg donor in order to avoid the health risks nested in their genes. Most prospective parents who use prenatal testing try to screen against salient medical conditions, but a few choose in favor of the deafness or dwarfism that parents themselves share. Bioethicists Stephanie Chen and David Wasserman give another example:

> Some older couples might well find the prospect of raising a child with a severe intellectual disability but a normal life expectancy more burden-some than raising a child with no intellectual impairments but a much shorter life expectancy. They would regard their inability to make adequate provisions for that child when it became an orphaned adult as a failure to fulfill their parental duties. Younger couples might have the reverse prefer-ence, confident that at least one of them would live long enough to make secure arrangements for a child with severe intellectual disabilities, but re-garding the near certainty of outliving their child as unacceptable.[5]

So the diverse values and circumstances that patients bring to the repro-ductive process can shape their prenatal preferences. Of course it's hard to predict how offspring will turn out. Even conditions that can be detected before birth often manifest themselves in ways that can't be known until much later. People on the autism spectrum range from high functioning to low. Cystic fibrosis confines some individuals to a wheelchair or even the hospital, while others stay active and play sports. A person with Down syndrome "may be profoundly mentally retarded and severely restricted in motor functioning," or fully "capable of meaningful employment, relationships, and community engagement."[6] The variable expression of such conditions ratchets up the guesswork to forecast how a defendant's negligence that thwarted their prenatal selection can be expected to affect the plaintiff's lives.

But all this uncertainty—and that's just the beginning—needn't keep courts from assessing how serious confounded procreation is in particular cases. Just because any such determination is bound to admit of some ar-bitrariness doesn't mean that injury severity can't be worked out in a rea-sonable and systematic way. For health conditions, courts should start with the foreseeable range of implications for offspring lifespan, impairment, medical care, and treatment options. How long does a person with the condition usually live? In what ways does it tend to impair the body or mind? What kind of medical care does living with the condition typically require? To what extent is therapy likely to mitigate its hardships? What are the practical impacts of pursuing that intervention? The answers to these questions will vary case to case, based on the specific facts in each. But a few generalizations are possible about the sorts of answers that usually make confounded procreation more severe, or less.

The reproductive injury will tend to be less serious for conditions whose symptoms are milder, treatable, and uncertain to manifest—or virtually certain to, but only later in life. That injury will be more serious when misconduct results in a child's being born with an incapacitating or life-threatening ailment. At one extreme lies degenerative, untreatable conditions that limit a child's ability to function or participate in family life. One state justice—dissenting from an Illinois Supreme Court dismissal of claims for negligent fetal testing—detailed the suffering a child can expect if he's born with a fatal nervous-system disorder like Tay-Sachs.

> Between 12 and 24 months the child becomes blind, experiences petit mal seizures lasting for several seconds, is unable to eat because of the deterioration of his respiratory and digestive systems, and loses muscle strength. By the beginning of the third year, the child is blind, retarded, deaf, and completely paralyzed. By 40 months, most Tay-Sachs children will die of infections.[7]

The corresponding challenges a Tay-Sachs diagnosis poses for parents are predictably crushing. Less ruthless conditions may still impair a child's learning, vision, hearing, or mobility, or demand agonizing medical interventions and lifestyle modifications. Lab technicians in Virginia missed a positive fetal test for Cooley's anemia, a life-threatening disorder requiring "frequent hospitalizations" for "extensive, lifelong blood transfusions" that cause "excruciating pain."[8] Florida doctors failed to catch a couple's carrier status for a brain-damaging condition that makes their child eat through a tube and prevents him from "being able to live on his own or function in society without constant care."[9] In Alaska, OB/GYNs overlooked a spinal cord defect in utero that led a boy to be born without his right leg, testicle, or kidney, and with a fluid buildup in his brain that took his life early and "required a colostomy bag for all six of those years."[10]

Not every medical condition so consumes and ravages families. Children born with Marfan syndrome can't be cured. The curved spine and heart murmurs common among people with Marfan can impair their activities. The connective-tissue disorder can also shorten the lives of those affected. But the forty years they live on average are often altogether normal and rewarding. Other incurable disorders like phenylketonuria (PKU) cause learning and behavior problems, plus a risk of seizures and even brain damage. But these symptoms and complications can be largely relieved, but only if people with PKU follow a strict diet that limits protein intake. Then there are genetic susceptibilities for cancers of the colon, prostate, or breast that can cut life short—or never manifest at all. Neurodegenerative diseases like Huntington's or Alzheimer's are ultimately fatal, but their symptoms usually don't appear until adulthood.[11] The injury of confounded procreation will typically be a great deal weaker for skin-deep or nonmedical traits, as when reproductive negligence frustrates efforts to choose an egg donor who isn't short, colorblind, or nearsighted—or a sperm donor without a big nose, male-pattern baldness, or "bat" ears that stick out to the side. These are characteristics that don't usually impede normal functioning, obstruct basic capacities, or require medical treatment.[12] Most incur modest or negligible harms at best. Plaintiffs who sue for their negligently thwarted selection would have a chance to rebut this presumption of lesser injury and lower damages. But they'd have to substantiate their reasons for choosing that particular trait and the uncommon harm that the mix-up wreaked on their lives.

B. Unconditional Love

Defendants ask what plaintiffs are complaining about—they wanted a child and got one. They came to the fertility clinic, sperm bank, or surrogacy agency asking for help having a baby. Though these services were carried out negligently, they're also what made it possible for them to be parents at all. What does it matter that the particular traits weren't exactly what they had in mind? Won't their lives be enriched by this child's presence in it anyway? Professor Carol Sanger argues along these lines that the perceived "loss of control" over procreation can often shade into "acceptance" of the reproductive fate that people are dealt.[13] Not always, but sometimes, even often. If so, defendants argue, how can plaintiffs claim to have been harmed in any real way by the very (mis)conduct that made them the parents they had wanted to become?

Parents may indeed derive profound satisfaction from raising a child whose features were unexpected and unfamiliar to them. A striking depiction emerges from author Andrew Solomon's *Far from the Tree*. Solomon paints a portrait of three hundred families whose children "are deaf or dwarfs; they have Down syndrome, autism, schizophrenia or multiple severe disabilities; they are prodigies [or] transgender." His book bears witness to the varied evolutions that bring parents "to tolerate, accept and finally celebrate children who are not what they originally had in mind." Solomon reveals how these parents find themselves "falling in love with someone they didn't yet know enough to want," ultimately grateful for the very experiences they once would have given anything to prevent.[14] But the undeniable tenacity of parental love doesn't diminish the legitimacy of reproductive interests in offspring selection, or the loss that their frustration can incur to life plans, outcomes, and identities. Solomon doesn't spare readers the episodic despair, isolation, and indignation of even the most big-hearted and resilient parents. And our law doesn't ordinarily condition recourse for wrongfully inflicted adversities on whether injured parties abide them. Nor should it immunize blameworthy defendants from liability just because plaintiffs tough it out or find consolation in how things turned out in the end. That parents often come to value a relationship that's not what they'd hoped for doesn't make confounded procreation harmless.

And this loss might be more serious still if the whole point of embryo screening or fetal testing is to decide whether to reproduce or not. Some patients—often those at risk of passing along a dire condition—are explicit with their doctor or specialist that the only way they want to have a child is if he or she would be born condition-free. These are patients who, if it weren't possible to have a healthy child, would have taken measures to avoid procreation altogether. The negligence victim in one Virginia Supreme Court case said there's no amount of money, indeed "nothing on this earth that would have made me have a baby with Tay Sachs Disease."[15] For her, any presumed benefits from getting to raise her child may be unwanted indeed. Reducing whatever compensation she's due for the sake of that benefit would make her pay for the very outcome that she'd sought to avoid. But for many, similar victims, confounded procreation was incidental to their decision to reproduce. The child they didn't anticipate getting still provides them with most of the parenting experience they'd hoped for when they set out to reproduce. Unmitigated damages would unjustly enrich them.[16]

The benefit-offset rule discussed in the last chapter was designed to address that very kind of circumstance. This is the tort doctrine that reduces dollar awards by however much a plaintiff's wrongfully inflicted injury ends up simultaneously benefiting her in a relevantly similar way. Recall the rule's same-interest limitation that emotional bright sides not play down the economic expenses required to treat a child's condition. That limitation means that any intangible or symbolic value associated with childrearing can't be taken to eclipse the financial cost of defeated selection interests. Instead, courts must weigh interest-specific costs and benefits using the best evidence available. A Maryland appeals court advised that this balancing inquiry might account for "family size and income, age of the parents and other relevant factors in determining the extent to which" confounded procreation nonetheless "represents a benefit to the parents."[17]

Some judges worry that after-the-fact viewpoints or incentives could skew parents' impressions of the costs and benefits associated with their child having been born one way rather than another. But a District of Columbia Circuit court was ready with a response: Parents' provable reasons for having chosen this or that trait in the first place may lend more reliable insight into the relative costs and benefits that some reproductive outcome can be expected to have for them. The court explained that this ex ante "calculation, untainted by bitterness and greed, or by a sense of duty to a child the parents have brought into the world, is usually the best available evidence of the extent to which" the negligent thwarting of their decision "has in fact been an injury to them."[18] Other judges have criticized this approach for "comparing apples and oranges" about "highly speculative and unquantifiable damages in contrast to intangible benefits."[19] They have a point. A Michigan appellate court put the point in terms that harkened back to classical antiquity:

> How would a hypothetical Grecian jury . . . measure the benefits to the parents of the whole life of Homer, the blind singer of songs who created the Iliad and the Odyssey? Absent the ability to foretell the future and to quantify the value of the spoken and then the written word, how, exactly, would the jury do that?[20]

There's no easy or precise way to work out and tally up the ways in which parenthood's virtues soften the blow of confounded procreation. But these complexities don't warrant refusing awards outright. It's better to identify these trade-offs with all practicable clarity and care, as a Tennessee court affirmed, than "to permit the law to be blinded to the realities of the plaintiff's concrete situation for the sake of indefinite abstractions."[21]

Chaya and Menachem Grossbaum were devout newlyweds eager to start a family. Both had attended Jewish high school, where standard genetic screening informed them that they were carriers of cystic fibrosis (CF), a recessive disorder that affects many Jews of Eastern European descent. The Grossbaums didn't suffer any symptoms of the disease themselves. Only a person with two mutated genes does. They each had one, making them both carriers. That meant any child they had together would have a one-in-four chance of suffering the consequences that come with having both mutations.[22] Cystic fibrosis clogs the lungs with thick mucus that restricts mobility due to wheezing and eventually deadly infections. People with CF can still lead full and happy lives, longer all the time thanks to improved medication and physiotherapy. In 1962, a child with cystic fibrosis was expected to live just ten years. Those born today usually make it closer to fifty.[23]

But the disease poses undeniable tribulations. One mother whose doctor failed to diagnose her child's CF while she was pregnant described the demands the disease makes in terms of time investments:

> [H]ow many hours each day you spend on treatments (for my toddler son, two; for adults, up to four), how many weeks at a time you spend in the hospital (a couple, if you're having a "tune-up" for a lung infection), how many months since you last saw a doctor (during periods of relative health, three). How many years you can expect to live: In 2016, half of all reported deaths occurred before the age of 30. In the later stages of the disease, you might measure time between incidents of coughing up blood, keep track of how long you've been on oxygen full time, or, should you qualify for one, count the number of years you're expected to live after a double lung transplant (about five).[24]

The Grossbaums wanted a child who wouldn't suffer in ways they'd witnessed in their community. They were opposed to abortion, so they underwent IVF so they could check each embryo for the disease before deciding whether to implant it. Their genetic testing facility cleared an embryo as "OK for transfer," even though it had the two mutated genes that confer CF. Nine months later, Mrs. Grossbaum gave birth to a baby girl with the very condition they'd used reproductive technology to screen against.[25]

Courts err in denying plaintiffs like the Grossbaums any right to sue for confounded procreation on the ground that their affected child confers benefits that inescapably outweigh whatever harms her presence visits upon their lives.[26] These courts misunderstand this reproductive injury and misapply the offset rule. Parents aren't saying that they don't love their child. Their grievance concerns the wrongful frustration of their interest in choosing offspring particulars. Recovery for that harm of thwarted selection should be reduced by foreseeable benefits of the reproductive kind that parents had sought out. Washington is the only state that has entertained awarding damages to compensate for these intangible kinds of harms to family life, and trading them off against the corresponding "emotional benefits to the parents."[27] But the Wisconsin Supreme Court rejected this approach under circumstances in which parents made clear their decision to forgo whatever benefits having a child with a particular condition would have brought with it. "[I]t hardly seems equitable," that court explained, "to not only force this benefit upon them but to tell them they must pay for it as well by offsetting it against their proven [] damages."[28]

C. Prediction Problems

The *Grossbaum* case also raises hard questions about the statute of limitations. These are the deadlines that every state establishes for filing certain kinds of claims in court. The family had lost their home while sorting out medical care to treat their daughter's cystic fibrosis. She was two before their priorities turned to legal action. That was too late, the court said, in dismissing the couple's suit as untimely. The clock typically runs from the date of the harmful act or omission. States impose these cutoffs to let defendants move on with their lives and to press plaintiffs to pursue complaints with reasonable diligence, before reliable evidence deteriorates. But parents often won't discover until much later—when a child gets a DNA kit for the holidays, or undergoes a blood test for unrelated reasons—that one donor's sample had long ago been switched with another's, or that a spouse's material were swapped with a stranger's.[29]

Missed diagnoses of genetic disease may also go unnoticed until a condition manifests many years later. Affected offspring may develop normally . . . until they don't. A 2017 case involved two infertile couples who used the same egg donor from a Manhattan clinic that had assured them that it screens donors for "all known genetic conditions for which testing is available." Both couples had children born with Fragile X syndrome, which causes cognitive impairment and learning disabilities that delay development by age two. The disorder passes down from the female side alone, and carrier screening is reliable and routine. The clinic admitted that it had negligently failed to test this particular egg donor for the well-known Fragile X mutation. But none of this came out until after the couples discovered that their children had the condition, which wasn't until well after they were born. The question before the court was whether New York's two-and-a-half-year window to file had already expired.[30]

The clinic argued that the countdown began as soon as "the act, omission or failure complained of"—either the missed diagnosis or the transfer of embryos that it failed to check for Fragile X. The couples countered that it didn't make sense to start running the clock before they became aware of the negligence. The court found middle ground. It reasoned that the discovery date was unfair to providers because it left them on the hook indefinitely. By the same token, the pregnancy start-date was unfair to patients, whose injury took place behind a shroud of mystery that the plaintiffs couldn't reasonably have been expected to know about until after their kids were diagnosed. The court split the difference—holding that the thirty-month timer got under way from the date of birth—in recognition of "unique and unanticipated" circumstances when reproductive professionals confound procreation.[31]

This compromise approach should guide courts as they begin to face even thornier controversies related to the editing of human embryos. Chapter 2 noted that a technique called CRISPR/Cas9 can splice portions of genetic code into and out of an IVF embryo that's implanted and becomes a person. These "germline" changes won't start and end with the resulting person himself—they'll pass down to any children he has. Gene-edited babies are only a matter of time, now that healthy gene-edited twins have been announced in China—albeit by a rogue scientist, in contravention of international norms and ethical guidelines. But the CRISPR process is highly vulnerable to mistakes, even in plants and animals. And "off-target" gene edits of the wrong sequence can have serious health consequences that don't appear for decades or even generations down the road—not until resulting children are themselves adults, and may well have affected children, or indeed grandchildren, of their own.[32]

Causation puzzles related to multigenerational injuries have confronted courts before. A synthetic estrogen called diethylstilbestrol (DES) set off a national health crisis after it was prescribed to millions of American pregnant women in the 1940s, 50s, and 60s. The drug caused vaginal cancer in women and birth defects in offspring. But affected grandchildren have a hard time proving that it caused their injuries. And courts are reluctant to hold physicians and manufacturers (or their estates) liable for misconduct that took place long ago.[33] Balancing the equities between defendants and plaintiffs could involve a generational cutoff for CRISPR-caused injuries, allowing suits by children but not grandchildren, or grandchildren but no later offspring. The statute of limitations should reflect gene editing's distinctive dangers, while giving practitioners a reasonable period of closure when they no longer have to worry about being sued.

It's not just the fact of a prenatal mix-up but also its consequences that can be indeterminate or hard to know for years to come. Even when it's clear that specialists have mislabeled donors or misdiagnosed embryos, genetic testing gives no guarantee of how, or sometimes whether, a particular medical disorder will manifest. Some are caused by variants in a single, identifiable region of a person's DNA—examples are cystic fibrosis, sickle cell anemia, Fragile X syndrome, muscular dystrophy. But multiple variants and nongenetic factors are responsible for the vast majority of serious maladies, like diabetes, heart disease, and most mental illnesses. And many other valued traits come from scores of genes working in concert with myriad other forces in ways yet unknown. These include susceptibilities to the likes of obesity, cancer, and alcoholism. Just because a donor is overweight or drinks too much doesn't tell us much about the chances that any resulting offspring will too.

Despite these layers of uncertainty, courts err to deny recovery for switched donors or embryos on the ground that no offspring condition can ever be "reliably predicted,"[34] or that whatever disease prenatal screening failed to detect resulted from "genetic[s] and not . . . any injury negligently inflicted."[35] Those were reasons that the supreme courts of Utah and Kentucky gave for refusing compensation to victims of confounded procreation. These red herrings about causation misunderstand what the plaintiffs in these cases are claiming. It isn't that the negligence took a healthy child and made him sick. Rather, as Nevada's supreme court explained, the plaintiff-parent "claims that her physicians' negligence kept her ignorant of [material] defects" that led her to reproduce in a way likely to produce children born with certain traits.[36] Genetic uncertainty doesn't absolve reproductive specialists of the harm their wrongdoing inflicts. Courts should just reduce damages in proportion to the rough-and-ready contribution of causes other than professional misconduct. Proportional recovery would apply the same loss-of-chance principles as medical malpractice cases involving health problems whose causes are tricky to sort out. It's enough for patients to show that the negligent mix-up is probably what thwarted their interest in choosing offspring particulars. Award totals for confounded procreation should then be adjusted downward based on however much non-negligence factors played a part in causing that injury. These remedy determinations aren't clear-cut. But neither are sound estimates too much for judges and juries to handle.[37]

Suppose a husband and wife decide to have kids. The wife's father was recently diagnosed with Alzheimer's, a partially heritable disease that usually arrives on late in life with dementia and eventually death. The wife undergoes a risk analysis for herself. She tests positive for a variant of the APOE gene that makes her four times as likely to develop Alzheimer's. Other unidentified genes also affect a person's chances of the disease, as do environmental factors like head trauma, pesticide exposure, and heart disease. And if she does have it, then any genetic child she has would be three times as likely to have it too. The woman and her husband decide to use IVF and preimplantation screening to weed out the APOE mutation from any future child they might have. But the clinic negligently implants an affected embryo instead. That error increases the likelihood that the resulting child will develop Alzheimer's. But his genetic history doesn't seal the boy's fate.[38]

Damages should reflect his chances of developing the disease and the relative role of professional wrongdoing in bringing it about. That percentage would trim the award total from what it would be if negligence alone made it all but certain that the condition would materialize. Some courts have adopted this kind of probabilistic approach where doctors negligently delay the diagnosis of a cancer that may still have killed the patient, even had it been detected earlier.[39] Others have granted partial relief for misconduct that leaves the injured party more likely to come down with some painful or debilitating illness. This is better than redressing that reproductive loss either fully, or not at all, depending on whether "a plaintiff proves that a future consequence is more likely to occur than not." The Connecticut Supreme Court explained that an all-or-nothing approach is disposed to make two kinds of mistakes: It will deny damages "for consequences that later ensue from risks not rising to the level of probability" and award them "for future consequences that never occur." Better to compensate "fairly for all the consequences of the injuries they have sustained, while avoiding, so far as possible, windfall awards for consequences that never happen."[40]

This chapter has considered the magnitude and probability of frustrated interests in offspring particulars. How serious is that reproductive injury? Do its benefits outweigh its harms? What are the chances of it manifesting within certain windows of time and at varying levels of severity? How likely is it that misconduct is what caused procreation to be confounded? Is some other factor responsible in addition or instead? To what extent was genetic randomness or diagnostic uncertainty to blame? The next chapter asks: Even if negligence were to inflict excruciating and demonstrable setback, is this the sort of loss that warrants recovery? Or would judicial remedies violate public policy? The question for this final portion of the book isn't how much harm that injury exacts, but whether courts should redress it at all.

10

Fraught Remedies

A fig for equity—common law has nothing to do with it.
—James Kirke Paulding, *The Merry Tales
of the Three Wise Men of Gotham* (G. & C. Carvill 1826)

When negligence thwarts parental efforts to select for socially salient traits like sex, race, and disability, compensation risks cutting against public safety or morality. A judge's charge to be impartial and independent usually keeps her from declaring policy values from the bench. When judges do invoke policy to resolve disputes, they try to moor such appeals to time-honored precepts of legal culture, the kind that bind Americans together in something close to civic consensus.[1] Think of canonical interests in national security and election integrity, or foundational ideals like freedom of expression and equality before the law. Mandated cash payments for the wrongful defeat of attempts to choose a child to be deaf or male or white have the potential to undermine public commitments to newborn health, gender balance, or racial equality. This chapter argues that these concerns will only under exceptional circumstances rule out any remedy for confounded procreation. Even in rare cases for which recovery is not valid but void, courts should still award nominal damages for generalized reproductive injuries—to deter professional misconduct and vindicate broader interests in parental selection of offspring particulars.

A. Impairment and Identity

The most common complaints of confounded procreation involve foiled efforts to have a healthy baby. The plaintiffs in these cases envisioned a life that would be meaningfully different for them were it to include a child with certain impairments. Courts often balk at awarding damages out of concern for "the child who will learn that his existence was unwanted and that his parents sued to have the person who made his existence possible provide for his support."[2] Judges worry that offspring will be deeply pained to "f[i]nd out that their birth was attributable to a doctor's negligence rather than to their parents' desires."[3] Any impulse to protect children must be taken seriously. But this one's misplaced, and doesn't justify refusal to right a reproductive wrong. Chances are, "[b]y the time the child is old enough to understand the nature of the legal issues surrounding its birth, [his] position in the family will already be secure."[4] And the Rhode Island Supreme Court has suggested it "may in fact alleviate the child's distress" to learn "that someone other than the parents" was "pay[ing] for the cost of rearing him." It concluded that parents are better positioned than courts are "to decide whether a lawsuit would adversely affect the child and should not be maintained" for that reason.[5] Any self-doubt that a child may suffer upon discovering that his parents sued over the (mis)conduct that made him how he is may be less bad for him, on balance, than the family's struggle to provide for his basic medical and education needs without the financial relief they're entitled to.

Others may worry about the message that remedies would send to people with disabilities. For the law to specially protect reproductive strivings to prevent certain conditions enshrines the view that living with those conditions is bad, thereby demeaning people who take pride in or identify with having them—or so this argument goes. On this view, judicial recovery for thwarted preferences would trade on dubious assumptions about differently abled people in ways that risk denying them equal respect. This isn't about prospective parents being allowed to destroy embryos or fetuses based on anticipated health complications. Even many ardent disability advocates wouldn't forbid prenatal selection, despite their conviction that it overlooks the richness of life with varying gifts and aptitudes. But when it comes to remedies for the failure to screen or diagnose some offspring condition, then it's no longer just individuals or couples deciding what's best for their own lives. That verdict as to compensation reflects the binding conclusion that the judge or jury reaches in view of specific facts and applicable law.

Words can wound, whether they're meant to or not, especially when they come from respected authorities. And citizens living with those same conditions may hear the formal pronouncement of those words to impart that their very existence amounts to a legal harm.[6] Many don't see their own impairment in pejorative terms, but neutral ones—less disability than difference. They're right that disability isn't just a medical problem. External barriers exacerbate the isolation and exclusion that people with impairments face. And studies show that social support for disabled children improves family functioning and marital satisfaction on par with the general population. But impairments usually aren't merely social constructs either. Internal limitations associated with paraplegia or Down syndrome make it harder to navigate life in most plausible visions of modern society. However well society remakes its institutional practices and cultural attitudes to include and accommodate human variation, it can still break a parent's heart to witness his child founder at tasks that come easily to others, or suffer pain that no social restructuring could take away.[7]

In 2017, the Iowa Supreme Court acknowledged the possibility that "allowing wrongful-birth claims will stigmatize the disabled community."[8] But that risk doesn't "warrant closing the courthouse door to these parents," it held, any more than it justifies "'immuniz[ing] those in the medical field from liability for their performance in one particular area of medical malpractice,' namely, prenatal care and genetic counseling."[9] There are better ways to blunt the expressive sting of judicial insults. For one, courts should avoid singling out impairment among thwarted preferences worthy of remedy. "A policy that gave no special status to disabilities" could mitigate the indignity to those whose conditions are targeted for elimination, by implying that they're "just some among the myriad variations that might be relevant to some prospective parents in deciding whether to bring a child into the world."[10] A tort right that doesn't set impairment apart as distinctively bad could help mute its power to offend. On this equal opportunity approach to remedies for confounded procreation, recourse wouldn't be directed at this child or that condition—it'd respond to the negligent defeat of interests in offspring selection. Accordingly, recovery need only convey that some families wish to forgo whatever hospital visits or medical expenses they anticipate would be required to care for a child with special needs.[11]

There's a more convincing policy rationale against recovery for victims of reproductive negligence who sought to choose in *favor* of disabling conditions. One IVF doctor reports that one couple wanted him "to identify an embryo with Down's syndrome" for implantation to give their "Down's-affected child a similar sibling."[12] Other fertility clinics say that prospective parents with dwarfism or high-functioning autism have asked for a child with similar differences in size or social interaction.[13] Couples in which both partners have the most common form of dwarfism, called achondroplasia, often create IVF embryos. Any embryo that combines their egg and sperm will have a one in four chance of being destined to die shortly before or after it's born. And genetic diagnosis can distinguish viable embryos from ill-fated ones. Screening them before deciding which implant helps these couples dodge that 25 percent chance of a doomed pregnancy. Since their embryos are already being sent for analysis anyway, it just takes one more test if they also want to choose a little person like them. Some facilities decline these requests. Achondroplasia would make the resulting child's life too much harder, they say, than it would have been for a different child who wasn't selected to have that condition. But it's also possible that sharing those differences might enhance bonding and flourishing, both in the family unit and beyond it.

That's how many deaf parents explain their efforts to have children who are born, like them, unable to hear. These parents prize the traditions bundled up with American Sign Language and the sense of belonging and camaraderie among those who use it. They select for embryos or donors likely to produce a deaf child. One such couple "celebrated when we found out about [our daughter's] deafness . . . We're proud, not of the medical aspect of deafness, but of the language we use and the community we live in."[14] Another affirmed that "it is important that our culture is passed on from one generation to another . . . [T]he threat of losing our culture would be devastating because we have so much to show and to give."[15] While a "hearing baby would be a blessing," a third maintained, a "deaf baby would be a special blessing."[16] "[B]eing deaf is a positive thing, with many wonderful aspects," they explained, much like "being Jewish or black."[17] Deafness won't impair their child's capacity to flourish, these parents are saying, because the social and cultural advantages of growing up with that common family identity will outweigh any drawbacks associated with not being able to hear. "[S]hared language can serve to foster community," as the U.S. Supreme Court has affirmed in a different context.[18]

Many others see deafness as a disability, and believe that its prenatal selection, if it doesn't violate felony prohibitions against child abuse, then it at least defies social norms against moral offenses that come very close to criminal maltreatment. Were a sperm bank or fertility clinic to use the wrong donor or embryo, and these parents thereby ended up with a hearing baby instead, would public policy counsel courts against redressing their negligently defeated efforts to have one who's deaf? The answer has nothing to do with what's in the best interest of the resulting child. Choosing a deaf donor isn't like damaging a born child's existing ability to hear: That child could have gone right on hearing had he not been made deaf. By contrast, a would-be child who was selected to inherit some genetic disability, before implantation or even conception, then owes her very existence to that prenatal choice. This child, with his particular biological makeup, couldn't have been born without the condition that his DNA assures he will have. His lived experience—with deafness or dwarfism or Down syndrome—is nowhere near bad enough that it might be better for him never to have lived at all. I addressed this "non-identity problem" in Chapter 1. That objection would fall away only in fetal surgery errors introduced in Chapter 3 and the off-target gene editing discussed in Chapter 9. These cases involve the wrongful *manipulation* of a fetus or embryo, which can harm that genetically unique entity itself. They don't just *select* for one instead of another, to take or leave as they come. But in the vast majority of cases, the decision to remedy confounded procreation isn't about making the resulting child himself any better off or worse.

A better reason to consider barring recovery in these cases is the state's strong interest in promoting offspring born *with* basic capacities, and *without* medical risks. Having the next generation arrive with more "normal" abilities or "healthy" functioning might be thought to help produce a productive citizenry, or one that costs less for the government to educate, accommodate, or care for.[19] This policy of promoting newborn wellness is reflected in federal mandates that grain manufacturers add folic acid to their products to reduce the risk of offspring with neurological disorders. Other evidence of society's commitment to offspring health comes from "elaborate neonatal intensive care units that go to great expense to save all newborns, and norms for treating all newborns no matter the cost or scope of their handicaps."[20] Selecting for children to have incapacitating conditions like deafness, dwarfism, or Down syndrome works against this long-standing public policy. On the other hand, disability-favoring selection is relatively rare: Just 3 percent of 186 American IVF clinics in a recent survey reported having enabled couples "to select an embryo for the presence of a disability."[21] That infrequency diminishes whatever health implications the practice has for the general population. More important is that most parents who choose for traits like deafness don't see it as a disabling trait at all. They say that any deaf child they have will enjoy an even more meaningful upbringing than a hearing one would have had because only the deaf child would share his family's valuable identity, language, and community.

Philosopher Russell Blackford points out that deaf parents don't select to have a deaf child out of "ignorance or irresponsibility, but out of a conviction that they are better placed to nurture and socialize a deaf child than one with normal hearing" and to grant the child "access to a culture that they experience as rich, complex, and satisfying—and not available to those with normal hearing." Granted, the child "might not be in a position to assess the full richness of what they have missed out on by being cut off from the world of music," or the sweet sounds of a bird's song, stream's gurgle, or baby's laughter. But "the rest of us perhaps are no better placed to assess what can be substituted for it by the parents' own culture."[22] Immersion in that culture might help a deaf child to thrive, perhaps more than a hearing child could. Or maybe not—besides, a hearing child of deaf parents could still learn sign language and participate in deaf culture without being limited in other settings by his inability to hear. These brief reflections suggest that the effects of deafness on a child's wellbeing will vary considerably from child to child, family to family, context to context. But deaf parents who want offspring like themselves aren't, at any rate, perverse to choose for deafness—even as others are also reasonable to see it differently. Idiosyncratic preferences shouldn't go unprotected just because they aren't widely shared in a society unfamiliar with the experiences of parents from diverse backgrounds. Decisions about reproductive selection "are invariably affected by factors not readily apparent to outsider observers," notes ethicist Colin Gavaghan. Efforts to choose offspring for certain traits may evoke less sympathy than censure. "But they can all be assumed to mean something to the person making them, to reflect her values or priorities or view of what it is that makes life important."[23]

This isn't to say that courts should necessarily redress any and every thwarted effort to have a child with any disabling condition, whatever their reasons or consequences for the child. People have all sorts of motivations for having kids, from baby fever to "just didn't think about it." Most are altogether ordinary and legitimate; few are truly noble or selfless. Scarcer still are callous rationales to reproduce. It strains credulity to imagine prospective parents who'd wish delinquency or suffering on their future child. But suppose violent felons look for a donor who's specially disposed to psychopathy in in hopes of grooming their off-spring to share in a life of crime. Or someone with the mental illness, Munchausen syndrome by proxy—but instead of faking or introducing symptoms to make it look like her child is sick, she seeks to implant a sick embryo in order to attract sympathy or attention. Venal or malicious reasons to choose this or that offspring trait don't warrant recovery for confounded procreation. But these examples sound preposterous because they are. And just because offspring selection is eccentric or disquieting to many doesn't mean that professional wrongdoing should go scot-free, and victims left out of luck. Available remedy should be the default, so long as parents can paint a plausible picture of defensible motivations and consequences.

B. Biological Sex and Kin

The same goes for thwarted efforts to choose a child's sex. Some prospective parents may try to have a girl in order to avoid a sex-linked disorder that they risk passing along only if they were to have a boy. The book's introduction mentioned the 2009 case of IVF patients Eve Rubell and her husband, who selected a female embryo after learning that any male child they might have would inherit an enzyme deficiency called Fabry disease. A mix-up gave them a son. The court explained his likely future:

> From an early age, boys with Fabry may experience severe pain, particu-larly in their hands and feet. As they get older, men with Fabry may suffer from kidney failure, heart failure, and an increased risk of stroke. Without enzyme replacement treatment, men with Fabry disease are expected to live into their late 40's or early 50's. Although there is now an enzyme treatment that slows the progression of Fabry, there is not yet long-term data demonstrating how much the treatment will extend the life expect-ancy of men with the disease.[24]

The blood-clotting disorder hemophilia likewise affects boys more than girls, as does Lesch-Nyhan syndrome. Male babies born with the latter show signs of intellectual disability after a few months, and movement problems confine most to a wheelchair by two or three. Then comes self-mutilating behavior that ranges from banging their heads to biting lips, tongues, and fingers.[25] At-risk parents who select for a girl just to avoid conditions like these are actually choosing for offspring health, not sex.

But "venture into some closed online chat forums and you will find hundreds of . . . women who are sharing their disappointment over the sex of their children"—for reasons that have nothing to do with disease or disability.[26] For some, cultural or religious norms prize boys over girls. A 2008 study of Indian, Chinese, and Korean American couples—less than 2 percent of the U.S. population combined—found that couples whose eldest child was a daughter had second- and especially third-born male children at significantly higher rates. The researchers attribute the "deviation in favor of sons to be evidence of sex selection, most likely at the prenatal stage." They infer that a fraction of immigrants from those countries bring a bias for sons.[27] A fertility doctor who specializes in sex selection reports that "[s]ome families want only one child with a specific gender" less for cultural reasons than ones relating to their own upbringing—as an only child, or growing up closer with one's mother or father.[28]

Other families seek to diversify the representation of sexes among their existing children. One prominent clinic explains on its website that parents are "appropriate candidates for Family Balancing" if they already have "a son and desire a daughter, or there is an otherwise unequal representation of both genders among current siblings."[29] Alan and Louise Masterton had four boys and, until recently, a little girl too. The couple lost their only daughter in a fire when she was three. They set out to create and select among embryos in order to replace the girl in their family. "We tried for Nicole for 15 years," explained Mr. Masterton. "We were blessed with her and she was a fantastic child. We are looking for the opportunity to try for another daughter, not another Nicole, but to bring a female dimension to our family."[30]

When negligent sperm sorting, embryo screening, or fetal testing confounds efforts to select offspring sex, do policy concerns count out remedies for confounded procreation? A right to recover for frustrated sex selection would risk exacerbating patriarchies and birth imbalances in parts of Southeast Asia. Substantial benefits come with having boys in much of China, India, and South Korea—financial privileges accrue to sons; dowry payments are required to marry off daughters; and spouses live with or near the husband's parents to provide the joy of grandchildren and support in old age. These cultural and economic conditions make sexism and gender disparities alarming enough to disclaim a right against thwarted sex-selection in those countries. But these concerns are far less urgent in the United States, where sex ratios at birth have long fallen squarely within population norms, and fertility clinics report that 80 percent of sex-selecting parents are trying to have a girl.[31]

Critics who object to gender-balancing in the United States argue that alternative grounds for sex selection are still "steeped in the same kind of gendered social norms and expectations" that impose "male" and "female" roles.[32] To assume that biological sex determines one's place in life, this argument goes, is to reduce a future child's identity, interests, personality, and values to the chromosomal or anatomical markers. Serious though these concerns are, many sex-selecting Americans won't ascribe such hard-and-fast character traits or life pursuits to boys or girls at birth. And even families who indulge or traffic in sex stereotypes can't realistically expect that getting a baby with an XX chromosome will guarantee them a dainty follower who enjoys domestic caretaking; or that an XY baby will be a tough leader drawn to sports and high-powered work outside the house. Couples like the Mastertons are probably just hoping for a better chance at whatever dispositions remind them of the men or women in their lives. Reasonable disagreement about the meaning of sex selection warrants against categorically barring recovery for its wrongful thwarting.

More common than the preference for a boy or girl is prenatal selection for a child of one's own "flesh and blood." Is there a stronger policy objection to deny a remedy for reproductive negligence that dashes hopes for a baby who shares his parents' DNA? Even those resigned to the private fertility industry could oppose codifying its protection by a state-sanctioned tort. Some scholars argue that elevating IVF or surrogacy to the designation of a right valorizes genetic affinity over the real work of parenthood. When courts treat "biogenetic forms of relationship and identity" as what matters most between parents and children, they risk disrespecting not only the relationship that fathers have with children they didn't sire, or mothers have with those they didn't give birth to. They could also demean the role of same-sex couples and adoptive or step-parents whose families flourish in the absence of biological ties. This critique challenges judicial redress of mix-ups that frustrate parental efforts to embody or replicate a "bionormative" conception of what it means to be a parent.[33]

Americans rarely question that parental bonds of biology are good. Infertile couples who use donors to conceive say it's hard not to feel inadequate and incomplete as parents when "one of the first things people always ask [] with the baby is 'Who does she look like?'" Many same-sex partners field similar skepticism about their parental status: "People always ask, 'Who are you? Are you his dad?'"[34] It's not just cultural norms and social pleasantries that presume the naturalness of genetic affinity. The legal system also uses heredity to anchor state determinations about child custody, visitation, and who counts as a parent. The primacy of blood ties forces nonbiological parents to labor for the family recognition that other parents enjoy as a matter of course. As lawyers argued before the Iowa Supreme Court, this privileging of genetics can also stigmatize adoptive and other children "who are not genetically related to their parents, whether because they were conceived through reproductive technology or [through] intercourse with a non-marital partner."[35]

But that doesn't mean that when negligence blocks efforts to share DNA with one's child, judicial recovery would demean adoptive, LGBT, or other families who defy traditional expectations of parenthood. Redress might simply recognize the cultural or religious meaning that the genetic tie can carry for groups that believe it joins them together across time or space. We met William Stern in Chapter 7. He was the father from the *Baby M* surrogacy case, and the only member of his extended family who wasn't killed in the Holocaust. Stern sought to "maintain[] [his] genetic line" in order to drive back "existential loneliness."[36] Compensation for confounded heredity could also speak to the loss felt by victims who longed to perceive a physical likeness in their baby. Or who hoped that shared features would strengthen emotional bonds with aunts, uncles, or grandparents. Or simply that the better chance for superficial resemblance would help to normalize everyday social exchanges.

An unnamed Singaporean couple—identified only as "the Appellant and her husband"—were struck by how little their newborn daughter looked like her father. Their IVF clinic confessed that it had swapped the husband's sperm with a stranger's, but shot back that the couple still got a child, a healthy one at that. The 2017 case reached the highest level of Singapore's Supreme Court, which called it "one of the most difficult" in its history. The Court found itself "at the crossroads" between "undercompensat[ing] the Appellant for the wrong which has been done to her"—one that left her "the mother of a child fathered by a complete stranger"—and "denigrat[ing] the worth of [the child's very] existence as a continuing source of loss to [her]." After wrestling for over fifty pages with the controversies implicated by this trade-off, a unanimous Court rejected the facility's protests of harmless error and public morality. It held the fertility center liable for negligently defeating the couple's plans to have a child with whom they would be "bound by ties of blood and share physical traits." This conclusion required setting forth a first-of-its-kind right of recovery for the wrongful denial of "genetic continuity and biological lineage."[37]

The portion of the Supreme Court's opinion that established this new tort relied on an essay I had published in the *Columbia Law Review* a few months earlier. The Court framed the injury, as I had, not just in terms of lost choices ("the frustration of . . . decisional autonomy") but also its consequences ("the substantive impact that [this frustration] has had on . . . well-being."). The justices adopted my proposal to evaluate the severity of that injury in practical terms of "the particular reasons fertility treatment was sought, the precise manner in which the negligence took place, and the personal circumstances of the plaintiff (such as the presence of other children or the familial and/or cultural histories particular to him or her)."[38] The Court highlighted the "deep socio-cultural significance" of "biological parenthood" that animated this couple's decision "to undergo IVF," and the "anguish, stigma, disconcertment, and embarrassment" they faced whenever someone asked about the "wife's fidelity and the paternity of [their] child."[39] The justices ultimately awarded the couple 30 percent of childrearing expenses, or about $78,000 in U.S. dollars. They made clear that this money wasn't for any out-of-pocket costs to raise their daughter. The Court merely benchmarked damages in childcare terms for want of a less arbitrary reference point for a dollar amount that more or less "reflects sufficiently the seriousness of the Appellant's loss" and doesn't "make a mockery of the value of the interest at stake."[40]

C. Resemblance and Race

The anonymous donor in that Singapore case was Indian. His skin complexion was conspicuously darker than that of the father and mother, whose families descended from Germany and China. The color clash pressed the Supreme Court to say just a word about "the complex role that physical resemblance, race, and cultural and ethnic identity have had and continue to have on our individual well-being." The wife's affidavit singled out the baby's "different skin tone" as the child's outstanding feature, which "never fails to draw curious looks from the public" and "turn joyous family time into depressing moments." The Court mentioned that being born conspicuously browner than her parents would leave the child susceptible to the "racist bullying" of "abusive and derogative comments and hurtful name calling." But the Court excused itself from grappling with these implications by focusing on the biological mismatch instead of the racial one. The couple's coinciding injury to genetic affinity softened any more divisive message that compensation might otherwise send by singling out confounded race, on its own. So, as in the New York *Andrews* case that opened Chapter 9, the Court didn't go there. This section does.[41]

First it distinguishes matters of race from resemblance. Some people who can't pass along their genes—so shared heredity isn't an option—still want their child to smack of them from the outside. They pick a donor who shares their build and appearance. But a mix-up switches that donor with one who looks nothing like them, even though their features signal a common racial ancestry. Other parents may want offspring who resemble the children they already have. Rachel and Aaron Halbert, both white, had previously adopted two black children. When they wanted more kids, this time with IVF, they used embryos donated from an African American couple so that "[t]he new babies would therefore 'match' their already existing siblings."[42] Race was part of it, but superficial likeness was more. Single mother Heidi Maher wanted her kids to share a common heredity, so she returned to the fertility clinic she'd used to have "a second child with the biological father of her first child."[43] In most cases, the loss of resemblance, on its own, inflicts a fairly small reproductive harm, one that warrants nominal damages. Lots of offspring look very different from their biological parents or siblings anyway. But the question that this section asks isn't how serious the injury is—it's whether that injury is compensable at all.

David and Stephanie Harnicher struggled to conceive for years. They learned that David's low sperm count and mobility made him all but sterile, so they'd need another man's semen to conceive. They still wanted to "believe and represent that any children born as a result of the treatment they received were David['s] biological offspring." The couple pored over donor profiles in search of one who "closely matched David's physical characteristics," and combined lucky No. 183's sample with David. The insemination process gave the couple not one but three healthy kids—except their ginger features didn't look anything like the donor who shared David's "curly dark hair and brown eyes." The triplets' "straight auburn hair and green eyes" reminded them of a different donor with a similar number, No. 83. DNA tests confirmed the switch. It hadn't cost David any real chance at genetic kinship. His grievance was that his kids "do not look as much like him as different children might have." The error kept him from holding himself out as their biological father.[44]

The Utah Supreme Court disparaged that complaint as the "destruction of a fiction." It wasn't just that the Harnichers "had not experienced any bodily harm as a result of the mistake," the three-justice majority reasoned. Or that it'd have been bad for the triplets not to be informed about the circumstances of their conception. Rather, the court avowed that "[e]xposure to the truth about one's own" genetic relationship with one's family "cannot be considered an injury" that's real or worthy enough for the law to recognize. Two dissenting justices painted the Harnichers' reproductive plans in a more flattering light. They would have redressed the couple's thwarted interest in having and raising their children how they saw fit.

> Had it not been for the University's negligence in mixing sperm from the wrong donor with David's, the "fiction" would never have been labeled a fiction; it would simply have been an "alternative reality" for the Harnicher family.[45]

The physical resemblance that the couple sought out would have afforded them the plausible presumption of offspring heredity that they longed for, thereby disguising the discomforting facts of David's infertility and their use of a donor to conceive.

Parents have aspired to conceal or cover genetic differences with their children since long before the advent of reproductive technology. The institution of adoption in the United States was designed to "unite children with parents who looked like them" in order to "obscure the fact that they had been born to others." Historian Ellen Herman recounts that adoption agencies and social workers matched adoptive parents with similar-looking children in the hope that perceived resemblances would facilitate emotional bonding, family belonging, and a sense of shared identity.[46] There's a Darwinian theory of parental love which supposes that people usually treat biological offspring better than stepchildren in their care. This "Cinderella effect," as it's called, has been hotly contested since the 1970s.[47] But even if stepmothers don't love genetic daughters more, it needn't traumatize children or demean nontraditional families to protect people's efforts to pass as bonded by DNA. The *Harnicher* majority erred in refusing to remedy foiled resemblance. Negligible though that injury may be, no opposing policy is strong enough to negate its recognition outright.

There's a more compelling case against redressing confounded ethnicity or national origin. Parents may have wanted an Asian child and got a Latino one, or sought the blue-blond coloring associated with Scandinavians, and ended up with Irish lime-strawberry. Truly tribal preferences aren't about having a kid who's genetic kin or free of disability. This doesn't include parents who try to select against African ancestry or Jewish heritage only in order to steer clear of an identified risk of correlated medical conditions like sickle cell anemia or Tay-Sachs disease. That would be like the sex selection the previous section discussed to avoid an X-linked disorder. It's not really about choosing a boy or girl at all, but rather a child born without some debilitating condition. Sex chromosomes are incidental to that superseding objective of having offspring of sound mind and body. In theory at least, it could also be like that for racial or ethnic groups afflicted by disproportionately high rates of disease. It's similar if a parent's point was to use one's own genetic material rather than someone else's, whatever his background, and it happened to be a different race or ethnicity. What might look like race selection is at least plausibly more about extending the family line. Precisely this ambiguity blurs the mix-ups in *Andrews* and the Singapore controversy, which switched a spouse's sperm with that of a stranger who had noticeably darker skin. Any selection goals imputed to race-matching can find ample cover behind overlapping aims to pass along one's own DNA. Case-specific facts might help to disentangle these objectives—but maybe not.

In other cases, efforts to select for some racial or ethnic affiliation—usually whiteness—is clear. Though Latin and African Americans suffer from higher rates of infertility, it's whites who predominantly access donor and IVF services—by and large, they want babies who are also white.[48] These are the circumstances that the Utah Supreme Court majority said it would have been *more* inclined to remedy, had the Harnichers instead complained of "racial or ethnic mismatch."[49] The physical difference between Mr. Harnicher and his kids wouldn't, in that case, simply have masked the fiction of heredity—they'd reflect the reality of color in modern America. Some parents, thwarted in their efforts to a have a child who's white like them, remark on the "disapproving looks" and "prying" questions that racial mismatches draw. Others want to spare their kids from racial taunts, confused identity, and cultural deficits. "What is going to happen when he comes home from school and says kids have been calling him 'the black one.' I'm white. I've never suffered racial discrimination and I won't know how to react properly."[50] Others still worry about the prejudice their child will face in a country that subjects many people of color to criminal suspicion and systematic inequality. For one white father whose donor-conceived baby was born with much darker features, his concern wasn't just that "[b]rown people have a smaller chance to get a decent job in our society" and "can't get a bank loan like white people." Even more, he worried that "[e]very time the right-wingers and racists in [government] open their mouths, I am frightened" for my son.[51]

Jennifer Cramblett was raised "around stereotypical attitudes about people other than those in her all-white community," according to the complaint she filed in 2014 with the Circuit Court of Cook County, Illinois. Her relatives spoke "openly and derisively about persons of color." By the time she left home for college, Cramblett "did not [even] know [any] African Americans." And then, by her account, she gave birth to one.[52] Cramblett knew a thing or two about not fitting in from having grown up a lesbian in a small conservative farm town. When she and her partner Amanda Zinkon decided to start a family, they wanted a sperm donor who resembled them—starting with one who was white like they are. Among hundreds of donors who identified themselves as Caucasian, Donor No. 380 stood out because he shared Zinkon's blond hair and blue eyes. Cramblett's features would already be reflected in the child, they figured, since she'd be contributing her DNA when she carried the pregnancy. After the first trimester, Cramblett called the sperm bank to order additional samples from the same donor, so their future child could have a biological sibling. "Okay, you want eight vials of sperm from Donor No. 330," the receptionist confirmed with Cramblett. "No, I said . . . No. 380." Asked if she'd "requested an African American donor," Cramblett replied, "Why would I? My partner and I are Caucasian." The technician who had retrieved their sperm sample from the lab misread the handwritten note that recorded their donor preference. A few months later, Cramblett gave birth to an "obviously mixed race[] baby girl."[53]

The switch didn't deny either of them any greater biological connection to their child that they otherwise would have enjoyed. If they'd gotten the donor they'd selected, half of the girl's genetics would still have come from Cramblett, while the other half wouldn't have come from Zinkon anyway, but an anonymous donor—just a different one. As far as they could tell, the only salient difference between the donor they chose and the one they got is that one identified as white, the other as black. Front and center in Cramblett's lawsuit was that she and Zinkon had expressed a clear preference for a white donor, and got a black one. What she objected to was getting a baby of color—one who is no less healthy or genetically related to her or her partner than the girl would have been if they'd gotten the donor they wanted.

Cramblett tried to frame her complaint about the racial mismatch in terms of what would be better for their daughter—or, more precisely, for the hypothetical white child who might otherwise have been born in her place. Cramblett argued that she and Zinkon lacked the "cultural competency" of personal experience or practical resources to navigate the "challenges [of] transracial parenting."[54] They'd never had to confront racist stereotypes themselves, or learn about African American history and culture, or even make black friends, let alone braid hair with kinks in it. How could they help their child develop a healthy racial identity or acquire the tools she would need to deal with discrimination and navigate a race-conscious society? One response is that it's not obviously better for a child to think about race as crucial to her identity than it is to see it as a less defining feature of herself. Another is to wonder whether Cramblett and Zinkon will actually be disadvantaged in raising their daughter-of-color by the fact that they themselves haven't experienced the racism that she is likely to. Professor Richard Banks asks:

> [W]hy would one conclude that [black parents] have been ennobled rather than damaged by such experiences? And why would white parents not have benefited from all their years spent on the white side of the racial divide? Who better than a white parent to explain to a black child how white people are likely to view and respond to him? It is as plausible that white parents might have useful knowledge about race that black people lack, as it is that black people may have developed unique and beneficial insights as a result of their experiences.[55]

Empirical evidence doesn't substantiate the intuition that a child's interests in identity formation or coping skills are better served by being raised in a same-race household than by parents of different race. There aren't any studies comparing mixed-race, donor-conceived children born to black parents as opposed to white ones. But the most searching analyses of black children adopted by white parents show that children raised in multiracial families fare as well as same-race adoptees on standard measures of self-esteem, educational achievement, and social and psychological adjustment.[56]

This suggests that Cramblett's complaint wasn't really about her daughter's welfare—that in actual fact it boiled down to Cramblett's own lost expectation of the comforts and convenience associated with her whiteness. Having a child of color marked Cramblett as yet another kind of outsider among her "insensitive family" and "all-white community" in which the "schools are much better." Cramblett had long sought to hide her own stigmatized same-sex orientation. But her daughter's unexpectedly African American features were "irrepressible." The girl's visibly mixed race disrupted Cramblett's vision of a normalizing family life that, notwithstanding its two moms, would improve her standing among relatives and neighbors who'd had a hard time accepting her lesbian relationship. Instead, the mix-up further alienated her from peers and loves one, driving her and Zinkon to move "far from where [they] live" to a more diverse neighborhood where the schools were worse and they had no support system—but at least they could find someone to cut their daughter's hair, and the three of them wouldn't be made to feel so unwelcome all the time.[57]

Cramblett's lawsuit was ultimately dismissed for violating state policy against "wrongful birth."[58] But that label mischaracterizes her grievance. She doesn't regret her daughter's existence, or wish that she hadn't been born. And she isn't saying that her daughter is illegitimate or unworthy of her love. Any implication that the girl's birth is any sense "wrongful" is a relic of unfortunate nomenclature. Cramblett's point is that the switch disadvantaged a family like hers that resides in a place which remains hostile to racial difference. Cramblett sued to affirm the residential, educational, and other privileges she had hoped to enjoy by parenting a child whose shared whiteness would have made it easier for her to assimilate and prosper. Her petition gives reason for pause, but not because it negates the aphorism that babies are blessings. The problem is that it sounds in the register of racial division. Specifically, she sought to offset the very harms that millions of black families endure every day without any legally recognized cause to quarrel. Only for Cramblett did the systemic injustices at issue result from medical negligence—unlike other minority families, she had never faced these racial challenges before. What makes her complaint so remarkable is how explicit it makes the social tax of being black in America—a tax that white people like Cramblett don't pay.[59]

The U.S. Supreme Court acknowledged this stubborn legacy of racism in a 1984 Florida family law dispute. Linda Sidoti had been awarded custody of her three-year-old daughter after she and her husband Anthony split. Anthony successfully sued to get his daughter back a year later, after Mrs. Sidoti got engaged to an African American man. The trial court was persuaded that the girl's staying in the multiracial household would lead her to "suffer from . . . social stigmatization."[60] On appeal, the Supreme Court conceded that the "reality of private biases and the possible injury they might inflict" may leave her better off with her father, explaining that "living with a stepparent of a different race may be subject to a variety of pressures and stresses not present if the child were living with parents of the same racial or ethnic origin." But that didn't make the custody transfer legitimate. Chief Justice Warren Burger held for a unanimous Supreme Court that constitutional commitments to racial equality forbid child-placement decisions based on the collateral effects of social prejudice. The law may not be able to force acceptance of interracial families, but neither may it elevate racial intolerance by "giv[ing] it effect."[61] Race plays an even more conspicuous role in assisted reproduction.

U.S. sperm banks cater to the racial preferences of prospective parents like Cramblett by supplying color-coded catalogs and drop-down menus to help them isolate only white donors with the flip of a page or click of a mouse. I have criticized these sorting practices for naturalizing the racial preferences they trade on and propping up the view that race deserves a prized place in family formation.[62] I compared those labeling practices to the 1960 ballot measure that the Supreme Court struck down in the case of *Anderson v. Martin*.[63] It involved a local election rule requiring that a candidate's race appear next to his name in the voting booth. My point wasn't that inviting people to exercise racial preferences in assisted reproduction is as bad as Louisiana's designating candidates by race in civil rights–era voting booths. It's not. What prompted the analogy was Justice Tom Clark's insight, writing for a unanimous Court, that racial identifiers portray "color [a]s an important—perhaps paramount—consideration" for how individuals think about and carry out a core function as citizens.[64] The prominence of race in assisted reproduction promotes a similarly divisive conception of what it means to be a parent, I argued, by credentializing the assumption that parents should have children of their same race. This focus on donor race risks sending a message that purely white babies are better, or more worth having, in a way that makes others less favorable.[65]

But sperm banks don't go so far as to classify donors along rankable terms, as by offering samples from white donors in gold vials and black ones in bronze, or by charging more for white gametes than black.[66] And I would still allow vendors and agencies to identify donor race as one among other factors for prospective parents to consider. So I don't go as far as scholars who would ban race-conscious donor selection because, they say, it "reflects the conviction that mixing 'blood' with those who are not white could sully or taint whiteness,"[67] thereby reinforcing this perceived "threat of racial contamination" that's been enlisted "to justify racial separation and subjugation."[68] Legal scholars have tied Cramblett's lawsuit to the vestiges of American slavery and Jim Crow. Professors Suzanne Lenon and Danielle Peers argue that what Cramblett is really claiming is that the mix-up denied her "the spoils of these inherited structural violences."[69] Professor Patricia Williams contends that Cramblett is asserting "racial deviance as a breach of birthright."[70] To Professor Dorothy Roberts, her suit implies that the "genetic trait (or taint) of race . . . overwhelm[s] the kinship bond that these mothers and their babies have in common."[71] Roberts maintains the Cramblett dispute evinces a "reproductive caste system" that seeks to keep the "white bloodline free from Black contamination."[72]

Until the civil rights era, American government enforced the doctrine of racial purity to maintain and sanction the domination of whites over blacks. At one time or another, thirty-eight states had anti-miscegenation laws that barred marriage between blacks and whites—that included every state in which blacks comprised at least 5 percent of the population.[73] It wasn't until 1967 that the U.S. Supreme Court struck down interracial marriage bans, calling out their purpose to promote "White Supremacy" by preventing "a mongrel breed of citizens, and the obliteration of racial pride."[74] Until the middle of the twentieth century, adoption agencies facilitated race-based family formation by classifying children into gradations of "racial admixture"—from fully white to not at all—based on their skin color, nose width, lip thickness, and hair texture.[75] Most states even authorized white parents to annul the adoption of any child they didn't realize was a different race.[76] This not-so-distant history of racial ordering across and within family units shores up the policy objection that equality norms operate to void complaints for confounded race.

But that shouldn't immunize reproductive specialists from liability for negligent switches just because prospective parents express interest in a donor of a different race. For plaintiffs like Cramblett, courts should provide limited recovery, with explicit caveats—enough to vindicate generic interests in offspring selection, while disclaiming any racial component. Compensation shouldn't be tied to any race-specific injury, or mark that more particular loss as a serious one. The law of remedies doesn't always insist that award levels align perfectly with the estimated severity of harm inflicted. Punitive damages are usually higher, for example, because they're designed to deter and punish wrongdoing.[77] The lower, baseline award in a case like Cramblett's would still allow for potentially greater damages when mix-ups keep interracial or minority couples from exercising their preference for a donor who shares their background. Even under these circumstances, race-conscious recovery would still risk casting racial discordance under suspicion. But by affirming the worth of black or brown families, redress would at least blur troubling racial hierarchies, rather than reinforce them.[78]

D. IQ, Height, Perfect Pitch

Reproductive negligence defeats efforts for more than health and heredity, sex and race. Single, LGBT, and infertile individuals who use reproductive material from other people can pick from among sperm or egg donors who boast quick wits, tall stature, and good looks. Misrepresentations or switches can thwart these attempts to choose offspring for whatever partly genetic traits prospective parents value, whether for their own sake (because that quality is good in itself) or because they confer social advantages (because it will help their child get ahead). Parents might go for a smart donor with the hope that their child would be more likely to find science and literature more rewarding and enjoy greater opportunities for education and employment. Or maybe they choose an athletic donor with the hope that natural strength or coordination would encourage their boy or girl to keep active, build character, or succeed in sports. Or they might look for perfect pitch because they think musical ability and appreciation enriches life and they want any kids they have to experience that joy. Should U.S. courts be open to compensating for negligently dashed interventions designed to produce children who would be disposed to such gifts?

Under the guise of "wrongful birth," a handful of state courts have connected prenatal misdiagnoses for genetic disease to less familiar mix-ups involving talented donors. These judges fervidly reject remedies for the thwarted selection of better-than-normal offspring. Some say that any legal claim to recover for such choosiness gone awry treats human procreation like "the breeding of prize cattle" and "smacks too much of a Hitlerian 'elimination of the unfit' approach." Others worry that judicial willingness to affirm parental preferences for a baby of one kind or another "could slide quickly into [an] applied eugenics" that "espouse[s] reproduction of the 'fit' and discourage[s] the birth of the 'unfit.'"[79] A Michigan court of appeals explained:

> If one accepts the premise that the birth of one "defective" child should have been prevented, then it is but a short step to accepting the premise that the births of classes of "defective" children should be similarly prevented, not just for the benefit of the parents but also for the benefit of society as a whole through the protection of the "public welfare." This is the operating principle of eugenics.[80]

Anxious judges foresee a future of selective reproduction to weed out every susceptibility to "hypertension, diabetes, early- and late-appearing cancers, degenerative disorders," and "various mental deficiencies." These judges recoil at the prospect of awarding damages to "the parents of every child" whose "perceived genetic" abnormality "was a foreseeable consequence of the defendant's negligence."[81] They conclude that setting down this path to tort recovery unduly "discriminates against disabled persons" and "condones the extermination of the weak by the strong or the more powerful."[82]

But the comparison to Nazi atrocities misunderstand what made eugenics so bad—and what distinguishes it from the fetal, embryo, and donor selection that's practiced in the United States today. Despite its monstrous history and menacing connotations, the term "eugenics" has been reclaimed by a school of left-leaning philosophers and ethicists who seek to carve out an innocuous core from the hateful motives and vicious methods with which the ideal has been carried out. Nazis gave eugenics a bad name, these scholars say, but there's nothing inherently wrong with trying to produce people of a particular type. Shorn of its racism and savagery, that ideal can affirm parental freedom and child welfare. Adding "the word 'liberal' to 'eugenics,'" they insist, "transforms an evil doctrine into a morally acceptable one."[83] This new "liberal eugenics" comes with none of the segregation, miscegenation, sterilization, or mass slaughter that enacted the racial hygiene of old. And the government doesn't promote any blueprint for what sorts of people there should be—no state agencies or experts devising some Aryan master race. Instead it's discrete families who make these decisions—for single offspring, rather than gene pools of broader groups.[84] That reproductive control was voluntary, individualistic, and state-neutral distinguishes modern prenatal selection from the horrors of eugenics that courts invoke to void remedies for negligently blocked endowments from intelligence to appearance to musicality. That's not to say these reproductive harms are serious—they're not. But the slippery slope to eugenics doesn't preclude modest recourse.

There are two other reasons that courts might resist the perceived exercise of "quality control" over the next generation. One objection concerns parental attitudes. Recovery for confounded procreation flouts a powerful social expectation that parents will embrace their offspring with open minds and hearts: regardless of their genetic particulars, no matter what traits they're born with, and however their lives appear positioned to unfold.[85] As Professor Michael Sandel puts it: "Parental love is not contingent" on the "talents and attributes a child happens to have." On this view, choosing offspring for straight teeth or athletic process goes against everything that parental love should be: patient, devoted, and unconditional. Sandel argues that "specifying the [] genetic traits of their children" disfigures the proper expression of that love.[86] And compensating for stymied efforts would embolden only more finicky shopping among donors or embryos for various features that parents find desirable. This is the first way that courts might try to refashion their concerns about eugenics. The second reframing has a more spiritual flavor. Those who espouse it bristle at the idea of courts backstopping the artificial means by which parents co-opt the function of natural evolution or heavenly creator. This unease is sometimes articulated in terms of misgivings that offspring selection amounts to "playing God."[87]

The policy argument against quality control is unconvincing, in either form, as a basis for refusing remedies for professional negligence. The problem isn't that the second version takes sides on religion in ways that the U.S. Constitution forbids—value judgments about human command over nature find expression in assorted moral and political sources, none of which need endorse any specific faith, or even religion more generally.[88] The reason that neither account justifies policy override is that their visions of parental love and playing God don't reflect social consensus about public morality or democratic ideals. Nor are they anchored in constitutional norms or common law. Whether it's voiced in terms of parental openness or divine humility, the principle of reproductive humility is essentially contested. Invoking it to void an otherwise justified tort would open judges to charges of legislating from the bench.

According to a recent survey conducted by the Pew Research Center, Americans greet the prospect of genetically editing enhancements for cognitive abilities or physical capacities with a healthy mix of enthusiasm and restraint.[89] Parental aspirations for offspring are more often reserved: sound health and shared heredity, nothing more. Bioethicists Stephanie Chen and David Wasserman explain:

> In the near future, at least, the fear of "genetic consumerism" seems greatly exaggerated. Not only is the detection of genetic variations predisposing to [desired] traits likely to remain elusive, but parental expectations for their children's biological endowment are generally modest—"as long as it has ten fingers and ten toes."[90]

But it's always possible that reproductive science will advance more rapidly, and parental expectations along with them. Chapter 1 noted Hank Greely's prediction that wider ranging embryo testing will become routine by the middle of the century—helped along by painless, low-cost ways of making IVF embryos.[91] Successful suits for negligently confounded height, intelligence, or perfect pitch would prompt judges to consider what's so wrong with trying to have a baby of this kind or that anyway.

Nothing really, according to philosopher Frances Kamm. Before a new child is born, "there is no person yet with certain characteristics that we have to accept if we love him and do not want to impose undue burdens necessary for changes." Kamm deems it "acceptable to seek good characteristics in a new person, even though we know that when the child comes to be and we love him or her, many of these characteristics may come and go and we will continue to love the particular person."[92] Professor Sandel might respond by appeal to reproductive attitudes more than actions. Parental love, at its best, takes hold before parents learn anything about the sort of person a future child might become. Recall from Chapter 1 how a parent's disposition toward his child characteristically differs from how he cares for a friend, partner, or anyone else in his life. A parent is supposed to love his child without reserve or qualification: That love is for whichever person comes to occupy that special role in the family, whether or not her attributes are ones that the parent wished for or comes to find desirable.[93] Kamm might reply that flourishing parent-child relationships are rich and resilient enough to accommodate a more discriminating prenatal posture.

My point isn't to resolve this dispute about the ethics of selecting progeny for nonmedical traits. I mean only to suggest that reasonable people can view that practice in very different ways. To some, like Sandel, donor browsing and embryo screening reflect a troubling dislocation of parental attachments. Others, like Kamm, see efforts to have children who are "more than healthy" or "better than normal" as innocuous expressions of the admirable impulse to want what's best for them. This reasonable moral disagreement supplies precarious footing to override legitimate interests and overlook professional negligence. But policy conclusions require case-sensitive analysis of the interests and policies at stake. This chapter has argued that, in modern American society, policy objections should seldom if ever exclude recovery for thwarted offspring selection. There's too little danger of gender imbalance, cohort contagion, or reproductive efforts to produce child slaves or partners in crime. Things might look different elsewhere or in the future. Matters of social interest and public morality aren't fixed or universal. And relevant facts and values—from sex ratios and newborn health to norms of racial equality and parental love—can vary across time and place. But for now, courts shouldn't hesitate to remedy confounded procreation.

Conclusion

We're used to blaming randomness or cosmic injustice when we don't get the child we want, or when we get the one we don't. Now cutting-edge interventions promise to deliver us from the vagaries of natural conception and the genetic lottery. Birth control and abortion prevent parenthood. Gamete donation and IVF make procreation possible. And prenatal testing can detect debilitating offspring diseases even before pregnancy. These undertakings are still riddled with uncertainty—sometimes things just don't work out. But that's no reason to turn a blind eye when bad behavior is at fault. The American legal system protects against professional negligence in other inherently risky activities, from riding a car to preparing a meal. Courts lay off when fate or accidents are responsible—when deer pop out onto dark roads, or homemade chicken is undercooked. But the law doesn't hesitate to respond when auto crashes are traced to defective brakes, or food poisoning to unsanitary farming. Reproductive medicine and technology shouldn't be any different—the stakes are high, and important interests hang in the balance. Just because would-be parents are accustomed to disappointment—because many of us have resigned ourselves to spontaneous miscarriage, or unplanned pregnancy, or an unexpected roll of the genetic dice—doesn't make those outcomes any less serious, or misconduct that produces them any less worthy of redress.

Different kinds of reproductive wrongs call for different kinds of rights. In some cases, procreation is *deprived*—as when a lab technician drops the tray of embryos that are an infertile couple's last chance to have biological children, or when a doctor leads an eagerly expecting pregnant woman to abort by misinforming her that her healthy fetus would be born with a fatal disease. In other cases, procreation is *imposed*—as when a pharmacist fills a woman's birth control prescription with prenatal vitamins, or when a surgeon botches the sterilization that parents of five had sought because they were already struggling to make ends meet. Procreation is *confounded* when an IVF clinic fertilizes a patient's eggs with sperm from a stranger instead of her spouse, or when a sperm bank neglects to inform prospective parents that the anonymous donor it called "perfect" had actually dropped out of college, been convicted of burglary, and diagnosed with schizophrenia. This brings us back to the Xytex case from the book's introduction.

Angie Collins and Beth Hanson are among the dozens of couples that Xytex Cryobank sold on Donor 9623. The sperm bank had touted his spotless record and sterling credentials without even asking him for so much as a diploma, drug test, or background check, let alone permission to see his medical records. Now their ten-year-old boy, like each of his thirty-five donor siblings, has been dealt a one-in-eight chance of serious mental illness. Odds are that four or five of them will develop schizophrenia. Collins and Hanson's son doesn't show any telltale signs so far—hallucinations and other symptoms of the disease wouldn't be expected to manifest until his late teens or early twenties. That's when Donor 9623, Chris Aggeles, started hearing "derogatory and demeaning" voices that "interrupted" his thoughts and derailed his goals. Some of the other families who used his sperm have lost the luxury of anxious uncertainty about whether their child will face the troubles Aggeles did.

Wendy and Janet Norman's fifteen-year-old son has already been in and out of psychiatric hospitals for years. The first time, he was committed because he had tried to take his own life. Other times, he had lashed out at his parents with a hammer or kitchen knife. When the Normans heard that other donor sibling families had filed complaints against Xytex, they left it to their son to decide whether they should too. He was torn: "[Y]ou sue over a product because it's faulty," he said. "If that product is a person, it feels like a terrible thing to do."[1] But he decided it was important to call out the badly behaving sperm bank and the regulatory vacuum that enables its misconduct. Two dozen other families also chose Donor 9623—ten used his sperm to have multiple offspring. Half of those brought suits against Xytex for legal claims ranging from negligence, fraud, and false advertising to products liability, breach of warranty, and battery-by-insemination. Every case that didn't settle was summarily dismissed.[2]

Courts got hung up on the fact that Donor 9623 siblings never would have existed if it hadn't been for the phony profile. Judges point out that had Xytex "been truthful with [families] about Aggeles' history, they would not have used his sperm." This means that "[a]voiding 'exposure' to Aggeles' various mental health problems" wouldn't have made their children any healthier, or mitigated the risk that they might develop mental illness. It just would have replaced the babies they ended up getting with different ones. The children they have never would have been born at all.[3] Framing the harm this way makes it sound as if parents are saying that they regret their own child's birth. And that's a message that courts refuse to send or sign off on. Wary of dignifying this existential insult, they're "unwilling to say that life, even life with severe impairments, may ever amount to a legal injury."[4] But lawsuits against Xytex aren't about abortion, or even embryo selection, where the choice is "life" versus "no life." In this sperm bank controversy, the choice is between "life without a significant risk of mental disease" and "life with it." These parents aren't saying that their children's lives "amount to a legal injury," or that their families would be better if they hadn't been born. They love their kids emphatically—it's not them that's the problem. The parents' grievance lies with the consequences of reproductive negligence on their valued identities, experiences, and relationships.

Chief Judge Robert McBurney heard the Normans' case in the Superior Court of Fulton County, a few miles from Xytex headquarters in Atlanta, Georgia. To Judge McBurney, it didn't seem fair to let Xytex off the hook or leave the Normans without recourse. "[T]here should be a way," he said as he shook his fist, "for parties aggrieved as these Plaintiffs are to pursue negligence claims." He nevertheless dismissed every claim the Normans brought against Xytex, lamenting that "[a]dvances in science have—as they always do—outstripped advances in law and policy."[5] These suits have fared no better in federal court or on second look. The U.S. Court of Appeals for the Eleventh Circuit condemned the sperm bank's conduct as "[r]eckless, reprehensible, and repugnant"—but not illegal. The three-judge panel admonished Xytex for doing "nothing to verify the validity of [its] representations" about Donor 9623. "It never requested Aggeles's medical records or asked him to sign a release so it could obtain" them, "never asked about his criminal history, never requested any proof of his identification, and never attempted to confirm his educational history." Yet the federal appeals court couldn't come up with any existing authority to "recognize as a private legal injury the birth of a child with actual or potential undesirable inherited characteristics."[6]

Adoptive parents have an easier time recovering when agencies misrepresent a child's medical records and family history.[7] In the adoption context, courts emphasize that "full disclosure" serves a "compelling need" "not only to secure timely and appropriate medical care for the child, but also to make vital personal, health and family decisions."[8] Judges point out that "the adoption agency is the only party with access to information about a child's medical and genetic background."[9] And it's not too much to expect it to disclose the information that it already "possesses or has reasonable ability to obtain or request."[10] Any professional who's in the business of family formation owes the individuals it serves better than hearsay and speculation. This is no less true for sperm banks—they shouldn't be immune from liability just because the offspring they help to make possible are still in the making.

It's not as if the resulting babies themselves stand to gain anything from sperm banks being less than forthcoming with people who are looking to become parents. That's the justification that some adoption agencies offer up: Learning about the health risks or traumatic past of actual children might dissuade would-be parents from adopting them. If agencies withhold potentially off-putting information about those difficult-to-place children, that deception could make it more likely for them to find the stable families and permanent homes they need. Noble though that goal is, keeping adoptive parents in the dark is hardly an ideal way to achieve it. In any case, no such defense plausibly applies to reproductive contexts in which there are only possible children, and no existing ones, with any present interests of their own. There is no cosmic orphanage. There's no difficult-to-place potential child, who might be made worse off by never having existed—if accurate profiles had steered prospective parents away from the donor whose sperm would have been used to create him, and instead toward another donor, used to create an altogether different child.

Sex cells aren't children. And there may be other reasons for holding sperm banks to a lower standard than adoption agencies. But whatever facts adoption agencies are required to disclose about an adoptive child's background or history, sperm banks should probably make known about a donor too. Xytex can't point to any child-centered reason why it failed to verify anything about Aggeles before vouching for sterling bill of health, among other talents and exploits. A right to recover for donor misrepresentation would serve parents' reproductive interests in offspring selection, without making any child less happy or cared for. The action for procreation confounded would compensate plaintiffs and hold defendants accountable. Successful claims require showing more than that specialists behaved badly. Plaintiffs like Collins and the Normans also must prove that professional negligence inflicted a real loss on them. Courts have to discern just what this harm is, its chances of coming about, how severely that injury will foreseeably impact family life, and the extent to which misconduct is responsible for causing it. Hanging over these determinations of magnitude and likelihood are nebulous issues of heritability. No one can know for sure whether, when, and to what extent complex traits like mental illness will express themselves in offspring. Policy defenses complicate matters further: Xytex can claim that awarding damages would exacerbate stigma against people with schizophrenia, or imply that donor-conceived children aren't blessings.

The principal injury to the parents who chose Donor 9623 is the undisclosed mental illness that his sperm could pass on to their offspring. Before unpacking that injury, there were also discrepancies involving Aggeles's run-of-the-mill intellect, which Xytex had boasted was as high as Stephen Hawking's, and his ho-hum appearance that the sperm bank airbrushed in his profile picture to pass off as a "Tom Cruise lookalike." The genetic contributions of cognitive aptitudes and physical features are substantial, albeit mysterious in their precise workings. And some parents will care a great deal that their future child has a less-than-advertised chance of genius-level acumen or movie star looks. But unremarkable endowments will tend to disrupt family life less than offspring conditions that incapacitate. Even if the most dazzling IQ or beauty would likely have conferred social and economic advantages, the multifarious causation and unpredictable expression of those traits make it extra hard to pin down the difference that it'd make instead to have a biological parent who's merely ordinary in those respects. The reproductive injury is probably graver and easier to estimate when it comes to a highly heritable disease like schizophrenia. How serious that injury is depends on the practical effects it has on the plaintiffs. When procreation is confounded, the harm isn't that would-be parents ended up with any child at all—it's that they got a child whose traits differ in a meaningful sense that negligence made substantially more likely. The most salient such difference in the Xytex case is the undisclosed psychiatric disorders that Aggeles suffers from.

Failure to disclose his schizophrenia made it twelve times more likely they'd have a child with the disease. Its symptoms can be devastating. Without effective treatment, it can cause people hear cruel voices, accompanied by haunting images and even foul odors that can make these illusions brutally real:

> I could find no rest, for horrible images assailed me, so vivid that I experienced actual physical sensations. . . . [M]y mouth was full of birds which

I crunched between my teeth, and their feathers, their blood and broken bones were choking me. Or I saw people whom I had entombed in milk bottles, putrefying, and I was consuming their rotten cadavers. Or I was devouring the head of a cat which meanwhile gnawed at my vitals. It was ghastly, intolerable.[11]

Hallucinations, paranoid delusions, and loose associations can thrust people with schizophrenia into a terrifying, topsy-turvy world of waking nightmares. These are the "positive" symptoms that the disease introduces to a person's psyche, so described because they intensify and exaggerate existing anxieties to the point that they become abnormal. Psychotic breaks may come and go—sometimes conspicuous, other times imperceptible—depending on how effective and consistent medical treatment is. Less vivid effects of the disease include dampened elements of personality and behavior. Lots of people with schizophrenia lose pleasure in the activities they used to enjoy, or grow isolated even from close family and friends. These "negative" symptoms manifest differently in different people, and often vary over time. Some have difficulty expressing emotions, or functioning well enough to hold a job or care for themselves. Others exhibit the monotone voice and flat facial expressions that psychologists refer to as a blunted emotional affect. Many drift through life more listless and apathetic than before: Vibrant children become withdrawn, high- achievers grow futile, and warm hearts turn cold.

What distinguishes schizophrenia from other offspring conditions is precisely this sense of loss for what was and might have been—for the one-time activities and shared memories that slip away, for the joys and successes so narrowly missed out on. A little girl who grows up full of promise and free from care, can fade—without warning or mercy—into an illness that transforms her beyond recognition. She becomes a stranger to those who know her best and love her most. Karen and David Yeiser's daughter Bethany was a gifted violinist and budding scientist who, as a college student, lead-authored multiple major articles in prestigious academic journals. But months before graduating, she dropped out and disappeared without a trace or explanation. She wouldn't answer the Yeisers' emails or return their calls, while constantly on the move. If they managed to track her down, she refused to see them—or anyone else she knew before her schizophrenic break. The Yeisers endured five years of agonizing estrangement, during which time Bethany had been mostly homeless. Then a hospital called with word that she was on seventy-two-hour psychiatric hold in an emergency room two thousand miles away.[12]

There's no cure for schizophrenia. Medication often treats both positive and negative symptoms, but not without side effects that can range from tics and tremors to weight gain and diabetes. Cognitive and behavioral therapy may be able to help manage manifestations of the disease that don't respond to antipsychotics. But many patients refuse treatment, too immersed in delusions to admit that they need help. Randye and Bill Kaye's son refused to accept that his prescriptions do him any good, even though each time he stopped taking them led him to regress to the point that it landed back him in the hospital. Each setback in turn lowered the ceiling for how well his functioning could improve in the future. When his symptoms began as a teenager, his mother recounts, "that baseline might have included the ability to get and keep a job," or to "return to college part-time." The first time he went off his meds,

> it might have meant he could learn to budget his money [or] rebuild friendships. After his two relapses, we reduced our hopes: maybe he could manage volunteer work, remember doctors' appointments, go out in public, and keep his response to "inner stimuli" under control while others are in the room.[13]

Author Andrew Solomon explains why caring for a child with schizophrenia can require such radical reshuffling of life: "The family must be a treatment center, an outpatient unit, a constellation of eyes to watch over, a series of hands to cook or clean or sooth or restrain."[14] Careers bend and marriages break under the weight of chaos at home and isolation outside it, as parents struggle to make sense of what's happening to their child, find out if he's a danger to himself or to his siblings, do whatever they can to make things better—and come to terms with what they can't.[15]

Symptoms of the disease express themselves in different ways that can incapacitate less, or more. The gravest effects usually emerge in young children. Starting at six, Michael and Susan Schofield's daughter suffered hallucinations that consumed 95 percent of her waking life. When voices commanded her to hurt her baby brother, the Schofields were forced to separate—one child with each kid, living in two homes they couldn't afford.[16] Schizophrenia is rarely this acute when it appears later in life, as it usually does—most frequently between sixteen and thirty, though as late as forty-five. The Normans' son suffered delusions and disorganization from an early age. Collins and Hanson's hasn't shown signs of any symptoms yet—maybe he never will. The indefinite age of onset and staggering range of severity make it hard to define, let alone measure, how Xytex has harmed these families. But that uncertainty alone doesn't make that injury any less real or serious. This isn't negligence "in the air"—like the drunk driver who makes it home from the bar without incident.

Ballparking this reproductive loss starts with how much greater chance the donor misrepresentation gave their child of having schizophrenia—from less than one in a hundred in the general population, to more than one in eight for a child who has a single genetic parent with the disease. Any damage awards associated with managing a child's potential symptoms must also be reduced by the possibility that he doesn't end up developing the disease at all. Most of the three dozen children conceived from Donor 9623 probably won't have schizophrenia, but no one knows which ones will—at least not by the time they're born, or negligence was exposed. It isn't just that scientists haven't isolated all of the genes related to schizophrenia. DNA is just one piece of a larger susceptibility that's also shaped by environmental factors including drug use, head injuries, and long-term trauma in utero or in infancy. Researchers have found much higher rates of the disease, for example, among children whose mothers suffered a military invasion or family tragedy while pregnant or nursing.[17] These other potential risk factors have nothing to do with Xytex. This indeterminate causation means that courts can't simply assume that the injury to plaintiffs like Hanson and Collins includes coping with a disease that may not, in fact, come to pass. A boy like theirs, with one schizophrenic parent and no other known risk factors, has roughly a 12 percent chance of developing the disease by the time he's a high school sophomore. So a court should reduce the absolute loss associated with their child's having schizophrenia by the 88 percent chance that he never will.

There are also two forms of harm that Xytex parents sustain in the here and now, whether their child is ultimately diagnosed or not. The first is anxiety, a species of emotional distress borne of fear and disquiet—in this case, a restless waiting for the other shoe to drop. Knowing that their "son's life could just turn on a dime," Collins said, would make any parent anxious about this peril of incapacity, isolation, even suicide.[18] No amount of surveillance is sure to shield their child from the clutches of schizophrenia. Avoiding triggers and catching warning signs may enable earlier interventions, but can't prevent schizophrenia or cure its symptoms.[19] There's nothing excessive or irrational about fearing your child's very real risk of suffering a sudden psychotic break from reality—one that could haunt them for the rest of their lives. Collins compared it to an endlessly "simmering pot on the back burner."[20]

The second immediate harm is the cost of managing risk through reasonable measures to detect or prepare for foreseeable dangers. Parents like Hanson and Collins will take their son to doctors to monitor his mental health, and invest time and energy keeping him away from risk factors like contact sports. They may also pay high health premiums to insure against the possibility that he'll require expensive treatment, or that they'll need to take long-term leave from work to care for him. Addressing the hazards of schizophrenia may also chill the family's ability to move homes, change jobs or schools, or undertake other life changes. Destabilizing events or circumstances risk accelerating onset of the disease, and that risk makes a healthy dose of parental vigilance and precaution entirely sensible.[21]

Xytex left parents with a particular baby, different from the one they chose. This case shares critical features with those that leave negligence victims with any baby, when they didn't want one—or with none, when they desperately did. In each category, misconduct goes undeterred and unreported, while medical errors inflict injuries that escape redress. Reproductive negligence metes out real-world consequences, separate and apart from abstract choices. These losses tend to fall hardest on women, LGBT couples, and others who already find themselves disadvantaged. In a moral and political culture allergic to meaningful regulation, American legal history gives glimpses of hope. It's time for courts to reclaim the legacy of personality torts to fashion remedies for those trespasses that confound, impose, and deprive procreation. This reproductive architecture equips us to right the controversies we've gotten wrong and meet the challenges on the horizon.

Notes

Preface

1. Davis Bushnell & Jack Mann, *Her Parents Rejoice and Critics Recoil as America's First Test-Tube Baby Is Delivered*, PEOPLE, Jan. 18, 1982, at 40.

2. Mitchel C. Schiewe et al., *Comprehensive Assessment of Cryogenic Storage Risk and Quality Management Concerns: Best Practice Guidelines for ART Labs*, 36 J. ASSISTED REPROD. & GENETICS 5, 5 (2019).

3. Zahava P. Michaelson et al., *Early Detection of Cryostorage Tank Failure Using a Weight-based Monitoring System*, J. ASSISTED REPROD. & GENETICS, Mar. 5, 2019 (10.1007/s10815-019-01402-3).

4. Elisha Brown, *California Fertility Clinic Sued over "Thousands" of Lost Embryos and Eggs*, DAILY BEAST (Mar. 15, 2018, 6:13 PM ET), https://www.thedailybeast.com/california-fertility-clinic-sued-over-thousands-of-lost-embryos-and-eggs [https://perma.cc/5ERZ-5545]; Kayla Webley Adler, *When Your Dreams of Motherhood Are Destroyed*, MARIE CLAIRE (Oct. 1, 2018), https://www.marieclaire.com/health-fitness/a23327231/egg-freezing-embryos-lack-of-regulation/ [https://perma.cc/76E2-UJUS].

5. Danielle Zoellner, *Second Fertility Clinic in the Last Week Has a Freezer Failure*, DAILY MAIL (Mar. 11, 2018, 6:05 PM EDT), https://www.dailymail.co.uk/news/article-5488507/Eggs-embryos-possibly-damaged-California-clinic.html [https://perma.cc/8QG5-F37Q]; Ariana Eunjung Cha, *These Would-be Parents' Embryos Were Lost. Now They're Grieving—And Suing*, WASH. POST (Aug. 24, 2018), https://www.washingtonpost.com/national/health-science/these-would-be-parents-embryos-were-lost-now-theyre-grieving--and-suing/2018/08/24/57040ab0-733c-11e8-805c-4b67019fcfe4_story.html?noredirect=on&utm_term=.80e17df7e769 [https://perma.cc/2SLA-VK8J].

6. Amy Goldstein, *Fertility Clinic Informs Hundreds of Patients Their Eggs May Have Been Damaged*, WASH. POST (Mar. 11, 2018), https://www.washingtonpost.com/national/health-science/fertility-clinic-informs-hundreds-of-patients-their-eggs-may-be-damaged/2018/03/11/b605ea82-2536-11e8-b79d-f3d931db7f68_story.html?utm_term=.1155a73dbbec [https://perma.cc/6ZDX-EMPV]; Natalie Lampert, *Their Embryos Were Destroyed: Now They Mourn the Children They'll Never Have*, GUARDIAN (May 13, 2018), https://www.theguardian.com/lifeandstyle/2018/may/13/their-embryos-were-destroyed-now-they-mourn-the-children-theyll-never-have [https://perma.cc/8B4F-YZNC].

Birth Rights and Wrongs. Dov Fox.
© Dov Fox 2019. Published 2019 by Oxford University Press.

7. Nathan Crabbe, *Mechanical Glitch Ruins Sperm Stored at UF Center*, GAINESVILLE SUN (Sept. 3, 2006, 12:01 AM EST), https://www.gainesville.com/news/20060903/mechanical-glitch-ruins-sperm-stored-at-uf-center [https://perma.cc/9H9A-YPGZ].

8. *See* Doe v. Nw. Mem'l Hosp., No. 2014L000869, at 2 (Ill. Cir. Ct. Aug. 20, 2013); Michelle Manchir, *Lawsuit: Northwestern Memorial Damaged Sperm Samples*, CHI. TRIB. (Aug. 21, 2013), http://www.chicagotribune.com/news/ct-xpm-2013-08-21-ct-met-40-northwestern-frozen-sperm-lawsuits-20130821-story.html [https://perma.cc/4ECV-6VYT].

9. *See* Doe v. Airgas USA, No. 2014-L-000869 (Ill. Cir. Ct. Cook Cty. dismissed Oct. 2, 2018).

10. *See* Rachel K. Jones & Jenna Jerman, *Population Group Abortion Rates and Lifetime Incidence of Abortion: United States 2008–2014*, 107 AM. J. PUB. HEALTH 1904, 1904–06, 1907 tbl. 2 (2017).

11. *See Fast Stats—Contraceptive Use*, CTRS. DISEASE CONTROL & PREVENTION: NAT'L CTR. FOR HEALTH STATISTICS, http://www.cdc.gov/nchs/fastats/contraceptive.htm [http://perma.cc/UXM3-RCD2].

12. *See* Saswati Sunderam et al., *Assisted Reproductive Technology Surveillance—United States, 2015*, CTRS. DISEASE CONTROL & PREVENTION (Feb. 16, 2018), https://www.cdc.gov/mmwr/volumes/67/ss/ss6703a1.htm [https://perma.cc/97YF-RJ57].

13. Stephen K. v. Roni L., 164 Cal. Rptr. 618, 642–43 (Cal. Ct. App. 1980).

Introduction

1. Emily Landau, *The Sperm Donor Who Lied—And the Couple That's Fighting Back*, CHATELAINE (Oct. 19, 2016), http://www.chatelaine.com/living/sperm-donor-lied-couple-fighting-back/ [https://perma.cc/P996-MU43].

2. Theresa Boyle, *He Was the Perfect Sperm Donor. Then 26 Families Found Out He Wasn't*, THE STAR (Apr. 9, 2016), https://www.thestar.com/life/health_wellness/2016/04/09/he-was-the-perfect-sperm-donor-then-26-families-found-out-he-wasnt.html [https://perma.cc/JS82-PJF4].

3. Landau, *supra* note 1.

4. XYTEX CRYO INTERNATIONAL, THE BANK THAT PAYS YOU, http://xytexdonor.com [https://perma.cc/ZU5D-QD3W].

5. Boyle, *supra* note 2.

6. Yanan Wang, *This Couple Says Everything They Were Told about Their Sperm Donor Was a Lie*, WASH. POST (Apr. 15, 2006), https://www.washingtonpost.com/news/morning-mix/wp/2016/04/15/this-couple-says-everything-they-were-told-about-their-sperm-donor-was-a-lie/?utm_term=.a4107ace6374 [https://perma.cc/WU2Z-8R2Y].

7. Landau, *supra* note 1.

8. *See* Boyle, *supra* note 2.

9. *Id.*

10. *See* Kahyee Hor & Mark Taylor, *Suicide and Schizophrenia: A Systematic Review of Rates and Risk Factors*, 24 J. PSYCHOPHARM. 81, 81 (2010).

11. Wang, *supra* note 6.

12. Boyle, *supra* note 2.

13. Christine Hauser, *Sperm Donor's Profile Hid Mental Illness and Crime, Lawsuits Say*, N.Y. TIMES (Apr. 17, 2016), https://www.nytimes.com/2016/04/18/world/americas/sperm-donors-profile-hid-mental-illness-and-crime-lawsuits-say.html   [https://perma.cc/C3XR-HBGZ].

14. Boyle, *supra* note 2.

15. Ariana Eunjung Cha, *Fertility Fraud: People Conceived Through Errors, Misdeeds in the Industry Are Pressing for Justice*, WASH. POST (Nov. 22, 2018), https://www.washingtonpost.com/national/health-science/fertility-fraud-people-conceived-through-errors-misdeeds-in-the-industry-are-pressing-for-justice/2018/11/22/02550ab0-c81d-11e8-9b1c-a90f1daae309_story.html?utm_term=.1be6d3801c27 [https://perma.cc/A5BP-3E3V].

16. Tamar Lewin, *In Business of Sperm Banks, It's Buyer Beware*, N.Y. TIMES, July 23, 2016, at A1.

17. *See Lost Samples, Poor Screening: Sperm Bank Industry Oversight Examined*, CBS NEWS (Oct. 3, 2016, 6:40 AM), http://www.cbsnews.com/news/advocates-sperm-bank-industry-lacks-federal-oversight/ [http://perma.cc/KKJ6-V49W].

18. Jennifer Wolff, *The Truth about Donor 1084: Angry Mothers Say Sperm Banks Are Hiding Evidence of Donors' Genetic Defects*, SELF MAG., Oct. 2006, at 204.

19. Jacqueline Mroz, *From One Sperm Donor, 150 Children*, N.Y. TIMES, Sept. 6, 2011, at D1. *See also* JACQUELINE MROZ, SCATTERED SEEDS: IN SEARCH OF FAMILY AND IDENTITY IN THE SPERM DONOR GENERATION (2017).

20. Boyle, *supra* note 2.

21. Landau, *supra* note 1.

22. Jacqueline Mroz, *In Choosing a Sperm Donor, A Roll of the Genetic Dice*, N.Y. TIMES, May 15, 2012, at D1.

23. *See* Pamela Callum et al., *Gonosomal Mosaicism for an NF1 Deletion in a Sperm Donor: Evidence of the Need for Coordinated, Long-term Communication of Health Information Among Relevant Parties*, 27 HUMAN REPROD. 1223, 1224–25 (2012).

24. *See* Barry J. Maron et al., *Implications of Hypertrophic Cardiomyopathy Transmitted by Sperm Donation*, 302 J. AM. MED. ASS'N 1681, 1681 (2009).

25. *See* Laurence A. Boxer et al., *Strong Evidence for Autosomal Dominant Inheritance of Severe Congenital Neutropenia Associated with ELA2 Mutations*, 148 J. PEDIATRICS 633, 633 (2006).

26. *See* Fourth Amended Complaint for Fraud, Negligent Misrepresentation/Suppression, Professional Negligence, Unfair Business Practices, at ¶¶ 63–64, 69, Johnson v. Cal. Cryobank, Inc., No. SC043434 (Cal. Super. Ct. Apr. 2, 2003); Plaintiffs' Brief in Support of Petition Approve Compromise of Claim at 1–2, Johnson v. Cal. Cryobank, Inc., No. SC043434 (Cal. Super. Ct. June 13, 2003).

27. *See* Johnson v. Superior Court, 124 Cal. Rptr. 2d 650, 666 (Cal. Ct. App. 2002); Johnson v. Superior Court, 95 Cal. Rptr. 2d 864, 868 (Cal. Ct. App. 2000).

28. *See* Susannah Baruch, David Kaufman, & Kathy L. Hudson, *Genetic Testing of Embryos: Practices and Perspectives of U.S. In Vitro Fertilization Clinics*, 89 FERTILITY & STERILITY 1053, 1055 (2008).

29. Beth Daley, *Oversold Prenatal Tests Spur Some to Choose Abortions*, BOSTON GLOBE (Dec. 14, 2014), https://www.bostonglobe.com/metro/2014/12/14/oversold-and-unregulated-flawed-prenatal-tests-leading-abortions-healthy-fetuses/aKFAOCP5N0Kr8S1HirL7EN/story.html [https://perma.cc/G948-L6L7].

30. *FertilityIQ Protocol: How to Pick a Fertility Doctor*, FERTILITYIQ, https://www.fertilityiq.com/ivf/fertilityiq-protocol-how-to-pick-a-fertility-doctor [https://perma.cc/YL9T-SUM3].

31. *See* SHARON MORTIMER & DAVID MORTIMER, QUALITY AND RISK MANAGEMENT IN THE IVF LABORATORY 118–25 (2d ed. 2015); J. P. W. Vermeiden, *Laboratory-Related Risks in Assisted Reproductive Technologies*, *in* ASSISTED REPRODUCTIVE TECHNOLOGIES: QUALITY AND SAFETY 127, 128–29 (Jan Gerris, Francois Olivennes, & Petra De Sutter eds., 2004); Deborah Bartz & James A. Greenberg, *Sterilization in the United States*, 1 REV. OBSTET. & GYNECOL. 23, 27 (2008).

32. *See* HOWARD W. JONES, JR. ET AL., INT'L FED'N OF FERTILITY SOCIETIES, IFFS SURVEILLANCE 2010, at 10 (2010), http://www.infertilitynetwork.org/files/IFFS_Surveillance_2010.pdf [http://perma.cc/TW4T-24HW].

33. Human Fertilisation & Embryology Auth., *How We Regulate*, https://www.hfea.gov.uk/about-us/how-we-regulate/ [https://perma.cc/7WT5-U276].

34. *See* HUMAN FERTILISATION AND EMBRYOLOGY AUTHORITY, STATE OF THE FERTILITY SECTOR: 2016–17, at 24–26 (Dec. 2017), https://www.hfea.gov.uk/media/2437/hfea_state_of_the_sector_report_tagged.pdf [https://perma.cc/PW96-QRQ2].

35. The exceptions come from two prescient law students and a recent graduate. *See* Ingrid H. Heide, *Negligence in the Creation of Healthy Babies: Negligent Infliction of Emotional Distress in Cases of Alternative Reproductive Technology Malpractice Without Physical Injury*, 9 J. MED. & L. 55, 65 (2005); Joshua Kleinfeld, Comment, *Tort Law and In Vitro Fertilization: The Need for Legal Recognition of "Procreative Injury,"* 115 YALE L.J. 237, 239 (2005); Fred Norton, Note, *Assisted Reproduction and the Frustration of Genetic Affinity: Interest, Injury, and Damages*, 74 N.Y.U. L. REV. 793, 810 (1999).

36. JANET L. DOLGIN, DEFENDING THE FAMILY: LAW, TECHNOLOGY, AND REPRODUCTION IN AN UNEASY AGE 32 (1997).

37. JUDITH DAAR, REPRODUCTIVE TECHNOLOGIES AND THE LAW 366–70, 500–19 (2013). *See* MARTHA CHAMALLAS & JENNIFER B. WRIGGINS, THE MEASURE OF INJURY: RACE, GENDER, AND TORT LAW 96 (2010); SUSAN FRELICH APPLETON & D. KELLY WEISBERG, ADOPTION AND ASSISTED REPRODUCTION 294 (2009); MELISSA MURRAY & KRISTIN LUKER, CASES ON REPRODUCTIVE RIGHTS AND JUSTICE 439 (2015).

38. *See* I. Glenn Cohen, *The Constitution and the Rights Not to Procreate*, 60 STAN. L. REV. 1135 (2008); Kaiponanea T. Matsumura, *Binding Future Selves*, 75 LA. L. REV. 71 (2014); Alyssa Yoshida, Note, *The Modern Legal Status of Frozen Embryos*, 68 HASTINGS L.J. 711 (2017).

39. *See* Michele Goodwin, *A View from the Cradle: Tort Law and the Private Regulation of Assisted Reproduction*, 59 Emory L.J. 1039 (2010); Kirsten Rabe Smolensky, *Creating Children with Disabilities: Parental Tort Liability for Preimplantation Genetic Interventions*, 60 Hastings L.J. 299 (2008); Sara Weinberger, Sharon Nakar, & Dov Greenbaum, *A Novel Cause of Action to Discourage Detrimental Genetic Selection*, 43 Am. J.L. & Med. 107 (2017).

40. Hollman v. Saadat, No. BC555411, at 3 (Cal. Super. Ct. Aug. 21, 2014).

41. Nell v. Froedtert & Cmty. Health, West Bend Clinic, Inc., 829 N.W.2d 175, 176–77 (Wis. Ct. App. 2013).

42. Bergero v. Univ. of S. Cal. Keck Sch. of Med., No. B200595, 2009 WL 946874, at *1–4 (Cal. Ct. App. Apr. 9, 2009).

43. Rye v. Women's Care Ctr. of Memphis, MPLLC, 477 S.W.3d 235, 238–39, 271–72 (Tenn. 2015).

44. Nell v. Froedtert & Cmty. Health, West Bend Clinic, Inc., 829 N.W.2d 175, 181 (Wis. Ct. App. 2013).

45. *See* Michael T. Murtaugh, *Wrongful Birth: The Courts' Dilemma in Determining a Remedy for a "Blessed Event,"* 27 Pace L. Rev. 241, 250, 251–59 (2007).

46. Pub. Health Trust v. Brown, 388 So. 2d 1084, 1085 (Fla. Dist. Ct. App. 1980).

47. Atl. Obstetrics & Gynecology Grp. v. Abelson, 398 S.E.2d 557, 561 (Ga. 1990) (quoting Azzolino v. Dingfelder, 337 S.E.2d 528, 534 (N.C. 1985)).

48. Carey v. Population Servs. Int'l, 431 U.S. 678, 685 (1977).

49. *See Overview of Abortion Laws*, Guttmacher Inst. (July 1, 2018), https://www.guttmacher.org/state-policy/explore/overview-abortion-laws [https://perma.cc/B4JW-KXG2]; *Insurance Coverage of Contraceptives*, Guttmacher Inst. (July 1, 2018), https://www.guttmacher.org/state-policy/explore/insurance-coverage-contraceptives [https://perma.cc/ZEG8-7CNC].

50. *See* Smith v. Cote, 513 A.2d 341, 344, 348 (N.H. 1986).

Chapter 1

1. *See* Griswold v. Connecticut, 381 U.S. 479 (1965); Eisenstadt v. Baird, 405 U.S. 438 (1972); Roe v. Wade, 410 U.S. 113 (1973); Planned Parenthood v. Danforth, 428 U.S. 52 (1976); Carey v. Population Servs. Int'l, 431 U.S. 678 (1977).

2. Skinner v. Oklahoma *ex rel.* Williamson, 316 U.S. 535, 541 (1942).

3. *See* Adam Cohen, Imbeciles: The Supreme Court, American Eugenics, and the Sterilization of Carrie Buck 74–75 (2016); Paul A. Lombardo, Three Generations, No Imbeciles: Eugenics, the Supreme Court, and *Buck v. Bell* 29, 85 (2008).

4. *See* Paul Popenoe & Ezra S. Gosney, Twenty-Eight Years of Sterilization in California 9–10 (1938); Nancy Ordover, American Eugenics: Race, Anatomy, and the Science of Nationalism 134 (2003).

5. *Skinner*, 316 U.S. at 536.

6. *See* THOMAS C. LEONARD, ILLIBERAL REFORMERS: RACE, EUGENICS & AMERICAN ECONOMICS IN THE PROGRESSIVE ERA 189–91 (2016).

7. FRANCIS GALTON, ESSAYS IN EUGENICS 42 (1909).

8. Henry Fairfield Osborn, *Birth Control vs. Birth Selection*, 76 SCIENCE 173, 174 (1932).

9. *See* ANNETTE K. VANCE DOREY, BETTER BABY CONTESTS: THE SCIENTIFIC QUEST FOR PERFECT CHILDHOOD HEALTH IN THE EARLY TWENTIETH CENTURY 209–10 (1999).

10. STEPHAN L. CHOROVER, FROM GENESIS TO GENOCIDE: THE MEANING OF HUMAN NATURE AND THE POWER OF BEHAVIOR CONTROL 98 (1979).

11. *See* HARRY BRUINIUS, BETTER FOR ALL THE WORLD: THE SECRET HISTORY OF FORCED STERILIZATION AND AMERICA'S QUEST FOR RACIAL PURITY 272–79 (2006).

12. Konrad Burchardi, *Why Hitler Says, "Sterilize the Unfit!,"* L.A. TIMES, Aug. 11, 1935, at F9.

13. Letter from Theodore Roosevelt to Charles B. Davenport (Jan. 13, 1913), *quoted in* EDWIN BLACK, WAR AGAINST THE WEAK: EUGENICS AND AMERICA'S CAMPAIGN TO CREATE A MASTER RACE 99 (2003).

14. Randy E. Barnett & Josh Blackman, CONSTITUTIONAL LAW: CASES IN CONTEXT 949 (2017); Jamal Greene, *The Anticanon*, 125 HARV. L. REV. 379, 389, 394, 462 n.554 (2011).

15. Buck v. Bell, 274 U.S. 200, 205–07 (1927).

16. *See* LOMBARDO, *supra* note 3, 171.

17. VICTORIA F. NOURSE, IN RECKLESS HANDS: SKINNER V. OKLAHOMA AND THE NEAR TRIUMPH OF AMERICAN EUGENICS 91 (2008).

18. Skinner v. Oklahoma *ex rel.* Williamson, 316 U.S. 535, 542 (1942).

19. *See* REBECCA M. KLUCHIN, FIT TO BE TIED: STERILIZATION AND REPRODUCTIVE RIGHTS IN AMERICA, 1950–1980, at 93–94, 177–79 (2009).

20. *See* Madrigal v. Quilligan, 639 F.2d 789, 781–82 (1981); Maya Manian, *Story of Madrigal v. Quilligan: Coerced Sterilization of Mexican-American Women*, *in* REPRODUCTIVE RIGHTS AND JUSTICE STORIES (Melissa Murray, Kate Shaw, & Reva Siegel (forthcoming 2019).

21. Bill Chappell, *California's Prison Sterilizations Reportedly Echo Eugenics Era*, NPR (July 9, 2013), https://www.npr.org/sections/thetwo-way/2013/07/09/200444613/californias-prison-sterilizations-reportedly-echoes-eugenics-era [https://perma.cc/U8EW-MJCU]; Corey G. Johnson, *Female Inmates Sterilized in California Prisons Without Approval*, NBC (July 8, 2013), http://www.nbcbayarea.com/news/california/Female-Inmates-Sterilized-in-California-Prisons-Without-Approval-214634341.html [http://perma.cc/6JHZ-22HS].

22. *See* Richard Craver, *Final Payment Goes Out to 220 Eugenics Victims*, WINSTON-SALEM J. (Feb. 9, 2018), https://www.greensboro.com/news/north_carolina/final-payment-goes-out-to-eugenics-victims/article_845880e6-9a34-5483-8b15-3f91dad62ff0.html [https://perma.cc/826Z-BECV].

23. *See, e.g.*, KHIARA M. BRIDGES, REPRODUCING RACE: AN ETHNOGRAPHY OF PREGNANCY AS A SITE OF RACIALIZATION 134–40 (2011); DOROTHY ROBERTS, KILLING THE BLACK BODY: RACE, REPRODUCTION, AND THE MEANING OF LIBERTY

305–11 (1997); Zakiya Luna & Kristin Luker, *Reproductive Justice*, 9 ANN. REV. L. & SOC. SCI. 327, 328–29 (2013).

24. Carey v. Population Servs. Int'l, 431 U.S. 678, 685 (1977).

25. Planned Parenthood of Se. Pa. v. Casey, 505 U.S. 833, 851 (1992) (plurality opinion) (O'Connor, Kennedy & Souter, JJ.).

26. *See* April L. Cherry, *Choosing Substantive Justice: A Discussion of "Choice," "Rights," and the New Reproductive Technologies*, 11 WIS. WOMEN'S L.J. 431, 432–36 (2991).

27. Harris v. McRae, 448 U.S. 297, 316 (1980); Maher v. Roe, 432 U.S. 464, 478 (1977). *See also* Williams v. Zbaraz, 435 U.S. 464 (1977); Poelker v. Doe, 432 U.S. 519 (1977).

28. *Ten Great Public Health Achievements—United States, 1900–1999*, MORBIDITY & MORTALITY WKLY. REP. (CDC, Atlanta, Ga.) (Apr. 2, 1999), http://www.cdc.gov/ mmwr/preview/mmwrhtml/00056796.htm [http://perma.cc/9XNK-6WMB].

29. Gonzales v. Carhart, 550 U.S. 124, 172 (2007) (Ginsburg, J., dissenting).

30. Brief for the Petitioner at 27, Struck v. Sec'y of Def., 409 U.S. 1071 (1972) (No. 72-178), 1972 WL 135840, at *27.

31. Planned Parenthood v. Casey, 505 U.S. 833, 852–56 (1992) (plurality opinion) (O'Connor, Kennedy & Souter, JJ.).

32. Rebecca C. H. Brown et al., *Reframing the Debate Around State Responses to Infertility: Considering the Harms of Subfertility and Involuntary Childlessness*, 9 PUBLIC HEALTH ETHICS 290, 294 (2016).

33. Carol Sanger, *Developing Markets in Baby-Making: In the Matter of Baby M*, 30 HARV. J.L. & GENDER 67, 72–75 (2007).

34. ELLEN LEWIN, LESBIAN MOTHERS: ACCOUNTS OF GENDER IN AMERICAN CULTURE 48 (1993).

35. Michael Boucai, *Is Assisted Procreation an LGBT Right?*, 2016 WISC. L. REV. 1065, 1085–86 (2016).

36. *See* JENNIFER M. DENBOW, GOVERNED THROUGH CHOICE: AUTONOMY, TECHNOLOGY, AND THE POLITICS OF REPRODUCTION 14 (2015); JEANETTE EDWARDS ET AL., TECHNOLOGIES OF PROCREATION: KINSHIP IN THE AGE OF ASSISTED CONCEPTION 1 (2d ed. 1999).

37. *See* Ruth F. Chadwick, *Having Children*, *in* ETHICS, REPRODUCTION AND GENETIC CONTROL 3, 6–11, 30–40 (Ruth F. Chadwick ed., 1992); JOHN A. ROBERTSON, CHILDREN OF CHOICE: FREEDOM AND THE NEW REPRODUCTIVE TECHNOLOGIES 108–09 (1994); I. Glenn Cohen, *The Constitution and the Rights Not to Procreate*, 60 STAN. L. REV. 1135, 1139-40 (2008); Kimberly M. Mutcherson, *Procreative Pluralism*, 30 BERKELEY J. GENDER L. & JUST. 22, 39 (2015).

38. *See* Steve Rukavina, *Couple Sues Fertility Clinic over Paternity Test Mix-up*, CBC NEWS (Dec. 22, 2016), http://www.cbc.ca/news/canada/montreal/quebec-couple-sues-fertility-clinic-over-paternity-test-mix-up-1.3908440 [https://perma.cc/GRC5-WVXH].

39. THE ALAN GUTTMACHER INSTITUTE, FULFILLING THE PROMISE: PUBLIC POLICY AND U.S. FAMILY PLANNING CLINICS 10 (2000), https://www.guttmacher.org/sites/ default/files/pdfs/pubs/fulfill.pdf [https://perma.cc/59QB-W3Y9].

40. *See* KRISTIN LUKER, ABORTION AND THE POLITICS OF MOTHERHOOD 168–69 (1984). *See also* EILEEN L. MCDONAGH, BREAKING THE ABORTION DEADLOCK: FROM CHOICE TO CONSENT 89–91 (1996); JEAN E. VEEVERS, CHILDLESS BY CHOICE 3–6 (1980).

41. Erickson v. Bartell Drug Co., 141 F. Supp. 2d 1266, 1273 (W.D. Wash. 2001).

42. Barbara J. Berg, *Listening to Voices of the Infertile*, *in* REPRODUCTION, ETHNICS, AND THE LAW: FEMINIST PERSPECTIVES 80, 83–84 (Joan C. Callahan ed., 1995).

43. Denise Grady, *National Briefing | Midwest; Ohio: Uterus Transplant Is First in United States*, N.Y. TIMES, Feb. 25, 2016, at A13.

44. Jed Rubenfeld, *The Right of Privacy*, 102 HARV. L. REV. 737, 788–90 (1989).

45. Brief Amici Curiae, Roe v. Wade, 410 U.S. 113 (1973) (No. 70-18) 1972 WL 126045, at *23.

46. Reva Siegel, *Reasoning from the Body: A Historical Perspective on Abortion Regulation and Questions of Equal Protection*, 44 STAN. L. REV. 261, 374 (1992) (footnotes omitted).

47. Young v. United Parcel Service, Inc., 135 S. Ct. 1338, 1349–50 (2015).

48. R. v. Morgentaler, [1988] 1 S.C.R. 30, 37 (Can.) (Wilson, J., concurring).

49. Khiara M. Bridges, *When Pregnancy Is an Injury: Rape, Law, and Culture*, 65 STAN. L. REV. 457, 488 (2013).

50. KHIARA M. BRIDGES, THE POVERTY OF PRIVACY RIGHTS 179 (2017).

51. *See* Gary L. Brase & Sandra L. Brase, *Emotional Regulation of Fertility Decision Making: What Is the Nature and Structure of "Baby Fever"?*, 12 EMOTION 1141, 1151–52 (2012).

52. *See* Onora O'Neill, *Begetting, Bearing, and Rearing*, *in* HAVING CHILDREN: PHILOSOPHICAL AND LEGAL REFLECTIONS ON PARENTHOOD 25, 26 (Onora O'Neill & William Ruddick eds., 1979); Nicolas DiDomizio, *11 Brutally Honest Reasons Why Millennials Don't Want Kids*, MIC (July 30, 2015), https://mic.com/articles/123051/why-millennials-dont-want-kids#.tijiRkNbf [https://perma.cc/6UJU-YZ44].

53. JOHN STEINBECK, BURNING BRIGHT 29 (1950).

54. *See* Patricia K. Jennings, *"God Had Something Else in Mind": Family, Religion and Infertility*, 39 J. CONTEMP. ETHNOGRAPHY 215 (2010); MAYBE BABY: 28 WRITERS TELL THE TRUTH ABOUT SKEPTICISM, INFERTILITY, BABY LUST, CHILDLESSNESS, AMBIVALENCE, AND HOW THEY MADE THE BIGGEST DECISION OF THEIR LIVES 15 (Lori Leibovich ed., 2006).

55. *See* Tracey L. Meares, *The Increasing Significance of Genes: Reproducing Race*, 92 NW. U. L. REV. 1046, 1063–64 (1998) (book review).

56. *See* Harry Brighouse & Adam Swift, *The Goods of Parenting*, *in* FAMILY-MAKING: CONTEMPORARY ETHICAL CHALLENGES 11, 16–17 (Françoise Baylis & Carolyn McLeod eds., 2014).

57. *See* Kenneth Alpern, *Genetic Puzzles and Stork Stories*, *in* THE ETHICS OF REPRODUCTIVE TECHNOLOGY 147, 151–52, 157 (1992).

58. Parkinson v. St. James & Seacroft Univ. Hosp. NHS Tr. [2001] EWCA (Civ) 530 [71], [2002] QB 266 [283] (Eng.).

59. *See* Claire M. Kamp Dush et al., *What Are Men Doing while Women Perform Extra Unpaid Labor? Leisure and Specialization at the Transitions to Parenthood*, 78 SEX ROLES 715, 726–27 (2018).

60. *In re* Marriage of Witten, 672 N.W.2d 768, 778 (Iowa 2013) (quoting Carl H. Coleman, *Procreative Liberty and Contemporaneous Choice: An Inalienable Rights Approach to Frozen Embryo Disputes*, 84 MINN. L. REV. 55, 97 (1999)).

61. *See* I. Glenn Cohen & Eli Y. Adashi, *Embryo Disposition Disputes: Controversies and Case Law*, 46 HASTINGS CTR. REP., July–Aug. 2016, at 13, 17–18.

62. Louise Farr, *Whose Egg Is It, Anyway? An Embryo-Custody Battle*, MORE MAG., Sept. 2006 (quoting husband from Roman v. Roman, 193 S.W.3d 40 (2006)).

63. Niko Kolodny, *Which Relationships Justify Partiality? The Case of Parents and Children*, 38 PHIL. & PUB. AFF. 37, 66 (2010). For discussion, *see* I. Glenn Cohen, *The Right Not to Be a Genetic Parent?*, 81 S. CAL. L. REV. 1115, 1124–25, 1137 (2008).

64. Davis v. Davis, No. E-14496, 1989 Tenn. App. LEXIS 641, at *59–*60 (Ct. App. Sept. 21, 1989).

65. Kass v. Kass, 663 N.Y.2d 581, 601 (App. Div. 1997). *See also* Appellee/Cross-Appellant's Brief, *In re* Marriage of Witten, 672 N.W.2d 768 (Iowa 2003).

66. Allen Goldberg, Opinion, *Select a Baby's Health Not Eye Color*, L.A. TIMES (Feb. 17, 2009), http://www.latimes.com/opinion/la-oe-mgoldberg17-2009feb17-story.html [http://perma.cc/LTM2-UH6G]; Rob Stein, *"Embryo Bank" Stirs Ethics Fears*, WASH. POST (Jan. 6, 2007), http://www.washingtonpost.com/wp-dyn/content/article/2007/01/05/AR2007010501953.html [http://perma.cc/D38R-V2GL].

67. SIDDHARTHA MUKHERJEE, THE GENE: AN INTIMATE HISTORY 456 (2016).

68. HENRY T. GREELY, THE END OF SEX AND THE FUTURE OF HUMAN REPRODUCTION 105, 128 (2016).

69. *See* Susannah Baruch, David Kaufman, & Kathy L. Hudson, *Genetic Testing of Embryos: Practices and Perspectives of U.S. In Vitro Fertilization Clinics*, 89 FERTILITY & STERILITY 1053, 1055 (2008).

70. Amy Dockser Marcus, *Is It Ethical to Choose Your Baby's Eye Color?*, WALL ST. J., Oct. 3, 2018, at A11.

71. Ariana Eunjung Cha, From Sex Selection to Surrogates, American IVF Clinics Provide Services Outlawed Elsewhere, WASH. POST (Dec. 30, 2018), https://www.washingtonpost.com/national/health-science/from-sex-selection-to-surrogates-american-ivf-clinics-provide-services-outlawed-elsewhere/2018/12/29/0b596668-03c0-11e9-9122-82e98f91ee6f_story.html?utm_term=.74e422aee6d9 [https://perma.cc/5X3A-ET67]; Clare Wilson, *Exclusive: A New Test Can Predict IVF Embryos' Risk of Having a Low IQ*, NEW SCIENTIST (Nov. 15, 2018), https://www.newscientist.com/article/mg24032041-900-exclusive-a-new-test-can-predict-ivf-embryos-risk-of-having-a-low-iq [https://perma.cc/V8V4-NH7U];

72. Sarah M. Capelouto et al., *Sex Selection for Non-medical Indications: A Survey of Current Pre-implantation Genetic Screening Practices Among U.S. ART Clinics*, 3 J. ASSIST. REPROD. GENET. 409, 416 (2018)..

73. *See* Dov Fox, *Safety, Efficacy, and Authenticity: The Gap Between Ethics and Law in FDA Decisionmaking*, 2005 MICH. ST. L. REV. 1135, 1142–43 (2005).

74. *See* Rene Almeling, Sex Cells: The Medical Market for Eggs and Sperm 64 (2011); Dov Fox, *Racial Classification in Assisted Reproduction*, 118 Yale L.J. 1844, 1850 (2009); Nick Allen, *Ben Affleck Tops Celebrity Look-a-Like Sperm Donors List*, Telegraph (Dec. 25, 2009, 2:26 PM GMT), http://www.telegraph.co.uk/news/celebritynews/6884489/Ben-Affleck-tops-celebrity-look-a-like-sperm-donorslist.html.

75. *See* Ananya Bhattacharya, *Tinder for Dads: Swipe Right for a Sperm Donor*, Quartz (Sept. 27, 2016), http://qz.com/793067/the-london-sperm-bank-created-a-tinder-esque-app-to-help-women-find-donors/ [http://perma.cc/B4A8-KDKM].

76. *Informed Consent for GenePeeks*, GenePeeks, http://www.genepeeks.com/consent [http://perma.cc/U5L3-VPNR].

77. John A. Robertson, *Genetic Selection of Offspring Characteristics*, 76 B.U. L. Rev. 421, 427 (1996).

78. *See* Jaime King, *Predicting Probability: Regulating the Future of Preimplantation Genetic Screening*, 8 Yale J. Health Pol'y L. & Ethics 283, 285–86, 293–96 (2008).

79. Thomas J. Bouchard, Jr. et al., *Sources of Human Psychological Differences: The Minnesota Study of Twins Reared Apart*, 250 Science 223, 227–28 (1990). For more recent research on the influence of genetics on psychological and behavioral traits, *see* Robert Plomin et al., *Top 10 Replicated Findings from Behavioral Genetics*, 11 Persp. on Psychol. Sci. 3 (2016); Tinca J. Polderman et al., *Meta-analysis of the Heritability of Human Traits Based on Fifty Years of Twin Studies*, 47 Nat. Genetics 702 (2015).

80. *See generally* Marc D. Ginsberg, *How Much Anguish Is Enough? Baby Switching and Negligent Infliction of Emotional Distress*, 13 DePaul J. Health Care L. 255 (2010).

81. *See* Derek Parfit, Reasons and Persons 351–79 (1984); David Heyd, *Parfit on the Non-Identity Problem, Again*, 8 L. & Ethics Hum. Rts. 1, 4–7 (2014).

82. *See, e.g.*, Hogle v. Hall, 916 P.2d 814, 816–17 (Nev. 1996); Reilly v. U.S., 665 F. Supp. 976, 978–89 (R.I. 1987); Group Health Ass'n v. Blumenthal, 453 A.2d 1198, 1206–07 (Md. 1983).

83. *See* Hong Ma et al., *Correction of a Pathogenic Gene Mutation in Human Embryos*, 548 Nature 413, 419 (2017); Pam Belluck, *Scientists Repair a Risky Mutation in Human Embryo*, N.Y. Times, Aug. 2, 2017, at A1.

84. Colin Gavaghan, *Reproductive Technologies and the Search for Regulatory Legitimacy*, *in* The Oxford Handbook of the Law and Regulation of Technology 992, 1010 (Roger Brownsword, Eloise Scotford, & Karen Yeung eds., 2017).

85. Michael H. v. Gerald D., 491 U.S. 110, 130–31 (1988). *See also* Troxel v. Granville, 530 U.S. 57, 66 (2000).

86. *See* Palmore v. Sidoti, 466 U.S. 429, 433 (1984).

87. *See, e.g.*, Pemberton v. Tallahassee Med. Ctr., 66 F. Supp. 2d 1247, 1250 (N.D. Fla. 1999); Schreiber v. Physicians Ins. Co., 579 N.W.2d 730, 735–36 (Wis. Ct. App. 1998).

88. *See* Sheena Meredith, Policing Pregnancy: The Law and Ethics of Obstetric Conflict? (2005); John Seymour, Childbirth and the Law (2000).

89. *See* Jamie R. Abrams, *Distorted and Diminished Tort Claims for Women*, 34 Cardozo L. Rev. 1955, 1979 (2013).

90. *See, e.g.*, McLean v. Lilling, 529 N.Y.S.2d 975, 977 (Sup. Ct. Kings County 1988); Ferrara v. Bernstein, 582 N.Y.S.2d 673 (1st Dep't 1992). Other courts decline to recognize birthing women as direct victims, treating them as bystanders to their fetuses' suffering. *See, e.g.*, Khan v. Hip Hospital, Inc., 487 N.Y.S.2d 700, 704 (Sup. Ct. Queens County 1985); Alberto v. Columbia Presbyterian Med. Ctr., N.Y.L.J., Sept. 10, 1993, at 21 (Sup. Ct. N.Y. County 1993).

91. Sheppard-Mobley v. King, 830 N.E.2d 301, 304 (N.Y. 2005). *See also* Broadnax v. Gonzalez, 809 N.E.2d 645, 649 (N.Y. 2004); Mendez v. Bhattacharya, 838 N.Y.S.2d 378, 384–85 (N.Y. Sup. Ct. 2007); Tanner v. Hartog, 696 So. 2d 705, 707–08 (Fla. 1997); Giardina v. Bennett, 545 A.2d 139, 140 (N.J. 1988).

92. Carey v. Lovett, 622 A.2d 1279, 1286 (N.J. 1993).

93. Johnson v. Superior Court, 177 Cal. Rptr. 63, 65 (Cal. Ct. App. 1981). *See also* Oswald v. LeGrand, 453 N.W.2d 634, 639–40 (Iowa 1990).

Chapter 2

1. *See* Andrew B. Coan, *Is There a Constitutional Right to Select the Genes of One's Offspring?*, 63 Hastings L.J. 233, 260 (2011).

2. *See* Clyde Haberman, *Scientists Can Design "Better" Babies. Should They?*, N.Y. Times (June 10, 2018), https://www.nytimes.com/2018/06/10/us/11retro-baby-genetics.html [https://perma.cc/YV7X-5MNL].

3. David Cyranoski & Heidi Ledford, *Genome-edited Baby Claim Provokes International Outcry*, 563 Nature 607, 607 (2018).

4. Alexandra Harney, *China Orders Halt to Gene-editing After Outcry over Babies*, Reuters (Nov. 28, 2018), https://www.reuters.com/article/us-health-china-babies-panel/china-orders-halt-to-gene-editing-after-outcry-over-babies-idUSKCN1NY0LQ [https://perma.cc/G723-7GAQ].

5. *E.g.*, Debora L. Spar, Opinion, *Fertility Industry Is a Wild West*, https://www.nytimes.com/roomfordebate/2011/09/13/making-laws-about-making-babies/fertility-industry-is-a-wild-west [https://perma.cc/8FFV-KFE6].

6. *See* Judith Daar, *Federalizing Embryo Transfers: Taming the Wild West of Reproductive Medicine?*, 23 Colum. J. Gender & L. 257, 273–76 (2012).

7. *See* Fertility Clinic Success Rate and Certification Act of 1992, Pub. L. No. 102-493, 106 Stat. 3146 (codified as amended in scattered sections of 42 U.S.C. (2012)).

8. *See* Elizabeth C. Price, *Does the FDA Have Authority to Regulate Human Cloning*, 11 Harv. J.L. & Tech. 619, 631 n.58 (1998).

9. *See* Vitaly A. Kushnir et al., *The Status of Public Reporting of Clinical Outcomes in ART*, 100 Fertility & Sterility 736, 737–39 (2013).

10. *See* FDA Human Cells, Tissues, and Cellular and Tissue-Based Products, 21 C.F.R. § 1271 (2016).

11. Fertility Clinic Success Rate and Certification Act of 1992, H.R. 4773, 102nd Cong., 138 Cong. Rec. 16,685 (1992); 138 Cong. Rec. 8210-11 (1992) (statement of Hon. Ron Wyden); *Fertility Clinic Services: Hearing on H.R. 3940 Before the*

Subcomm. on Health & the Env't of the H. Comm. on Energy & Commerce, 102nd Cong. 98-102 (1992) (statement of Robert D. Visscher, executive director, American Fertility Society).

12. In 2018, the FDA rejected as beyond its scope a petition to make it harder for sperm donors to sire dozens of genetic siblings who don't know they're related. The agency has so far weighed in only to discourage research on next-generation advances like mitochondrial transfer, human cloning, and germline embryo editing. *See* Myrisha S. Lewis, *How Subterranean Regulation Hinders Innovation in Assisted Reproductive Technology*, 39 CARDOZO L. REV. 1239, 1269 (2018).

13. *See* Ruth M. Farrell et al., *Online Direct-to-Consumer Messages About Non-invasive Prenatal Genetic Testing*, 1 REPROD. BIOMED. SOC. 88, 93 (2015).

14. *See* Tanja Schlaikjær Hartwig et al., *Discordant Non-Invasive Prenatal Testing (NIPT)—A Systematic Review*, 37 PRENATAL DIAGNOSIS 527, 528 (2017); *Prenatal Tests Have High Failure Rate, Triggering Abortions*, NBC NEWS (Dec. 14, 2014, 3:12 PM PST), http://www.nbcnews.com/health/womens-health/prenatal-tests-have-high-failure-rate-triggering-abortions-n267301 [https://perma.cc/QL6D-AA8U]; Brandy Zadrozny, *Parents Sue Doctors over "Wrongful Abortion,"* DAILY BEAST (Jan. 29, 2015, 5:55 AM EST), https://www.thedailybeast.com/parents-sue-doctors-over-wrongful-abortion [https://perma.cc/S4RF-CW5A].

15. *See* John A. Robertson, *Commerce and Regulation in the Assisted Reproduction Industry, in* BABY MARKETS: MONEY AND THE NEW POLITICS OF CREATING FAMILIES 191, 203 (Michele Bratcher Goodwin ed., 2010); Richard F. Storrow, *Surrogacy American Style, in* SURROGACY, LAW, AND HUMAN RIGHTS 191, 194 (Paula Gerber & Katie O'Byrne eds., 2015).

16. *See* ARIZ. REV. STAT. § 25-318.03 (LexisNexis 2018).

17. *See* UTAH CODE ANN. § 78B-15-708 (West 2015).

18. LA. REV. STAT. ANN. § 9:128 (2009).

19. *See* Ariana Eunjung Cha, *Embryo Storage Bill Seeks Oversight of Fertility Centers and Penalties for Those That Violate Safeguards*, WASH. POST (July 5, 2018), https://www.washingtonpost.com/news/to-your-health/wp/2018/07/05/embryo-storage-bill-seeks-oversight-of-fertility-centers-and-penalties-for-those-that-violate-safeguards/?noredirect=on&utm_term=.a9ac72972990 [https://perma.cc/PU2L-ZQ9U].

20. Rodriguez v. Salem, No. BC626618 (Cal. Super. Ct. Jan. 12, 2017); Sills v. Pacific Reproductive Medical Center, Inc., No. 30-2015-00812947-CU-WT-CJC (Cal. Super. Ct. Oct. 2, 2015); Lumanlan-Domingo v. Rosenberg, No. BC563660 (Cal. Super. Ct. Nov. 12, 2014); Said v. Pacific Reproductive Center, No. PC040905, 2009 WL 9095786 (Cal. Super. Ct. Apr. 9, 2008); Young v. Salem, No. YC050743 (Cal. Super. Ct. Apr. 13, 2005).

21. *See* Request for Dismissal, Pineda v. Salem, No. BC571805 (Cal. Super. Ct. Oct. 20, 2018); Kacey Montoya, *Lawsuit: Torrance Doctor Terminated Woman's Pregnancy Without Consent after Embryo Mix-up*, KTLA (Nov. 24, 2015, 2:10 AM), http://ktla.com/2015/11/24/lawsuit-torrance-doctor-terminated-womans-pregnancy-without-consent-after-embryo-mix-up/ [http://perma.cc/8GJM-E3DW].

22. *See* Bernice Yeung & Jonathan Jones, *When Pregnancy Dreams Become IVF Nightmares*, Reveal (June 1, 2017), https://www.revealnews.org/article/when-pregnancy-dreams-become-ivf-nightmares/ [https://perma.cc/JMW8-MFQ7].

23. Am. Soc'y for Reprod. Med. et al., *Revised Minimum Standards for Practices Offering Assisted Reproductive Technologies: A Committee Opinion*, 102 Fertility & Sterility 682 (2014), http://www.asrm.org/globalassets/asrm/asrm-content/news-and-publications/practice-guidelines/for-non-members/revised_minimum_standards_for_practices_offering_assisted_reproductive_technologies-noprint.pdf [https://perma.cc/34U7-GB9X].

24. *See* Ellie Kincaid, *A Booming Medical Industry in the US Is Almost Totally Unregulated*, Bus. Insider (July 7, 2015, 3:50 PM), https://www.businessinsider.com/assisted-reproduction-ivf-industry-regulation-2015-6 [https://perma.cc/3PMS-ACZ9].

25. Andrea Preisler, *Assisted Reproductive Technology: The Dangers of an Unregulated Market and the Need for Reform*, 15 DePaul J. Health Care L. 213, 220, 213 (2013).

26. *FertilityIQ Protocol: How to Pick a Fertility Doctor*, FertilityIQ, https://www.fertilityiq.com/ivf/fertilityiq-protocol-how-to-pick-a-fertility-doctor [https://perma.cc/YL9T-SUM3].

27. *See* Dov Fox, *Transparency Challenges in Reproductive Health Care*, *in* Transparency in Health and Health Care: Legal and Ethical Possibilities and Limits 286, 293–94 (I. Glenn Cohen, Holly Fernandez Lynch, & Barbara Evans eds., 2019).

28. Sujatha Jesudason, Opinion, *Regulations Can Hurt the Vulnerable*, N.Y. Times (Sept. 13, 2011), https://www.nytimes.com/roomfordebate/2011/09/13/making-laws-about-making-babies/regulations-can-hurt-the-vulnerable [https://perma.cc/HZ6R-NSRF].

29. *See* Surrogacy Bill 2010 (N.S.W.), pt 2 div 2 s 8 (Austl.); Surrogacy Act 2008 (W. Austl.), pt 2 div 2 ss 8–9 (Austl.); Law No. 94-654 of July 29, 1994, J.O., July 30, 1994, p. 11,062; D.S.L. 1994, 29, 411 (Fr.).

30. *See* Departments of Labor, Health and Human Services, and Education and Related Agencies Appropriations Act of 1998, § 513 Pub. L. No. 105-78, 1997 U.S.C.C.A.N. (111 Stat.) 1467, 1517.

31. *See* Anne Drapkin Lyerly, *Marking the Fine Line: Ethics and the Regulation of Innovative Technologies in Human Reproduction*, 11 Minn. J.L. Sci. & Tech. 685, 697–701 (2010); Michael Ollove, *Lightly Regulated In Vitro Fertilization Yields Thousands of Babies Annually*, Wash. Post (Apr. 13, 2015), https://www.washingtonpost.com/national/health-science/lightly-regulated-in-vitro-fertilization-yields-thousands-of-babies-annually/2015/04/13/f1f3fa36-d8a2-11e4-8103-fa84725dbf9d_story.html?utm_term=.366a1ca3f9c5 [https://perma.cc/Q5P8-LWJ2].

32. *See* RESOLVE: The National Infertility Association, *Convio Case Study* (2009), http://www.convio.com/files/RESOLVE.pdf [https://perma.cc/E63Y-BXK3].

33. *See* Elizabeth Nash et al., *Laws Affecting Reproductive Health and Rights: State Policy Trends at Midyear, 2017*, Guttmacher Inst. (July 13, 2017), https://www.guttmacher.org/article/2017/07/laws-affecting-reproductive-health-and-rights-state-policy-trends-midyear-2017 [https://perma.cc/3R6J-3U6Q].

34. *See* Dov Fox, *Retracing Liberalism and Remaking Nature: Designer Children, Research Embryos, and Featherless Chickens*, 24 Bioethics 170, 174 (2010).

35. *Compare* Dov Fox, *Racial Classification in Assisted Reproduction*, 118 YALE L.J. 1844, 1881–83 (2009), *with* Courtney Megan Cahill, *Reproduction Reconceived*, 101 MINN. L. REV. 617, 638–41, 656–57, 665–66 (2016).

36. *See* June Carbone & Naomi Cahn, *Embryo Fundamentalism*, 18 WM. & MARY BILL RTS. J. 1015, 1032 (2010); Heather Silber Mohamed, *Embryonic Politics: Attitudes about Abortion, Stem Cell Research, and IVF*, 11 POL. & RELIGION 459, 479–81 (2018).

37. *See* ROBERT H. BLANK, REGULATING REPRODUCTION 223–24 (1992).

38. *See* Marsha Saxton, *Disability Rights and Selective Abortion, in* THE DISABILITY STUDIES READER 105, 112 (Lennard J. Davis ed., 2006).

39. HENRY T. GREELY, THE END OF SEX AND THE FUTURE OF HUMAN REPRODUCTION 167–68, 274 (2016).

40. *See* JOHN FABIAN WITT, THE ACCIDENTAL REPUBLIC: CRIPPLED WORKINGMEN, DESTITUTE WIDOWS, AND THE REMAKING OF AMERICAN LAW 31–40 (2004).

41. RALPH NADER, UNSAFE AT ANY SPEED: THE DESIGNED-IN DANGERS OF THE AMERICAN AUTOMOBILE (1965). For discussion, *see* Nora Freeman Engstrom, *When Cars Crash: The Automobile's Tort Legacy*, 53 WAKE FOREST L. REV. 293, 312–13 (2018).

42. *See* KEN OLIPHANT & RICHARD W. WRIGHT, MEDICAL MALPRACTICE AND COMPENSATION IN GLOBAL PERSPECTIVE 555–57 (2013). *See also* Robert L. Rabin, *The Politics of Tort Reform*, 26 VAL. U. L. REV. 709, 710–11 (1992); Stephen D. Sugarman, *Doing Away with Tort Law*, 73 CAL. L. REV. 555, 627 (1985); Peter H. Schuck, *Tort Reform, Kiwi-Style*, 27 YALE L. & POL'Y REV. 187, 203 (2008).

43. *See* VA. CODE ANN. § 38.2-5014 (2007); FLA. STAT. § 766.302 (2007). For discussion, *see* Gil Siegal et al., *Adjudicating Severe Birth Injury Claims in Florida and Virginia: The Experience of a Landmark Experiment in Personal Injury Compensation*, 34 AM. J.L. & MED. 493, 533 (2008).

44. *See* JOINT LEGISLATIVE AUDIT AND REVIEW COMM'N OF THE VA. GEN. ASSEMBLY, REVIEW OF THE VIRGINIA BIRTH-RELATED NEUROLOGICAL INJURY COMPENSATION PROGRAM 25 (2003), http://www.vabirthinjury.com/wp-content/uploads/2012/08/rpt2841.pdf [https://perma.cc/6BHU-C8ZH]; *NICA-Florida's Innovative Alternative to Costly Litigation*, FLA. BIRTH-RELATED NEUROLOGICAL INJ. COMPENSATION ASS'N [NICA], https://www.nica.com/what-is-nica.html [https://perma.cc/PH3V-PHFF].

45. *See* Nora Freeman Engstrom, *Exit, Adversarialism, and the Stubborn Persistence of Tort*, 6 J. TORT LAW 1, 35–36 (2015).

46. *See* Samuel Issacharoff & John Fabian Witt, *The Inevitability of Aggregate Settlement: An Institutional Account of American Tort Law*, 57 VAND. L. REV. 1571, 1614 (2004).

47. *See* John C. Coffee, Jr., *Class Wars: The Dilemma of the Mass Tort Class Action*, 95 COLUM. L. REV. 1343, 1384–86, 1404–09 (1995).

48. *See* Hebert v. Ochsner Fertility Clinic, 102 So. 3d 913, 919–20 (La. Ct. App. 2012).

49. *Id.* at 921.

50. DAVID M. ENGEL, THE MYTH OF THE LITIGIOUS SOCIETY: WHY WE DON'T SUE 5 (2016).

51. *See* WILLIAM HALTOM & MICHAEL MCCANN, DISTORTING THE LAW: POLITICS, MEDIA, AND THE LITIGATION CRISIS 183–226 (2004); William McCann, William Haltom, & Anne Bloom, *Java Jive: Genealogy of a Juridical Icon*, 56 U. MIAMI L. REV. 113, 130 (2001).

52. *See* ENGEL, *supra* note 50, at 13.

53. *See* Troyen A. Brennan et al., *Incidence of Adverse Events and Negligence in Hospitalized Patients: Results of the Harvard Medical Practice Study I*, 324 NEW ENG. J. MED. 370, 371 (1991); David M. Studdert et al., *Claims, Errors, and Compensation Payments in Medical Malpractice Litigation*, 354 NEW ENG. J. MED. 2024–33 (2006); David M. Studdert et al., *Negligent Care and Malpractice Claiming Behavior in Utah and Colorado*, 38 MED. CARE 250, 251 (2000).

54. *See* David M. Studdert, Michelle M. Mello, & Troyen A. Brennan, *Medical Malpractice*, 350 N. ENG. J. MED. 283, 287–88 (2004); Charles Vincent et al., *Why Do People Sue Doctors?*, 343 LANCET 1609, 1609–13 (1994).

55. *See* Rebecca J. Cook & Bernard M. Dickens, *Reducing Stigma in Reproductive Health*, 125 INT'L J. OBSTET. & GYNECOL. 89, 89 (2014).

56. GAY BECKER, THE ELUSIVE EMBRYO: HOW WOMEN AND MEN APPROACH NEW REPRODUCTIVE TECHNOLOGIES 148 (2000).

57. *See* Pauline Slade et al., *The Relationship Between Perceived Stigma, Disclosure Patterns, Support and Distress in New Attendees at an Infertility Clinic*, 22 HUMAN REPRODUCTION 2309, 2309 (2007).

58. Paula Abrams, *The Bad Mother: Stigma, Abortion and Surrogacy*, 43 J.L. MED. & ETHICS 179, 179 (2015).

59. Sigrid Nunez, *The Most Important Thing*, *in* SELFISH, SHALLOW, AND SELF-ABSORBED: SIXTEEN WRITERS ON THE DECISION NOT TO HAVE KIDS 97, 109 (Meghan Daum ed., 2015).

60. BECKER, *supra* note 56, at 39.

61. ELAINE TYLER MAY, BARREN IN THE PROMISED LAND: CHILDLESS AMERICANS AND THE PURSUIT OF HAPPINESS 219 (1995).

62. *Id.* at 255.

63. *See id.* at 142–43.

64. *Id.* at 129.

65. *Id.* at 3.

66. *See id.* at 183.

67. *See id.* at 10, 19.

68. *Id.* at 16–17, 183.

69. Y.G. v. Jewish Hosp. of St. Louis, 795 S.W.2d 488, 491–93 (Mo. Ct. App. 1990).

70. *See* Alice Clapman, Note, *Privacy Rights and Abortion Outing: A Proposal for Using Common-Law Torts to Protect Abortion Patients and Staff*, 112 YALE L.J. 1545, 1545–47 (2003). *See also* CAROL SANGER, ABOUT ABORTION: TERMINATING PREGNANCY IN TWENTY-FIRST CENTURY AMERICA 62–73 (2017).

71. *Y.G.*, 795 S.W.2d at 500, 503.

72. *See, e.g.*, Jodi Kantor, *Lawsuits' Lurid Details Draw an Online Crowd*, N.Y. TIMES, Feb. 23, 2015, at A1; Lior Jacob Strahilevitz, *Pseudonymous Litigation*, 77 U. CHI. L. REV. 1239, 1243 (2010).

73. *See* DANIEL J. SOLOVE, THE FUTURE OF REPUTATION: GOSSIP, RUMOR, AND PRIVACY ON THE INTERNET 94 (2007).

74. *See* FED. R. CIV. PRO 10(a); Sealed Plaintiff v. Sealed Defendant, 537 F.3d 185, 188–89 (2d Cir. 2008).

75. MAY, *supra* note 61, at 255.

76. *See* JUDITH DAAR, THE NEW EUGENICS: SELECTIVE BREEDING IN AN ERA OF REPRODUCTIVE TECHNOLOGIES 64–69 (2017).

77. *Induced Abortion in the United States (2018)*, GUTTMACHER INST. (Jan. 2018), https://www.guttmacher.org/fact-sheet/induced-abortion-united-states [https://perma.cc/ASV8-UDTW].

78. The price is about $5,000 less if using donated embryos, $20,000 more if buying eggs, and another $75,000 to $150,000 if assisted reproduction involves a gestational surrogate. *See* Jessica Ravitz, *Two Dads, an Egg Donor and a Surrogate: How a Freezer Failure Changed Everything*, CNN (June 29, 2018, 3:41 PM ET), https://www.cnn.com/2018/06/28/health/embryos-egg-donor-surrogate/index.html [https://perma.cc/HCR9-NFEY].

79. *See* JODY LYNEÉ MADEIRA, TAKING BABY STEPS: HOW PATIENTS AND FERTILITY CLINICS COLLABORATE IN CONCEPTION 10 (2018).

80. *See* MERCER HEALTH & BENEFITS, EMPLOYER EXPERIENCE WITH, AND ATTITUDES TOWARD, COVERAGE OF INFERTILITY TREATMENT 2 (2006).

81. *See* Megan Jula, *4 Lesbians Sue over New Jersey Rules on Fertility Treatment*, N.Y. TIMES (Aug. 8, 2016), http://www.nytimes.com/2016/08/09/nyregion/lesbian-couple-sues-over-new-jersey-rules-for-fertility-treatment.html [https://perma.cc/A3PU-RYFT].

82. Allison K. Hoffman, *Review of The New Eugenics: Selective Breeding in an Era of Reproductive Technologies*, 4 J. LAW BIOSCIENCES 671, 674 (2017) (book review).

83. *See* Ilene Prusher, *New IVF Policy Have Israeli Women Worried About Being Left Behind*, HAARETZ (Feb. 21, 2014, 2:13 AM), http://www.haaretz.com/news/features/.premium-1.575442 [http://perma.cc/K4GH-NCJH].

84. Ralston v. Conn. Gen. Life Ins., 617 So. 2d 1379, 1382 (La. Ct. App. 1993), *rev'd and remanded*, 625 So. 2d 156, 157 (La. 1993). Courts have also upheld a range of reproductive restrictions. These include (1) probate conditions not to procreate, *see* U.S. v. Harris, 794 F.3d 885, 887 (2015); State v. Oakley, 629 N.W.2d 200, 202 (Wis. 2001); State v. Kline, 963 P.2d 697 (Or. Ct. App. 1998); (2) judicial orders barring drug-using parents from having additional children, *see In re* V.R., No. 5616-04, 2004 WL 3029874, at *1 (N.Y. Fam. Ct., Monroe Cty. Dec. 22, 2004); (3) federal bans on donating unscreened gametes, *see* Doe v. Hamburg, No. C-12-3412 EMC, 2013 WL 3783749, at *1 (N.D. Cal. July 16, 2013); and (4) penal rules that forbid prisoners from mailing their sperm to inseminate their wives. *See* Gerber v. Hickman, 291 F.3d 617, 619 (9th Cir. 2002); Goodwin v. Turner, 908 F.2d 1395, 1399 (8th Cir. 1990).

85. Castles v. Sec'y to the Dep't of Justice (2010) 28 VR 141, para. 123 (Austl.).

Chapter 3

1. *See, e.g.,* Deborah S. Mazer, *Born Breach: The Challenge of Remedies in Surrogacy Contracts,* 28 YALE J.L. & FEMINISM 211, 218–19 (2017).

2. Wilczynski v. Goodman, 391 N.E.2d 479, 488 (Ill. App. Ct. 1979); Lovely v. Percy, 826 N.E.2d 909, 913 (Ohio Ct. App. 2005).

3. *See* Hawkins v. McGee, 146 A. 641, 643, 644 (N.H. 1929); THE PAPER CHASE (Twentieth Century Fox Film Corp. 1973).

4. *See* Jacob & Youngs, Inc. v. Kent, 129 N.E. 889, 890–91 (N.Y. 1921).

5. Editorial, *Fertility Clinic Is Sued over the Loss of Embryos,* N.Y. TIMES, Oct. 1, 1995, at A26.

6. *Selecting a Sperm Bank,* CAL. CRYOBANK, https://cryobank.com/why-use-us/selecting-a-sperm-bank/ [https://perma.cc/8LZX-VTPH].

7. *Donor Semen Services Agreement,* CAL. CRYOBANK, http://cryobank.com/uploadedFiles/Cryobankcom/_forms/pdf/documents/PurchaseStorageAgreement.pdf [http://perma.cc/J6JG-84TH].

8. Tunkl v. Regents of the Univ. of Cal., 383 P.2d 441, 446–47 (Cal. 1963).

9. *See* Ash v. N.Y. Univ. Dental Ctr., 564 N.Y.S.2d 308, 310 (App. Div. 1990); Olson v. Molzen, 558 S.W.2d 429, 430, 432 (Tenn. 1977).

10. Scalisi v. N.Y. Univ. Med. Ctr., 805 N.Y.S.2d 62, 63 (App. Div. 2005).

11. Jim Hawkins, *Doctors as Bankers: Evidence from Fertility Markets,* 84 TUL. L. REV. 841, 873 (2010).

12. JODY LYNEÉ MADEIRA, TAKING BABY STEPS: HOW PATIENTS AND FERTILITY CLINICS COLLABORATE IN CONCEPTION 2 (2018).

13. *See* Jennifer Arlen, *Contracting over Liability: Medical Malpractice and the Cost of Choice,* 158 U. PA. L. REV. 957, 1022 (2010).

14. *See* Ronen Perry, *It's a Wonderful Life,* 93 CORNELL L. REV. 329, 382 (2008).

15. *See* DAN B. DOBBS, PAUL T. HAYDEN, & ELLEN M. BUBLICK, THE LAW OF TORTS §§ 283–84 (2d ed. 2011).

16. Ball v. Mudge, 391 P.2d 201, 203 (Wash. 1964).

17. *See* Roberts v. Tardif, 417 A.2d 444, 448–49 (Me. 1980); Sinclair v. Block, 633 A.2d 1137, 1141–42 (Pa. 1993). For discussion, *see* Michelle Oberman, *Mothers and Doctors' Orders: Unmasking the Doctor's Fiduciary Role in Maternal-Fetal Conflicts,* 94 Nw. U. L. REV. 451, 489 (2000); Philip G. Peters, Jr., *The Quiet Demise of Deference to Custom: Malpractice Law at the Millennium,* 57 WASH. & LEE L. REV. 163, 180–85 (2000).

18. Nowatske v. Osterloh, 543 N.W.2d 265, 271–72 (Wis. 1996), *abrogated by* Nommensen v. Am. Cont'l Ins., 629 N.W.2d 301 (Wis. 2001).

19. *See* Navid Esfandiari, Megan E. Bunnell, & Robert F. Casper, *Human Embryo Mosaicism: Did We Drop the Ball on Chromosomal Testing?,* 33 J. ASSISTED REPROD. GEN. 1439, 1443 (2016).

20. Tochi Amagwula et al., *Preimplantation Genetic Diagnosis: A Systematic Review of Litigation in the Face of New Technology,* 98 FERTILITY & STERILITY 1277, 1279–80 (2012).

21. *See* Leeanda Wilton et al., *The Causes of Misdiagnosis and Adverse Outcomes in PGD*, 24 Hum. Reprod. 1221, 1222 (2009); Matts Wikland & Cecilia Sjöblom, *The Application of Quality Systems in ART Programs*, 166 Molecular & Cellular Endocrinology 3, 5 (2000).

22. *See* Sergi Novo et al., *Barcode Tagging of Human Oocytes and Embryos to Prevent Mix-ups in Assisted Reproduction Technologies*, 29 Hum. Reprod. 18, 20 (2014).

23. *See* Cristina Gutiérrez-Mateo et al., *Validation of Microarray Comparative Genomic Hybridization for Comprehensive Chromosome Analysis of Embryos*, 95 Fertility & Sterility 953, 955 (2011).

24. Huddleston v. Infertility Ctr. of Am., Inc., 700 A.2d 453, 460 (Pa. Super. Ct. 1997).

25. Daniel Grossman et al., *Induced Abortion Provision Among a National Sample of Obstetrician–Gynecologists*, 133 Obstet. & Gynecol. (forthcoming 2019).

26. *See* U.S. Dep't of Health & Human Servs., Overview of Federal Statutory Healthcare Provider Conscience Protections (2016), http://www.hhs.gov/ocr/civilrights/faq/providerconsciencefaq.html [http://perma.cc/5T4H-SXKZ]; N. Coast Women's Care Med. Grp. v. San Diego Cty. Superior Court, 189 P.3d 959, 962 (Cal. 2008); Mark R. Wicclair, Conscientious Objection in Health Care: An Ethical Analysis 95–98 (2011).

27. *See* Andrea D. Gurmankin et al., Screening Practices and Beliefs of Assisted Reproductive Technology Programs 61, 65 tbl.6 (2005); Alanna Weissman, *Doctors Fail Women Who Don't Want Children*, N.Y. Times, Dec. 2, 2017, at SR10; Sharon Kirkey, *Doctors Denying "Tubals" to Women Under 30 Opting Out of Motherhood*, Nat'l Post (Sept. 6, 2017), https://nationalpost.com/health/doctors-denying-tubals-to-women-under-30-opting-out-of-motherhood [https://perma.cc/59LF-2ADS].

28. *See* Mark A. Hall, Ira M. Ellman, & David Orentlicher, Health Care Law and Ethics in a Nutshell 78 (3d ed. 2011); Jolene S. Fernandes, Note, *Perfecting Pregnancy via Preimplantation Genetic Screening: The Quest for an Elusive Standard of Care*, 4 U.C. Irvine L. Rev. 1295, 1320 (2014).

29. Shaffer v. Icely, 16 So. 3d 282, 283 (Fla. Dist. Ct. App. 2d Dist. 2009), *dismissed*, 21 So. 3d 813 (Fla. 2009).

30. Schloss v. Miriam Hosp., No. C.A. 98-2076, 1999 WL 41875, at *3 (R.I. Super. Ct., Jan. 11, 1999).

31. Restatement (Third) of Torts: Liability for Physical & Emotional Harm § 4 (Am. Law Inst. 2012).

32. *See* Doe v. Lai-Yet Lam, 701 N.Y.S.2d 347, 348 (App. Div. 2000).

33. *See* Haymon v. Wilkerson, 535 A.2d 880, 881 (D.C. 1987); Naccash v. Burger, 290 S.E.2d 825, 827 (Va. 1982); Keel v. Banach, 624 So. 2d 1022, 1029 (Ala. 1993); Flanagan v. Williams, 623 N.E.2d 185, 190 (Ohio Ct. App. 1993). For discussion, *see* Kate Wevers, Note, *Prenatal Torts and Pre-Implantation Genetic Diagnosis*, 24 Harv. J.L. & Tech. 257, 267 (2010).

34. *See* Alexander Morgan Capron, *Tort Liability in Genetic Counseling*, 79 Colum. L. Rev. 618, 634–36 & 635 n.67 (1979). For the legal history of wrongful birth actions in the United Kingdom, *see* J. K. Mason, The Troubled Pregnancy: Legal Wrongs and Rights 53–99 (2007).

35. Moorman v. Walker, 773 P.2d 887, 889 (Wash. Ct. App. 1989) (citing McKernan v. Aasheim, 687 P.2d 850, 855 (Wash. 1984)).

36. *See* Doherty v. Merck & Co., No. 17-1997, 2018 WL 3016909 (1st Cir. June 18, 2018); Tillman v. Goodpasture, No. 117,439, 2018 WL 2994343 (Kan. Ct. App. June 15, 2018).

37. *See* ME. REV. STAT. ANN. tit. 24, § 2931(3) (2015); Stewart-Graves v. Vaughn, 170 P.3d 1151, 1160 (Wash. 2007); Moscatello v. Univ. of Med. & Dentistry, 776 A.2d 874, 878–79 (N.J. Super. Ct. App. Div. 2001); Galvez v. Frields, 107 Cal. Rptr. 2d 50, 57–59 (Cal. Ct. App. 2001).

38. *See* Berman v. Allan, 404 A.2d 8, 14 (N.J. 1979); Cailin Harris, *Statutory Prohibitions on Wrongful Birth Claims and Their Dangerous Effects on Parents*, 34 B.C.J.L. & SOC. JUST. 365, 383–84 (2014).

39. DAVID BOONIN, THE NON-IDENTITY PROBLEM AND THE ETHICS OF FUTURE PEOPLE 275–76 (2014); I. Glenn Cohen, *Regulating Reproduction: The Problem with Best Interests*, 96 MINN. L. REV. 423, 471–74 (2011).

40. *See* Paola Frati, *Preimplantation and Prenatal Diagnosis, Wrongful Birth and Wrongful Life: A Global View of Bioethical and Legal Controversies*, 23 HUMAN REPROD. UPDATE 338, 344–46 (2017).

41. Schloss v. Miriam Hosp., No. C.A. 98-2076, 1999 WL 41875, at *4 (R.I. Super. Ct., Jan. 11, 1999).

42. *See* Janet L. Dolgin, *Embryonic Discourse: Abortion, Stem Cells, and Cloning*, 31 FLA. ST. U. L. REV. 101, 130 (2003); Robert Post & Reva Siegel, *Roe Rage: Democratic Constitutionalism and Backlash*, 42 HARV. C.R.-C.L. L. REV. 373, 420 (2007).

43. Carol Sanger, *The Lopsided Harms of Reproductive Negligence*, 117 COLUM. L. REV. ONLINE 1, 9–10 (2017), http://columbialawreview.org/content/the-lopsided-harms-of-reproductive-negligence/ [http://perma.cc/W5MD-27RC].

44. Gonzales v. Carhart, 550 U.S. 124, 159 (2007).

45. *See* Clare Huntington, *The Empirical Turn in Family Law*, 118 COLUM. L. REV. 227, 250–52 (2018); Mary Ziegler, *The Jurisprudence of Uncertainty: Knowledge, Science, and Abortion*, 2018 WIS. L. REV. 317, 361–66 (2018).

46. Roe v. Wade, 410 U.S. 113, 149 (1973).

47. *See Carhart*, 550 U.S. at 161–65.

48. Whole Woman's Health v. Hellerstedt, 136 S. Ct. 2292, 2309–10 (2016) (citing Planned Parenthood of Se. Pa. v. Casey, 505 U.S. 833, 877 (1992)).

49. *See Abortion Bans in Cases of Sex or Race Selection or Genetic Anomaly*, GUTTMACHER INST. (Mar. 1, 2018), https://www.guttmacher.org/state-policy/explore/abortion-bans-cases-sex-or-race-selection-or-genetic-anomaly [https://perma.cc/A74S-QE3R].

50. *See* Dov Fox, *Selective Procreation in Public and Private Law*, 64 UCLA L. REV. DISC. 294, 301–08 (2016).

51. *See* Michael A. Belfort et al., *Fetoscopic Open Neural Tube Defect Repair: Development and Refinement of a Two-Port, Carbon Dioxide Insufflation Technique*, 129 OBSTET. & GYNECOL. 734, 743 (2017).

52. Denise Grady, *The Patient Within*, N.Y. TIMES, Oct. 23, 2017, at D1.

53. *See* Daily Mail Reporter, *Victory for Couple Who Said They "Would Have Aborted Daughter if They Knew She Had Down's Syndrome" as Jury Forces Hospital to Pay $2.9*

Million Following Botched Test, DAILY MAIL (Mar. 11, 2012, 3:31 AM ET), http://
www.dailymail.co.uk/news/article-2113342/Deborah-Ariel-Levy-Portland-couple-
wins-case-Legacy-Heath-wrongful-birth-daughter-born-Down-syndrome.html
[https://perma.cc/YG6D-CSQY]. *See also* ANDREW SOLOMON, FAR FROM THE TREE:
PARENTS, CHILDREN, AND THE SEARCH FOR IDENTITY 40 (2012); Wendy F. Hensel,
The Disabling Impact of Wrongful Birth and Wrongful Life Actions, 40 HARV. C.R.-
C.L. L. REV. 141, 172 (2005); Elizabeth Picciuto, *Parents Sue for "Wrongful Birth,"*
DAILY BEAST (Aug. 17, 2014, 6:45 AM), https://www.thedailybeast.com/parents-
sue-for-wrongful-birth [https://perma.cc/V5BD-VF7Z]; Sofia Yakren, *"Wrongful
Birth" Claims and the Paradox of Parenting a Child with a Disability*, 87 FORDHAM L.
REV 583, 622–24 (2018).

54. Cassy Fiano, *Couple Wins Down Syndrome "Wrongful Birth" Suit*, LIVE ACTION
(Mar. 11, 2012, 8:19 PM), https://www.liveaction.org/news/update-couple-wins-
down-syndrome-wrongful-birth-suit/ [https://perma.cc/C48L-2PWL]. *See also*
Jane Musgrave, *Jury Awards West Palm Beach Parents of Child Born with No
Arms, One Leg $4.5 Million*, PALM BEACH POST (Sept. 10, 2011), https://www.
palmbeachpost.com/news/jury-awards-west-palm-beach-parents-child-born-
with-arms-one-leg-million/E4pWBxRxQqGsj0wtzkPYsI/ [https://perma.cc/XPE4-
53Q4].

55. Jonathan V. Last, *From Blessing to Curse: The Evolution of "Wrongful Birth" Lawsuits*,
WKLY. STANDARD, Apr. 30, 2012, http://www.weeklystandard.com/from-blessing-
to-curse/article/640524 [https://perma.cc/5X5Y-JUMW].

56. Jen Gann, *Every Parent Wants to Protect Their Child. I Never Got the Chance*, N.Y.
MAG., Nov. 27, 2017, https://www.thecut.com/2017/11/raising-child-with-cystic-
fibrosis.html [https://perma.cc/3YYH-S82Q].

57. *See* Nicolette Priaulx, *Rethinking Reproductive Injury*, 39 FAM. L. 1161, 1161 (2009);
John A. Robertson, *In the Beginning: The Legal Status of Early Embryos*, 76 VA. L. REV.
437, 459 & n.61 (1990).

58. *See* Belcher v. T. Rowe Price Found., Inc., 621 A.2d 872, 884 (Md. 1993).

59. Complaint for Declaratory Judgment with Memorandum in Support, Penniman
v. University Hospitals Health System, Inc., No. CV 18 895503 (Ohio Ct. Com. Pl.,
Mar. 30, 2018), 2018 WL 1729440.

60. Thornburgh v. Am. Coll. of Obstetricians & Gynecologists, 476 U.S. 747, 792 (1986)
(White, J., dissenting).

61. Roe v. Wade, 410 U.S. 113, 161, 163 (1973).

62. *See* Wex S. Malone, *The Genesis of Wrongful Death*, 17 STAN. L. REV. 1043, 1062–66
(1965).

63. *See* WILLIAM PROSSER & W. PAGE KEETON, THE LAW OF TORTS § 127, at 945 (5th
ed. 1984).

64. *See, e.g.*, Carranza v. United States, 267 P.3d 912 (Utah 2011); Summerfield v. Superior
Court, 698 P.2d 712, 715, 724 (Ariz. 1985).

65. *See* McClain v. Univ. of Mich. Bd. of Regents, 665 N.W.2d 484, 486 (Mich. Ct.
App. 2003); Miccolis v. Amica Mut. Ins. Co., 587 A.2d 67, 71 (1991); Gentry
v. Gilmore, 613 So.2d 1241, 1244 (Ala. 1993); Jeter v. Mayo Clinic Ariz., 121 P.3d

1256, 1261–62 (Ariz. Ct. App. 2005); Miller v. Am. Infertility Grp. of Ill., 897 N.E.2d 837, 839–40 (Ill. App. Ct. 2008).

66. *Roe*, 410 U.S. at 151, 163.

67. Davis v. Davis, 842 S.W.2d 588, 602 (Tenn. 1992) (emphasis added).

68. *Id.* at 596–97.

69. *See, e.g.*, Jeter v. Mayo Clinic Ariz., 121 P.3d 1256, 1266–68 (Ariz. Ct. App. 2005); McQueen v. Gadberry, 507 S.W.3d 127, 148–49 (Mo. Ct. App. 2016).

70. *See* Doe v. Obama, 631 F.3d 157, 160 (4th Cir. 2011); Sarah Zhang, *Can Lost Embryos Give Rise to a Wrongful-Death Suit?*, ATLANTIC (Apr. 5, 2018), https://www.theatlantic.com/health/archive/2018/04/fertility-clinic-embryos/557258/ [https://perma.cc/VH39-2N88].

71. LA. REV. STAT. ANN. § 9:128 (2009).

72. *See* I. Glenn Cohen, *The Constitution and the Rights Not to Procreate*, 60 STAN. L. REV. 1135, 1139–41 (2008).

73. Hecht v. Superior Court, 20 Cal. Rptr. 2d. 275, 283 (Cal. Ct. App. 1993); Hecht v. Super. Ct., 59 Cal. Rptr. 2d 222, 222 (Cal. Ct. App. 1996), *depublished by* Hecht v. Super. Ct., 1997 Cal. LEXIS 131 (Cal. 1997).

74. York v. Jones, 717 F. Supp. 421, 425 (E.D. Va. 1989).

75. Kass v. Kass, 1995 WL 110368, *2 (N.Y. Sup. Ct. 1995), *rev'd on other grounds*, 663 N.Y.S.2d 581 (App. Div. 1997), *aff'd*, 696 N.E.2d 174 (N.Y. 1998).

76. *In re* Marriage of Dahl, 194 P.3d 834, 838–39 (Or. Ct. App. 2008).

77. *See* Judith D. Fischer, *Misappropriation of Human Eggs and Embryos and the Tort of Conversion: A Relational View*, 32 LOY. L.A. L. REV. 381, 419 (1999).

78. Frisina v. Women & Infants Hosp. of R.I., No. CIV. A. 95-4037, 2002 WL 1288784, at *9, *10 (R.I. Super. Ct. May 30, 2002).

79. *See* Sell v. Ward, 81 Ill. App. 675, 678 (App. Ct. 1898).

80. *See* United States v. Arora, 860 F. Supp. 1091, 1100 (D. Md. 1994).

81. *Frisina*, 2002 WL 1288784, at *9 (citing Hawkins v. Scituate Oil, 723 A.2d 771 (R.I. 1999)).

Chapter 4

1. *See* MARY ZIEGLER, BEYOND ABORTION: *ROE V. WADE* AND THE BATTLE FOR PRIVACY 19–31 (2018).

2. *See* DAVID J. GARROW, LIBERTY AND SEXUALITY: THE RIGHT TO PRIVACY AND THE MAKING OF *ROE V. WADE* 260–61 (1998).

3. *See* William L. Prosser, *Intentional Infliction of Mental Suffering: A New Tort*, 37 MICH. L. REV. 874, 875–77 (1939); Robert L. Rabin, *Pain and Suffering and Beyond: Some Thoughts on Recovery for Intangible Loss*, 55 DEPAUL L. REV. 359, 363–67 (2006).

4. E. L. Godkin, *The Rights of the Citizen. IV.—To His Own Reputation*, SCRIBNER's, July 1890, at 59. For discussion, *see* Samantha Barbas, *The Social Origins of Personality Torts*, 67 RUTGERS U. L. REV. 393, 400–02 (2015).

5. Morissette v. United States, 342 U.S. 246, 253–54 (1952).

6. *See* William L. Prosser, *The Assault upon the Citadel (Strict Liability to the Consumer)*, 69 YALE L.J. 1099, 1100 (1960).

7. MacPherson v. Buick Motor Co., 111 N.E. 1050, 1053 (N.Y. 1916).

8. *Id.* at 1052.

9. *See* David G. Owen, *The Evolution of Products Liability Law*, 26 Rev. Litig. 955, 967–69 (2007); Robert L. Rabin, *Restating the Law: The Dilemmas of Products Liability*, 30 U. Mich. J.L. Reform 197, 199–200 (1997).

10. *See* Frank Michelman, *Property, Utility and Fairness: Comments on the Ethical Foundation of "Just Compensation" Law*, 80 Harv. L. Rev. 1165, 1192 (1967).

11. Sydney Ember, *In Bankruptcy, Gawker Offers Itself for Sale*, N.Y. Times, June 11, 2016, at A1.

12. *See* Robert William Jones, Journalism in the United States 248 (1947).

13. *See* Sarah E. Igo, The Known Citizen: A History of Privacy in Modern America 9–25 (2018).

14. *See* Michael Lynch, The Internet of Us 89 (2016).

15. *See* Jennifer E. Rothman, The Right of Publicity: Privacy Reimagined for a Public World 12–27 (2018).

16. Thomas M. Cooley, The Law of Torts 29 (2d ed. 1888). The expression previously appeared in the copyright case Wheaton v. Peters, 33 U.S. 591, 634 (1834) ("The defendant asks nothing—wants nothing, but to be let alone until it can be shown that he has violated the rights of another.").

17. Samuel D. Warren & Louis D. Brandeis, *The Right to Privacy*, 4 Harv. L. Rev. 193, 196–98 (1890).

18. *The Right of Privacy: Georgia's Highest Court Makes Ruling Adverse to that of Judge Parker*, L.A. Times, July 28, 1905, at 4; *The Right of Privacy*, N.Y. Times, Aug. 23, 1902, at 8.

19. Roberson v. Rochester Folding Box Co., 64 N.E. 442, 547, 544 (N.Y. 1902).

20. Pavesich v. New England Life Ins. Co., 50 S.E. 68, 70 (Ga. 1905).

21. *See* William L. Prosser, Handbook of the Law of Torts 1050 (1st ed. 1941).

22. Dov Fox, *Reproductive Negligence*, 117 Colum. L. Rev. 149 (2017).

23. Gregory C. Keating, *Response to Fox: Impaired Conditions, Frustrated Expectations, and the Law of Torts*, 117 Colum. L. Rev. Online 212, 214 (2017), http://columbialawreview.org/content/response-to-fox-impaired-conditions-frustrated-expectations-and-the-law-of-torts/ [http://perma.cc/T9VL-EQXF].

24. *Id.* at 215, 224.

25. John Gardner, From Personal Life to Private Law 179–80 (2018).

26. *See* Daniel Kahneman, Jack L. Knetsch, & Richard H. Thaler, *Anomalies: The Endowment Effect, Loss Aversion, and Status Quo Bias*, 5 J. Econ. Persp. 193, 195–97 (1991).

27. Keating, *supra* note 23, at 225.

28. Lucas v. S.C. Coastal Council, 505 U.S. 1003, 1024–26 (1992).

29. Arthur Ripstein, Equality, Responsibility, and the Law 55 (1999).

30. Seana Valentine Shiffrin, *Wrongful Life, Procreative Responsibility, and the Significance of Harm*, 5 Legal Theory 117, 123–24 (1999).

31. Keating, *supra* note 23, at 222–23 (citing Scott Hershovitz, *Two Models of Tort (and Takings)*, 92 Va. L. Rev. 1147 (2006)).

32. *See* Dov Fox, *Making Things Right When Reproductive Medicine Goes Wrong? Reply to Robert Rabin, Carol Sanger, and Gregory Keating*, 118 Colum. L. Rev. Online 94 (2018), https://columbialawreview.org/content/making-things-right-when-reproductive-medicine-goes-wrongreply-to-robert-rabin-carol-sanger-and-gregory-keating/ [https://perma.cc/9ES4-X3NQ].

33. Joel Feinberg, *Wrongful Life and the Counterfactual Element in Harming*, in Freedom and Fulfillment 3, 7 (1992).

34. *Id.* at 225 (citing Seana Shiffrin, *Harm and Its Moral Significance*, 18 Legal Theory 357 (2012)).

35. Steven D. Smith, *Missing Persons*, 2 Nev. L.J. 590, 598, 602–03 (2002).

36. Justus v. Atchison, 565 P.2d 122, 133 (Cal. 1977) (en banc).

37. Smith v. Mercy Hosp. & Med. Ctr., 560 N.E.2d 1164, 1171 (Ill. App. Ct. 1990). *See also* Porter v. Lassiter, 87 S.E.2d 100, 103 (Ga. Ct. App. 1955); Danos v. St. Pierre, 402 So. 2d 633, 638 (La. 1981); Connor v. Monkem Co., 898 S.W.2d 89, 93 (Mo. 1995); Wiersma v. Maple Leaf Farms, 543 N.W.2d 787, 790–91 (S.D. 1996); Farley v. Sartin, 466 S.E.2d 522, 533 (W. Va. 1995).

38. Keating, *supra* note 23, at 221–22.

39. Lord v. Lovett, 770 A.2d 1103, 1104–06 (N.H. 2001); Petriello v. Kalman, 576 A.2d 474, 476–77, 484 (Conn. 1990). For discussion, *see* Claire Finkelstein, *Is Risk a Harm?*, 151 U. Pa. L. Rev. 963, 985–86 (2003); Nancy Levit, *Ethereal Torts*, 61 Geo. Wash. L. Rev. 136, 181–83 (1992).

40. *See* Dickhoff v. Green, 836 N.W.2d 321, 325–26 (Minn. 2013); Cast Art Industries v. KPMG, 36 A.3d 1049, 1051–52 (N.J. 2012); Greyhound Lines, Inc. v. Sutton, 765 So. 2d 1269, 1276–77 (Miss. 2000).

41. Metro-North Commuter R.R. Co. v. Buckley, 521 U.S. 424, 446, 427 (1997).

42. *Id.* at 444, 433 (quoting Consol. Rail Corp. v. Gottshall, 512 U.S. 532, 557 (1994)). *See also* Norfolk & W. Ry. Co. v. Ayers, 538 U.S. 135, 157–58 (2003); Dov Fox & Alex Stein, *Dualism and Doctrine*, 90 Ind. L.J. 975, 985–86 (2015).

43. Rodrigues v. State, 472 P.2d 509, 520 (Haw. 1970).

44. *See* Nancy Levit, *Ethereal Torts*, 61 Geo. Wash. L. Rev. 136, 144–45 (1992); Robert L. Rabin, *Emotional Distress in Tort Law: Themes of Constraint*, 44 Wake Forest L. Rev. 1197, 1202–03 (2009).

45. Thing v. La Chusa, 771 P.2d 814, 829–30 (Cal. 1989) (en banc).

46. Garrison v. Med. Ctr. of Del., 581 A.2d 288, 293 (Del. 1990); Arche v. United States, 798 P.2d 477, 482 (Kan. 1990).

47. *See* Lawson v. Mgmt. Activities, Inc., 81 Cal. Rptr. 2d 745, 756 (Cal. Ct. App. 1999); Restatement (Third) of Torts: Physical & Emotional Harm § 46 (Am. Law Inst. 2012).

48. *See* "The Handmaid's Tale," *Nolite Te Bastardes Carborundorum* (Hulu television broadcast, May 3, 2017); "Sisters," *Episode 1.1* (Netflix television broadcast, Sept. 1, 2018); "Law & Order: Special Victims Unit," *Inconceivable* (NBC television broadcast, Jan. 22, 2008).

49. *See* Rowlette v. Mortimer, No. 4:18-cv-00143-DCN, 2018 WL 5305538, **1–2 (D. Idaho Oct. 25, 2018); Ken Kusmer, *Donald Cline, Indianapolis Fertility Doctor, Used*

Own Sperm to Impregnate Women: Affidavit, WASH. TIMES (Sept. 12, 2016), http://
www.washingtontimes.com/news/2016/sep/12/donald-cline-indianapolis-fertility-
doctor-used-ow/ [https://perma.cc/29KG-XLUP]; *Lawsuit Claims Former Fertility
Doctor Used His Own Sperm*, BBC NEWS: U.S. & Can. (Nov. 3, 2016), http://www.
bbc.com/news/world-us-canada-37842458   [https://perma.cc/MCK5-7TN5];
Matthew Piper, *Report: Utah Kidnapper Is Woman's Father Due to Semen Switch*,
SALT LAKE TRIB. (Jan. 10, 2014, 10:18 AM), http://archive.sltrib.com/story.php?ref=/
sltrib/news/57372964-78/lippert-says-family-daughter.html.csp   [http://perma.cc/
89DN-GHTH]; *Conviction Upheld in Fertility Case*, N.Y. TIMES, Sept. 8, 1993, at
B11. For discussion, *see* Jody Madeira, Steven R. Lindheim, & Mark V. Sauer, *Against
Seminal Principles: Ethics, Hubris, and Lessons to Learn from Illicit Inseminations*, 110
FERTILITY & STERILITY 1003, 1005 (2018).

50. *See* Saleh v. Hollinger, 335 S.W.3d 368, 371 (Tex. App. 2011); Del Zio v. Presbyterian
Hosp., No. 74 Civ. 3588 (CES), 1978 U.S. Dist. LEXIS 14450, at *3–4 (S.D.N.Y. Nov.
9, 1978).

51. The scandal made international news and triggered state senate hearings. The
school shelled out over $24 million to settle complaints by more than 137 families.
See Prato-Morrison v. Doe, 126 Cal. Rptr. 2d 509, 511 (Cal. Ct. App. 2002); MARY
DODGE & GILBERT GEIS, STEALING DREAMS: A FERTILITY CLINIC SCANDAL 190
(2003); Kimi Yoshino, *UCI Settles Dozens of Fertility Suits*, L.A. TIMES (Sept. 11,
2009),   http://articles.latimes.com/2009/sep/11/local/me-uci-fertility11   [https://
perma.cc/THM5-5BJA].

52. Dillon v. Legg, 441 P.2d 912, 918 (Cal. 1968).

53. *See, e.g.*, Hedgepeth v. Whitman Walker Clinic, 22 A.3d 789 (D.C. 2011) (en banc);
Chizmar v. Mackie, 896 P.2d 196, 203–05 (Alaska 1995).

54. *See, e.g.*, W. Union v. Smith, 227 S.W. 1111, 1113 (Tex. Civ. App. 1921); Young v. W.
Union Tel. Co., 11 S.E. 1044, 1045 (N.C. 1890).

55. *See* Smith v. Telophase Nat. Cremation Soc., Inc., 471 So. 2d 163 (Fla. Dist. Ct.
App. 2d Dist. 1985); Akins Funeral Home, Inc. v. Miller, 878 So. 2d 267 (Ala. 2003);
Guth v. Freeland, 28 P.3d 982, 990 (Haw. 2001).

56. *See* Gregory C. Keating, *Is Negligent Infliction of Emotional Distress a Freestanding
Tort?*, 44 WAKE FOREST L. REV. 1131, 1173–74 (2009).

57. Witt v. Yale-New Haven Hosp., 977 A.2d 779, 791 (Conn. Super. Ct. 2008).

58. Rowlette v. Mortimer, No. 4:18-cv-00143-DCN, 2018 WL 5305538, at *15, *1 (D.
Idaho Oct. 25, 2018).

59. *Witt*, 977 A.2d at 791.

60. RESTATEMENT (THIRD) OF TORTS: PHYSICAL & EMOTIONAL HARM § 47 & cmt. b
(Am. Law Inst. 2012).

61. *See, e.g.*, Miranda v. Said, 836 N.W.2d 8, 27–28 (Iowa 2013).

62. Andrews v. Keltz, 38 N.Y.S.2d 363, 368 (N.Y. Sup. Ct. 2007); *see Witt*, 977 A.2d at
787; Chamberland v. Physicians for Women's Health, No. CV010164040S, 2006 WL
437553, at *6 (Conn. Super. Ct. Feb. 8, 2006).

63. *See* Canesi v. Wilson, 730 A.2d 805, 815 (N.J. 1999); Cauman v. George Washington
Univ., 630 A.2d 1104, 1109 (D.C. 1993); Becker v. Schwartz, 386 N.E.2d 807, 814 (N.Y.

1978); Nicolette Priaulx, The Harm Paradox: Tort Law and the Unwanted Child in an Era of Choice 32–33, 64–68, 144–48, 161–64 (2007).

64. Shelton v. St. Anthony's Medical Center, 781 S.W.2d 48, 50 (Mo. 1989).

65. Perry-Rogers v. Obasaju, 723 N.Y.S.2d 28, 29–30 (App. Div. 2001).

66. See Stanley Ingber, Rethinking Intangible Injuries: A Focus on Remedy, 73 Cal. L. Rev. 772, 779 (1985); Louis L. Jaffe, Damages for Personal Injury: The Impact of Insurance, 18 Law & Contemp. Probs. 219, 224–25 (1953).

67. Gleitman v. Cosgrove, 227 A.2d 689, 692 (N.J. 1967).

68. Willis v. Wu, 607 S.E.2d 63, 72 (S.C. 2004).

69. Spokeo, Inc. v. Robins, 136 S. Ct. 1540, 1548–49 (2016). This was a case about standing to sue in federal court under Article III of the U.S. Constitution, as opposed to the substance of tort claims under state law. The requirements for standing doctrine and substantive claims differ, but courts tend to think about the concept of harm almost identically in both.

70. Story Parchment Co. v. Paterson Parchment Paper Co., 282 U.S. 555, 563 (1931).

71. Id. at 561, 565. For discussion in the context of wrongful life claims, see Berman v. Allan, 404 A.2d 8, 14 (N.J. 1979).

72. Wycko v. Gnodtke, 105 N.W.2d 118, 123 (Mich. 1960).

73. See Campbell v. Delbridge, 670 N.W.2d 108, 113 (Iowa 2003); Callison v. Hillcrest Healthcare Sys., No. CJ-2010-3197, 2011 WL 7990001 (Okla. Dist. Ct. Tulsa Cnty. Apr. 14, 2011).

74. See Omri Ben-Shahar & Ariel Porat, 118 Colum. L. Rev. 1901, 1915–17 (2018).

75. Naccash v. Burger, 290 S.E.2d 825, 831 (1982).

76. Id. at 827–28.

77. Id. at 832–33.

78. See Ben-Shahar & Porat, supra note 74, at 1918 (footnotes and citations omitted).

79. Serena Scurria et al., Professional Liability Insurance in Obstetrics and Gynaecology, BMC Res. Notes, June 17, 2011, at 1, 2.

80. Borer v. Am. Airlines, Inc., 563 P.2d 858, 862 (Cal. 1977).

Chapter 5

1. See Paul Schwartz & Karl-Nikolaus Pfeifer, Prosser's Privacy and the German Right of Personality: Are Four Privacy Torts Better than One Unitary Concept?, 98 Cal. L. Rev. 1925, 1937–47, 1981–84 (2010).

2. See Ronald J. Krotoszynski, Jr., The Polysemy of Privacy, 88 Ind. L.J. 881, 883 (2013).

3. See William L. Prosser, Privacy, 48 Cal. L. Rev. 383, 392–98, 398–401 (1960).

4. Vassiliades v. Garfinckel's, Brooks Bros., Miller & Rhoades, Inc., 492 A.2d 580, 585–86, 594–95 (D.C. 1985); Catsouras v. Dep't of the Cal. Highway Patrol, 104 Cal. Rptr. 3d 352, 359, 385 (Cal. Ct. App. 2010); Douglas v. Stokes, 149 S.W. 849, 849–50 (Ky. 1912); Daily Times Democrat v. Graham, 162 So.2d 474, 475–76, 478 (Ala. 1964).

5. *See* Peoples Bank & Trust Co. v. Globe Int'l Publ'g, Inc., 978 F.2d 1065, 1068 (8th Cir. 1992).

6. *See* Spahn v. Julian Messner, Inc., 221 N.E.2d 543, 545 (N.Y. 1966), *vacated on other grounds*, 387 U.S. 239 (1967).

7. *See id.* at 401–07, 409–21.

8. *See* Robert L. Rabin, *Dov Fox on Reproductive Negligence: A Commentary*, 117 COLUM. L. REV. ONLINE 228, 233–35 (2017), http://columbialawreview.org/content/dov-fox-on-reproductive-negligence-a-commentary/ [http://perma.cc/E7X6-7HDZ].

9. Planned Parenthood of Se. Pa. v. Casey, 505 U.S. 833, 897 (1992).

10. *See* C.A.M. v. R.A.W., 568 A.2d 556, 556 (N.J. Super. Ct. App. Div. 1990); Barbara A. v. John G., 193 Cal. Rptr. 422, 428 (Cal. Ct. App. 1983). For discussion, *see* A. Rachel Camp, *Coercing Pregnancy*, 21 WM. & MARY J. WOMEN & L. 275, 282–83 (2015).

11. *See* Dubay v. Wells, 506 F.3d 422, 424 (6th Cir. 2007); Erwin Wallis v. Smith, 22 P.3d 682, 682–83 (N.M. Ct. App. 2001); Henson v. Sorrell, No. 02A01-9711-CV-00291, 1999 WL 5630, at *6 (Tenn. Ct. App. 1999); Murphy v. Myers, 560 N.W.2d 752, 756 (Minn. Ct. App. 1997); Erwin L.D. v. Myla Jean L., 847 S.W.2d 45, 47 (Ark. Ct. App. 1993); Jose F. v. Pat M., 586 N.Y.S.2d 734, 735–36 (N.Y. Sup. Ct. 1992); Beard v. Skipper, 451 N.W.2d 614, 614 (Mich. Ct. App. 1990); Douglas R. v. Suzanne M., 487 N.Y.S.2d 244, 246 (App. Div. 1985); Linda D. v. Fritz C., 687 P.2d 223, 226–27 (Wash. Ct. App. 1984); Hughes v. Hutt, 455 A.2d 623, 624–25 (Pa. 1983); Inez M. v. Nathan G., 451 N.Y.S.2d 607, 611 (N.Y. Fam. Ct. 1982).

12. Phillips v. Irons, 2005 WL 4694579, at *1 (Ill. Ct. App. Feb. 22, 2005).

13. *Id.* at *5–6. For discussion, *see* Preston D. Mitchum, *Male Reproductive Autonomy: Unplanned Fatherhood and the Victory of Child Support*, 7 MOD. AM. 10, 15–16 (2011).

14. *See* Conley v. Romeri, 806 N.E.2d 933, 935 (2004).

15. *See* Perry v. Atkinson, 240 Cal. Rptr. 402, 403 (Cal. Ct. App. 1987).

16. *See* State of Wisconsin v. Manishkumar M. Patel, No. 2007-CF-001002 (Wis. Cir. Ct. Aug. 1, 2018) (decision per no contest plea agreement); Commonwealth of Virginia v. Sikander S. Imran, No. CR17001209-00 (Va. Cir. Ct. May 18, 2018) (decision per guilty plea); U.S. v. Welden, Docket No. 8:13-cr-00252 (M.D. Fla. May 14, 2013).

17. Leventhal v. Liberman, 186 N.E. 675, 677 (1933).

18. *See* Alexandra Brodsky, *"Rape-Adjacent": Imagining Legal Responses to Nonconsensual Condom Removal*, 32 COLUM. J. GENDER & L. 183, 201–02 (2017); Athena Katsampes, *A Rape by Any Other Name: The Problem of Defining Acts of Protection Deception and the University as a Solution*, 24 VA. J. SOC. POL'Y & L. 157, 160–61 (2017).

19. David Margolick, *Serpico in Court*, N.Y. TIMES, May 23, 1982, § 1, at 28, col. 2.

20. *See* Paula C. Murray & Brenda J. Winslett, *The Constitutional Right to Privacy and Emerging Tort Liability for Deceit in Interpersonal Relationships*, 1986 U. ILL. L. REV. 779, 817 (1986).

21. R.A.P. v. B.J.P., 438 N.W.2d 103 (Minn. Ct. App. 1988); Doe v. Roe, 660 So. 2d 350 (Fla. Dist. Ct. App. 1995); Hogan v. Tavzel, 333 S.E.2d 852 (Ga. Ct. App. 1985);

Long v. Adams, 267 Cal. Rptr. 564 (Cal. Ct. App. 1990); B.N. v. K.K., 538 A.2d 1175 (Md. 1988).

22. L. Pamela P. v. Frank S., 449 N.E.2d 713, 716 (N.Y. 1983).

23. Stephen K. v. Roni L., 164 Cal. Rptr. 618, 621 (Cal. Ct. App. 1980).

24. Planned Parenthood of Central Mo. v. Danforth, 428 U.S. 52, 71 (1976).

25. Planned Parenthood of Se. Pa. v. Casey, 505 U.S. 833, 846, 851, 896 (1992).

26. Danforth, 428 U.S. at 70; Casey, 505 U.S. at 897–98.

27. Griswold v. Connecticut, 381 U.S. 479, 486 (1965); Eisenstadt v. Baird, 405 U.S. 438, 453 (1972); Carey v. Population Srvcs. Int'l, 431 U.S. 678, 685 (1977).

28. *See* Nancy Levit, The Gender Line: Men, Women, and the Law 170 (1998); Carol Sanger, About Abortion: Terminating Pregnancy in Twenty-First Century America 205–09 (2017); Jean Strout, *Dads and Dicta: The Value of Acknowledging Fathers' Interests*, 21 Cardozo J.L. & Gender 135, 150 (2014).

29. Parvin v. Dean, 7 S.W.3d 264, 279 (Tex. Ct. App. 1999) (quoting Krishnan v. Sepulveda, 916 S.W.2d 478, 483 (Tex. 1995) (Gonzales, J., dissenting)).

30. *See* Stiver v. Parker, 975 F.2d 261, 270 (6th Cir. 1992); Tamar Lewin, *Surrogate Mother Able to Sue for Negligence*, N.Y. Times, Sept. 20, 1992, § 1, at 36.

31. Rowlette v. Mortimer, No. 4:18-cv-00143-DCN, 2018 WL 5305538, *8 (D. Idaho Oct. 25, 2018).

32. *See* Reisner v. Regents of Univ. of California, 31 Cal. App. 4th 1195, 1199 (Cal. Ct. App. 1995); Renslow v. Mennonite Hosp., 367 N.E.2d 1250, 1251 (Ill. 1977).

33. Jacoves v. United Merch. Corp., 11 Cal. Rptr. 2d 468, 482 (Ct. App. 1992).

34. *See* Dehn v. Edgecombe, 865 A.2d 603, 622 (Md. 2005).

35. Adams v. Cavins, No. B163375, 2003 WL 22456117, at *5 (Cal. Ct. App. Oct. 30, 2003).

36. Meleney-Distassio v. Weinstein, No. FSTCV136018746S, 2014 WL 7462584, at *1, *13 (Conn. Super. Ct. Nov. 20, 2014).

37. *See id.* at *16.

38. *Id.* at *13, *11.

39. *Id.* at *12, *9, *16.

40. *See, e.g.*, Eldon v. Sheldon, 758 P.2d 582, 586–87 (Cal. 1988).

41. Miller v. Rivard, 585 N.Y.S.2d 523, 526–27 (N.Y. App. Div. 1992).

42. John Gardner, From Personal Life to Private Law 52 (2018).

43. Seana Shiffrin, *The Moral Neglect of Negligence, in* 3 Oxford Studies in Political Philosophy 197, 197 (David Sobel, Peter Vallentyne, & Steve Wall eds., 2017).

44. *See* Gardner, *supra* note 42, at 164–65.

45. State Farm Mut. Auto. Ins. Co. v. Campbell, 538 U.S. 408, 416 (2003) (quoting Cooper Industries, Inc. v. Leatherman Tool Group, Inc., 532 U.S. 424, 432 (2001)).

46. *See* Frank A. Sloan & Lindsey M. Chepke, Medical Malpractice 85 (2008).

47. Valerie P. Hans & Theodore Eisenberg, *The Predictability of Juries*, 60 DePaul L. Rev. 375, 379 (2011).

48. Valerie P. Hans, Business on Trial: The Civil Jury and Corporate Responsibility 216 (2000).

49. State v. Briggs, 776 P.2d 1347, 1355 (Wash. Ct. App. 1989); Spaziano v. Florida, 468 U.S. 447, 461 (1984).

50. *See* Dov Fox, *Neuro-Voir Dire and the Architecture of Bias*, 65 HASTINGS L.J. 999, 1006–09 (2014).

51. *See* JoEllen Lind, *The End of Trial on Damages? Intangible Losses and Comparability Review*, 51 BUFF. L. REV. 251, 252–53 (2003).

52. *See* Patton v. TIC United Corp., 77 F.3d 1235, 1247 (10th Cir. 1996); Catherine M. Sharkey, *Unintended Consequences of Medical Malpractice Damages Caps*, 80 N.Y.U. L. REV. 391, 396 (2005); Stephen C. Yeazell, *Unspoken Truths and Misaligned Interests: Political Parties and the Two Cultures of Civil Litigation*, 60 UCLA L. REV. 1752, 1786 (2013).

53. *See, e.g.*, Moore v. Mobile Infirmary Ass'n, 592 So. 2d 156 (Ala. 1991); Estate of McCall v. United States, 134 So. 3d 894 (Fla. 2014); Atlanta Oculoplastic Surgery, P.C. v. Nestlehutt, 691 S.E.2d 218 (Ga. 2010); Lebran v. Gottlieb Mem'l Hosp., 930 N.E.2d 895 (Ill. 2010); Brannigan v. Usitalo, 587 A.2d 1232 (N.H. 1991); Lakin v. Senco Prods., Inc., 987 P. 2d 463 (Or. 1999); Sofie v. Fibreboard Corp., 771 P.2d 711 (Wash. 1989).

54. *See, e.g.*, Miller v. Johnson, 289 P.3d 1098 (Kan. 2012); Act of Apr. 17, 2014, ch. 84, 2014 Kan. Sess. Laws 632; Watts v. Lester E. Cox Med. Ctrs., 376 S.W.3d 633 (Mo. 2012); SB 239, 2015 Mo. Laws 62; WIS. STAT. ANN. §§ 893.04, 893.55 (West 2016); Act of Mar. 24, 2016, Pub. L. No. 182, 2016 Ind. Acts 1984.

55. *See* Ronen Avraham, *Putting a Price on Pain-and-Suffering Damages: A Critique of the Current Approaches and a Preliminary Proposal for Change*, 100 Nw. U. L. REV. 87, 92–106 (2006).

Chapter 6

1. *See* Margaret Jane Radin, *Compensation and Commensurability*, 43 DUKE L.J. 56, 60 (1993).

2. *See* NAT'L ASS'N OF INS. COMM'RS, MALPRACTICE CLAIMS: MEDICAL MALPRACTICE CLOSED CLAIMS 1975–1978, at 304 (M. Patricia Sowka ed., 1980).

3. *See* Amy Baron-Evans & Kate Stith, *Booker Rules*, 160 U. PA. L. REV. 1631, 1681 (2012).

4. *See* THE REPORT OF THE NATIONAL COMMISSION ON STATE WORKMEN'S COMPENSATION LAWS 31–35 (1972).

5. *See* Murray B. Rutherford, Jack L. Knetsch, & Thomas C. Brown, *Assessing Environmental Losses: Judgments of Importance and Damage Schedules*, 22 HARV. ENVTL. L. REV. 51, 53 (1998).

6. Ellen S. Pryor, *Compensation and a Consequential Model of Loss*, 64 TUL. L. REV. 783, 808 (1990).

7. *See* Posey v. State Workmen's Compensation Comm'r, 201 S.E.2d 102, 106–07 (W. Va. 1973); Woodman v. Georgia–Pacific Corp., 614 P.2d 1162, 1164 (Or. 1980);

Pima County Bd. of Supervisors v. Industrial Comm'n, 716 P.2d 407, 412 (Ariz. 1986) (en banc).

8. *See* David A. Logan, *Judges, Juries and the Politics of Tort Reform*, 83 U. Cin. L. Rev. 903, 942–43 (2015).

9. Randall R. Bovbjerg, Frank A. Sloan, & James F. Blumstein, *Valuing Life and Limb in Tort: Scheduling "Pain and Suffering,"* 83 Nw. U. L. Rev. 908, 930 (1989).

10. Emerson v. Magendantz, 689 A.2d 409, 418 (R.I. 1997) (Bourcier, J., dissenting in part).

11. Bennett v. Lembo, 761 A.2d 494, 496–97 (N.H. 2000).

12. Valence v. Louisiana Power & Light Co., 50 So.2d 847, 848, 849–50 (La. App. 1951).

13. *See, e.g.*, Ferriter v. Daniel O'Connell's Sons, Inc., 413 N.E.2d 690, 696 (Mass. 1980); Fernandez v. Walgreen Hastings Co., 968 P.2d 774, 782–83 (N.M. 1998).

14. Gallimore v. Children's Hosp. Medical Ctr., 617 N.E.2d 1052, 1058–59 (Ohio 1993). *See also* Frank v. Superior Ct. of Ariz., 722 P.2d 955, 956 (Ariz. 1986); Yordeo v. Savage, 279 So. 2d 844, 845 (Fla. 1973); Masaki v. General Motors Corp., 780 P.2d 566, 577 (Haw. 1989); Hayward v. Yost, 242 P.2d 971, 976 (Idaho 1952); Handeland v. Brown, 216 N.W.2d 574, 579 (Iowa 1974); Lee v. USAA Casualty Ins. Co., 540 So. 2d 1083, 1090 (La. Ct. App. 1989); Davis v. Elizabeth Gen. Medical Ctr., 548 A.2d 528, 528–30 (N.J. Super. Ct. Law Div. 1988); First Trust Co. v. Scheels Hardware & Sports, 429 N.W.2d 5, 9–11 (N.D. 1988); Norvell v. Cuyahoga County Hosp., 463 N.E.2d 111, 114–15 (Ohio Ct. App. 1983); Jannette v. Duprez, 701 S.W.2d 56, 61 (Tex. Ct. App. 1985); Adcox v. Children's Orthopedic Hosp., 864 P.2d 921, 932–33 (Wash. 1993); Harbeson v. Parke-Davis, Inc., 656 P.2d 483, 492–93 (Wash. 1983); Shockley v. Prier, 225 N.W.2d 495, 499–500 (Wis. 1975).

15. Fantozzi v. Sandusky Cement Products Co., 59f7 N.E.2d 474, 481 (Ohio 1992).

16. *See, e.g.*, Viccaro v. Milunsky, 551 N.E.2d 8, 11 (Mass. 1990); Greco v. United States, 893 P.2d 345, 350–51 (Nev. 1995); Glascock v. Laserna, 439 S.E.2d 380, 381 (Va. 1994).

17. *See, e.g.*, Snow v. Villacci, 754 A.2d 360, 364–65 (Me. 2000); Melford v. S. V. Rossi Const. Co., 303 A.2d 146, 148–49 (Vt. 1973); Turrietta v. Wyche, 212 P.2d 1041, 1043–44 (N.M. 1949).

18. *See, e.g.*, McAlister v. Carl, 197 A.2d 140, 142–46 (Md. 1964).

19. DiDonato v. Wortman, 358 S.E.2d 489, 492 (N.C. 1987).

20. Dunn v. Rose Way, Inc., 333 N.W.2d 830, 833 (Iowa 1980).

21. Burnham v. Miller, 972 P.2d 645, 647 (Ariz. Ct. App. 1998).

22. JoEllen Lind, *Valuing Relationships: The Role of Damages for Loss of Society*, 35 N.M. L. Rev. 301, 305 (2005).

23. Matsuyama v. Birnbaum, 890 N.E.2d 819, 828, 832 (Mass. 2008).

24. Dickhoff *ex rel.* Dickhoff v. Green, 836 N.W.2d 321, 326, 329 (Minn. 2013).

25. *See* Biondo v. City of Chicago, 382 F.3d 680, 688–89 (7th Cir. 2004); John C. P. Goldberg, *What Clients Are Owed: Cautionary Observations on Lawyers and Loss of a Chance*, 52 Emory L.J. 1201, 1208–13 (2003).

26. *See* Ariel Porat & Alex Stein, Tort Liability Under Uncertainty 73–76, 116–29 (2001); Joseph H. King, Jr., *Causation, Valuation, and Chance in Personal Injury*

Torts Involving Preexisting Conditions and Future Consequences, 90 YALE L.J. 1353, 1384–85 (1981).

Chapter 7

1. *See, e.g.*, Complaint at 3, Robertson v. Saadat, No. BC621038 (Cal. Super. Ct. May 26, 2016); Hollman v. Saadat, No. BC555411, at 3 (Cal. Super. Ct. Aug. 21, 2014); Kurchner v. State Farm Fire & Cas. Co., 858 So. 2d 1220, 1220 (Fla. Dist. Ct. App. 2003); Baskette v. Atlanta Ctr. for Reprod. Med., LLC, 648 S.E.2d 100, 102 (Ga. Ct. App. 2007); Doe v. Nw. Mem'l Hosp., No. 2014L000869, at 2 (Ill. Cir. Ct. Aug. 20, 2013).

2. *See, e.g.*, Kate Briquelet, *Aspiring Mom: Fertility Clinic Destroyed My Embryos and My Chance at Motherhood*, DAILY BEAST (Mar. 30, 2016), http://www.thedailybeast. com/articles/2016/03/30/fertility-clinic-destroyed-her-embryos.html [http://perma. cc/E9MV-NPGN]; Jose Martinez, *Lesbian Pair Sues for 3M After Sperm Bank Loses Embryos*, N.Y. DAILY NEWS (Mar. 6, 2007), http://www.nydailynews.com/news/ lesbian-pair-sues-3m-sperm-bank-loses-embryos-article-1.214041; SoCal Patch (Patch Staff), *Couple Accuses Pasadena Reproductive Center of Losing Embryos*, PASADENA PATCH (Aug. 11, 2016, 3:05 PM ET), http://patch.com/california/ pasadena-ca/couple-accuses-pasadena-reproductive-center-losing-embryos [http:// perma.cc/3N9A-V698].

3. *See, e.g.*, Jeter v. Mayo Clinic Ariz., 121 P.3d 1256, 1261–62 (Ariz. Ct. App. 2005); Kazmeirczak v. Reprod. Genetic Inst., Inc., No. 10 C 05253, 2012 WL 4482753, at *1 (N.D. Ill. Sept. 26, 2012); Miller v. Am. Infertility Grp. of Ill., 897 N.E.2d 837, 839 (Ill. App. Ct. 2008); Frisina v. Women & Infants Hosp. of R.I., Nos. CIV. A. 95-4037, CIV. A. 95-4469, CIV. A. 95-5827, 2002 WL 1288784, at *1 (R.I. Super. Ct. May 30, 2002); Inst. for Women's Health, P.L.L.C. v. Imad, No. 04-05-00555-CV, 2006 WL 334013, at *1 (Tex. Ct. App. Feb. 15, 2006).

4. *See* Creed v. United Hosp., 600 N.Y.S.2d 151, 151–52 (App. Div. 1993); Lubowitz v. Albert Einstein Medical Center, Northern Division, 623 A.2d 3, 4–5 (Pa. Super. Ct. 1993); Complaint at 4–5, Walterspiel v. Jain, No. BC467123 (Cal. Super. Ct. Aug. 17, 2011); Mike Celizic, *Genetic Parents of Embryo Felt "Powerless,"* TODAY (Sept. 23, 2009, 6:00 AM), https://www.today.com/health/genetic-parents-embryo-felt-powerless-1C9404873 [https://perma.cc/3K5D-QLAH]; Associated Press, *Woman Awarded $1 Million in Embryo Mix-Up*, NBC NEWS: WOMEN'S HEALTH (Aug. 4, 2004, 3:08 PM ET), http://www.nbcnews.com/id/5603277/ns/health-womens_health/t/woman-awarded-million-embryo-mix-up/#.V9sl2JMrJE4 [http://perma.cc/P4S9-7M6Z].

5. *See, e.g.*, Cohen v. Cabrini Med. Ctr., 730 N.E.2d 949, 950 (N.Y. 2000); Albala v. City of New York, 429 N.E.2d 786, 788–89 (N.Y. 1981); Chen v. Genetics & IVF Inst., Inc., No. L-153343, 1996 WL 1065627, at *1 (Va. Cir. Ct. Oct. 21, 1996); Terrie Morgan-Besecker, *Judge Refuses to Seal $4.25 Million Settlement in Baby Death Case*, TIMES-TRIB. (Aug. 23, 2016), http://thetimes-tribune.com/news/

judge-refuses-to-seal-4-25-million-settlement-in-baby-death-case-1.2081805 [http://perma.cc/ZF2P-7VB6].

6. *See, e.g.*, Elderkin v. Greater New Haven OB-GYN Grop, P.C., No. NNHCV156056190, LEXIS 1440, Conn., at *1–4 (Conn. Super. Ct. 2018); Johnson v. United States, 735 F. Supp. 1, 2 (D.D.C. 1990); Martinez v. Long Island Jewish Hillside Med. Ctr., 512 N.E.2d 538, 539 (N.Y. 1987); Breyne v. Potter, 574 S.E.2d 916, 919 (Ga. Ct. App. 2002); Alger v. Univ. of Rochester Med. Ctr., 980 N.Y.S.2d 200, 200–01 (App. Div. 2014).

7. *See* Matt Fountain, *Atascadero Woman Says Doctor Mistakenly Gave Her an Abortion Pill—Ending Her Pregnancy*, Sacramento Bee (Jan. 8, 2019, at 4:01 PM), https://www.sacbee.com/news/state/california/article224083755.html [https://perma.cc/Z7UA-H8BE].

8. Baker v. Gordon, 759 S.W.2d 87, 89–90, 94 (Mo. Ct. App. 1988). For discussion of similar cases, *see* Ronen Perry & Yehuda Adar, *Wrongful Abortion: A Wrong in Search of a Remedy*, 5 Yale J. Health Pol'y L. & Ethics 507, 512–14 (2005); Brandy Zadrozny, *Parents Sue Doctors over "Wrongful Abortion,"* Daily Beast (Jan. 29, 2015), http://www.thedailybeast.com/articles/2015/01/29/parents-sue-over-wrongful-abortion.html [http://perma.cc/JJR7-KZB8].

9. Complaint at 4–8, Robertson v. Saadat (Cal. Super. Ct. May 26, 2016) (No. BC621038); Cole Kazdin, *What Happened to Aaron Robertson's Sperm?*, Mel Mag. (Dec. 12, 2016), https://melmagazine.com/what-happened-to-aaron-robertsons-sperm-7473ec028c47 [https://perma.cc/348K-7YL6].

10. Doe v. Irvine Sci. Sales Co., 7 F. Supp. 2d 737, 739, 741, 743 (E.D. Va. 1998); Appellant's Opening Brief at 4, *id.*

11. Creed v. United Hosp., 600 N.Y.S.2d 151, 153 (App. Div. 1993).

12. Robinson v. Cutchin, 140 F. Supp. 2d 488, 493, 491 n.1 (D. Md. 2001).

13. Alice D. Domar et al., *The Psychological Impact of Infertility: A Comparison with Patients with Other Medical Conditions*, 14 J. Psychosomatic Obstet. & Gynecol. 45, 49 tbl. 1 (1993).

14. Daniel J. Solove & Danielle Keats Citron, *Risk and Anxiety: A Theory of Data-Breach Harms*, 96 Tex. L. Rev. 737, 756 (2018).

15. Witt v. Yale-New Haven Hospital, 977 A.2d 779, 781–82, 788, 795 (Conn. Super. Ct. 2008).

16. *See* Perry-Rogers v. Fasano, 715 N.Y.S.2d 19, 21–22, 29–30, 28–29 (App. Div. 2000); Perry-Rogers v. Fasano, Nos. 107068/99, 601218/99, 2000 WL 35534976 (N.Y. Sup. Mar. 2, 2000); Jim Yardley, *After Embryo Mix-Up, Couple Say They Will Give Up a Baby*, N.Y. Times (Mar. 30, 1999), http://www.nytimes.com/1999/03/30/nyregion/after-embryo-mix-up-couple-say-they-will-give-up-a-baby.html [https://perma.cc/B2KD-CFBR]; Jim Yardley, *Sharing Baby Proves Rough on 2 Mothers*, N.Y. Times (June 30, 1999), http://www.nytimes.com/1999/06/30/nyregion/about-new-york-sharing-baby-proves-rough-on-2-mothers.html?ref=topics [https://perma.cc/L9DM-8HTW].

17. *See* Perry-Rogers v. Fasano, Nos. 107068/99, 601218/99, 2000 WL 35534976 (N.Y. Sup. Mar. 2, 2000); Perry-Rogers v. Fasano, 715 N.Y.S.2d 19, 21–22, 29–30, 28–29 (App. Div. 2000).

18. PAUL MORELL & SHANNON MORELL, MISCONCEPTION: ONE COUPLE'S JOURNEY FROM EMBRYO MIX-UP TO MIRACLE BABY 119 (2010).

19. Mike Celizic, *Genetic Parents of Embryo Felt "Powerless,"* TODAY (Sept. 23, 2009, 6:00 AM), https://www.today.com/health/genetic-parents-embryo-felt-powerless-1C9404873 [https://perma.cc/3K5D-QLAH].

20. CAROLYN SAVAGE & SEAN SAVAGE, INCONCEIVABLE: A MEDICAL MISTAKE, THE BABY WE COULDN'T KEEP, AND OUR CHOICE TO DELIVER THE ULTIMATE GIFT 1 (2011); *Woman in Embryo Mix-up Gives Birth to Boy*, CNN (Sept. 26, 2009, 1:24 AM ET), http://www.cnn.com/2009/HEALTH/09/25/wrong.embryo.birth/ [http://perma.cc/R9PG-P2KP].

21. *See* Arthur L. Greil et al., *Variation in Distress Among Women with Infertility Evidence from a Population-Based Sample*, 26 HUMAN REPROD. 2101, 2112 (2011).

22. Reber v. Reiss, 42 A.3d 1131, 1138–40 (Pa. 2012).

23. Bilbao v. Goodwin, 2017 WL 5642280, at *4 (Conn. Super. Ct. 2017).

24. J.B. v. M.B., 783 A.2d 707, 717 (N.J. 2001).

25. *See* Family Size, By Race and Ethnicity, PEW RESEARCH CENTER (May 7, 2015), http://www.pewsocialtrends.org/2015/05/07/childlessness-falls-family-size-grows-among-highly-educated-women/st_2015-05-07_childlessness-12/ [https://perma.cc/ZZC8-9J5Z].

26. *See* Carey v. Lovett, 622 A.2d 1279, 1290 (N.J. 1993); Kammer v. Hurley, 765 So. 2d 975, 978 (Fla. Dist. Ct. App. 2000).

27. McCann v. ABC Ins. Co., 640 So.2d 865, 875 (La. Ct. App. 1994).

28. Skinner v. Oklahoma *ex rel.* Williamson, 316 U.S. 535, 541 (1942).

29. VICTORIA F. NOURSE, IN RECKLESS HANDS: SKINNER V. OKLAHOMA AND THE NEAR TRIUMPH OF AMERICAN EUGENICS 106, 108 (2008).

30. *See* CDC—NAT'L CTR. FOR CHRONIC DISEASE PREVENTION & HEALTH PROMOTION, 2012 ASSISTED REPRODUCTIVE TECHNOLOGY: FERTILITY CLINIC SUCCESS RATES REPORT 23 (2014), http://www.cdc.gov/art/pdf/2012-report/art-2012-fertility-clinic-report.pdf [http://perma.cc/J7XN-LL5V].

31. *See* William J. Stewart & Randi Lynn Scheinblum, *Deprivation of Parenthood—A New Tort?*, 6 WEST. ST. U. L. REV. 229, 244–45 (1979).

32. *See* Heather Murphy, *Held in Reserve: Too Few Mr. Rights Lead More Women to Freeze Their Eggs*, N.Y. TIMES, July 9, 2018, at D2.

33. *See* Natality Dashboard, *Age Specific Birth Rates*, CDC—NAT'L CTR. FOR HEALTH STATISTICS (last updated Jan. 30, 2018), https://www.cdc.gov/nchs/products/vsrr/natality-dashboard.htm# [https://perma.cc/6ZZG-M9X6].

34. *See* Siladitya Bhattacharya et al., *Factors Associated with Failed Treatment: An Analysis of 121,744 Women Embarking on Their First IVF Cycles*, 8 PLOS ONE 1, 12 (2013), http://journals.plos.org/plosone/article/asset?id=10.1371/journal.pone.0082249. PDF [http://perma.cc/9PP5-5USU].

35. Ariana Eunjung Cha, *She Championed the Idea That Freezing Your Eggs Would Free Your Career. But Things Didn't Quite Work Out*, WASH. POST (Jan. 27, 2018, 5:35 PM), https://www.washingtonpost.com/classic-apps/brigette-adams-became-the-poster-child-for-freezing-your-eggs-but-things-didnt-quite-work-out-how-she-imagined/

2018/01/27/ff55857a-e667-11e7-833f-155031558ff4_story.html?utm_
term=.473549865feb [https://perma.cc/Y2DZ-4NE8].

36. *See id.*

37. *See* Dara Purvis, *Expectant Fathers, Abortion, and Embryos*, 43 J.L. MED. & ETHICS
330, 337–38 (2015).

38. *See* Ian Sample, *Chances of IVF Success "Futile" for Women over 44, Says Study*,
GUARDIAN (June 16, 2015, 7:46 PM EDT), http://www.theguardian.com/society/
2015/jun/17/women-ivf-birth-donor-eggs [http://perma.cc/D8GL-M7TY].

39. Witt v. Yale-New Haven Hosp., 977 A.2d 779, 787–88 (Conn. Super. Ct. 2008).

40. *In re* Dunjee, 57 So. 3d 541, 551–52 (La. Ct. App. 2011).

41. Jane E. Brody, *I.V.F.'s Misleading Promise to Those over 40*, N.Y. TIMES (Oct. 17, 2016)
http://www.nytimes.com/2016/10/18/well/the-misleading-promise-of-ivf-for-
women-over-40.html [http://perma.cc/MM4V-VH6N].

42. AM. MED. ASS'N COUNCIL ON ETHICAL & JUDICIAL AFFAIRS & COUNCIL ON SCI.
AFFAIRS, ISSUES OF ETHICAL CONDUCT IN ASSISTED REPRODUCTIVE TECHNOLOGY
2 (1996). For discussion, *see* Keith Alan Byers, *Infertility and In Vitro Fertilization: A
Growing Need for Consumer-Oriented Regulation of the In Vitro Fertilization Industry*,
18 J. LEGAL MED. 265, 299–313 (1997).

43. Salgo v. Leland Stanford Jr. Univ. Bd. of Trs., 317 P.2d 170, 181 (Cal. Ct. App. 1957).

44. Jody Lyneé Madeira et al., *Inform and Consent: More Than Just "Sign Here,"* 108
FERTILITY & STERILITY 40, 41 (2007).

45. *See* Karlin v. IVF America Inc., 712 N.E.2d 662, 664–65, 666–67 (N.Y. 1999).

46. Karlsons v. Guerinot, 394 N.Y.S.2d 933, 939 (App. Div. 1977). For discussion, *see*
Marjorie M. Shultz, *From Informed Consent to Patient Choice: A New Protected
Interest*, 95 YALE L.J. 219, 233–36 (1985).

47. CHARLES FRIED, RIGHT AND WRONG 155 (1978).

48. JEAN-JACQUES ROUSSEAU, EMILE, OR ON EDUCATION 79, 38 (Allan Bloom ed. &
trans., 1978).

49. Smith v. Org. of Foster Families for Equal. & Reform, 431 U.S. 816, 843 (1977).

50. *See* Lalli v. Lalli, 439 U.S. 259, 275–76 (1978).

51. *See* Lehr v. Robertson, 463 U.S. 248, 262 (1983).

52. *See* Sara Randazzo, GAY CUSTODY FIGHTS REDEFINE LEGAL PARENTHOOD, WALL.
ST. J. (June 1, 2016, 10:48 PM ET), http://www.wsj.com/articles/gay-custody-fights-
redefine-legal-parenthood-1464818297 [http://perma.cc/GQV2-EQCN].

53. JUDITH S. MODELL, KINSHIP WITH STRANGERS: ADOPTION AND INTERPRETATIONS
OF KINSHIP IN AMERICAN CULTURE 95 (1994). *See also* Susan Frelich Appleton &
Robert A. Pollak, Response, *Exploring the Connections Between Adoption and
IVF: Twibling Analyses*, 95 MINN. L. REV. HEADNOTES 60, 67 (2011).

54. Henderson v. Adams, No. 1:15-cv-00220-TWP-MJD, 2016 WL 3548645, at *2 (S.D.
Ind. June 30, 2016).

55. ELIZABETH BARTHOLET, FAMILY BONDS: ADOPTION AND THE POLITICS OF
PARENTING 48 (1993).

56. *See* Sarah B. Dougherty, "Exploring Public Perceptions of Adoptive Families: The More Things Change," Ph.D. diss., Antioch University New England, 2009, ProQuest Dissertations Publishing (3357864).

57. I. Glenn Cohen & Daniel Chen, *Trading-Off Reproductive Technology and Adoption: Does Subsidizing IVF Decrease Adoption Rates and Should It Matter?*, 95 MINN. L. REV. 485, 550–54, 575 (2010).

58. Reber v. Reiss, 42 A.3d 1131, 1138 (Pa. Super. Ct. 2012).

59. *See Introduction to* FAMILIES BY LAW: AN ADOPTION READER 1, 3 (Naomi R. Cahn & Joan Heifetz Hollinger eds., 2004).

60. Leslie A. Baxter et al., *Narrating Adoption: Resisting Adoption as "Second Best,"* 14 J. FAM. COMM. 253, 255 (2014).

61. Allen P. Fisher, *Still "Not Quite as Good as Having Your Own"? Toward A Sociology of Adoption*, 29 ANN. REV. SOC. 336, 361 (2003).

62. *See* June Carbone, *Negating the Genetic Tie: Does the Law Encourage Unnecessary Risks?*, 79 UMKC L. REV. 333, 333–34 (2010).

63. *See* Janet L. Dolgin, *Biological Evaluations: Blood, Genes, and Family*, 41 AKRON L. REV. 347, 366–67 (2008).

64. Gregory E. Kaebnick & Thomas H. Murray, *Introduction: The Many-Stranded Tapestry of Parenthood, in* GENETIC TIES AND THE FAMILY: THE IMPACT OF PATERNITY TESTING ON PARENTS AND CHILDREN, at xiii, xiii (Mark A. Rothstein et al. eds., 2005).

65. MICHAEL GROSSBERG, GOVERNING THE HEARTH: LAW AND THE FAMILY IN NINETEENTH-CENTURY AMERICA 278 (1985).

66. Gay Becker et al., *Resemblance Talk: A Challenge for Parents Whose Children Were Conceived with Donor Gametes in the U.S.*, 61 SOC. SCI. & MED. 1300, 1301 (2005). For discussion, *see* Katharine K. Baker, *Legitimate Families and Equal Protection*, 56 B.C. L. REV. 1647, 1649–50 (2015).

67. Saskia Hendriks et al., *The Importance of Genetic Parenthood for Infertile Men and Women*, 32 HUM. REPROD. 2076, 2087 (2017).

68. *See* AVIAD E. RAZ, COMMUNITY GENETICS AND GENETIC ALLIANCES: EUGENICS, CARRIER TESTING, AND NETWORKS OF RISK 53–54, 62 (2010); DAVID M. SCHNEIDER, AMERICAN KINSHIP 23–25 (2d ed. 1980); KATH WESTON, FAMILIES WE CHOOSE: LESBIANS, GAYS, KINSHIP 35–36 (1991).

69. *In re* Baby M, 537 A.2d 1227, 1235 (N.J. 1988); Iver Peterson, *Baby M, Ethics and the Law*, N.Y. TIMES, Jan. 18, 1987, at A1.

70. Michelle Harrison, *Social Construction of Mary Beth Whitehead*, 1 GENDER & SOC'Y 300, 302 (1987).

71. Anna Goldfarb, *How to Leave a Legacy When You Don't Have Children*, N.Y. TIMES (July 17, 2018), https://www.nytimes.com/2018/07/17/well/how-to-leave-a-legacy-when-you-dont-have-children.html [https://perma.cc/V9AD-4CR4].

72. KAJA FINKLER, EXPERIENCING THE NEW GENETICS: FAMILY AND KINSHIP ON THE MEDICAL FRONTIER 10 (2000). *See also* John Lawrence Hill, *What Does It Mean to Be a "Parent"? The Claims of Biology as the Basis for Parental Rights*, 66 N.Y.U. L. REV. 353, 389 (1991).

73. Guido Pennings, *The Right to Choose Your Donor: A Step Towards Commercialization or a Step Towards Empowering the Patient?*, 15 HUM. REPROD. 508, 508–09 (2000).

74. MODELL, *supra* note 53, at 2. For discussion, *see* Dov Fox, *Racial Classification in Assisted Reproduction*, 118 YALE L.J. 1844, 1861–62 & n.87 (2009).

75. Rachel H. Farr & Charlotte J. Patterson, *Lesbian and Gay Adoptive Parents and Their Children*, *in* LGBT-PARENT FAMILIES: INNOVATIONS IN RESEARCH AND IMPLICATIONS FOR PRACTICE 39, 45 (Abbie E. Goldberg & Katherine R. Allen eds., 2013); GARY J. GATES, DEMOGRAPHICS OF MARRIED AND UNMARRIED SAME-SEX COUPLES: ANALYSES OF THE 2013 AMERICAN COMMUNITY SURVEY 1 (2015).

76. *See* KARÍN LESNIK-OBERSTEIN, ON HAVING AN OWN CHILD: REPRODUCTIVE TECHNOLOGIES AND THE CULTURAL CONSTRUCTION OF CHILDHOOD xii (2008); Dana Berkowitz, *Gay Men and Surrogacy*, *in* LGBT-PARENT FAMILIES: INNOVATIONS IN RESEARCH AND IMPLICATIONS FOR PRACTICE 71, 76 (Abbie E. Goldberg & Katherine R. Allen eds., 2013).

77. MAUREEN SULLIVAN, THE FAMILY OF WOMAN: LESBIAN MOTHERS, THEIR CHILDREN, AND THE UNDOING OF GENDER 44 (2004).

78. *See* LAURA MAMO, QUEERING REPRODUCTION 191–92 (2007); DEAN A. MURPHY, GAY MEN PURSUING PARENTHOOD THROUGH SURROGACY 152–53 (2015).

Chapter 8

1. Roe v. Wade, 410 U.S. 113, 153 (1973).

2. Lininger v. Eisenbaum, 764 P.2d 1202, 1204 n.2 (Colo. 1998).

3. *See, e.g.*, M.A. v. United States, 951 P.2d 851 (Alaska 1998); Stills v. Gratton, 127 Cal. Rptr. 652 (Ct. App. 1976); Nanke v. Napier, 346 N.W.2d 520 (Iowa 1984); Clapham v. Yanga, 300 N.W.2d 727 (Mich. 1981); Debora S. v. Sapega, 392 N.Y.S.2d 79 (App. Div. 1977); Miller v. Johnson, 343 S.E.2d 301 (Va. 1986); Rieck v. Medical Protective Co., 219 N.W.2d 242 (Wis. 1974).

4. *See, e.g.*, Lininger v. Eisenbaum, 764 P.2d 1202 (Colo. 1988); Hartke v. McKelway, 707 F.2d 1544 (D.C. Cir.), *cert. denied*, 464 U.S. 983 (1983); Bertrand v. Kudla, 139 So. 3d 1233 (La. Ct. App. 2014); Dehn v. Edgecombe, 865 A.2d 603 (Md. 2005); Cichewicz v. Salesin, 854 N.W.2d 901 (Mich. 2014); J.P.M. v. Schmidt Labs., Inc., 428 A.2d 515 (N.J. Super. App. Div. 1981); Provencio v. Wenrich, 261 P.3d 1089 (N.M. 2011); Miceli v. Ansell, 23 F. Supp. 2d 929 (N.D. Ind. 1998).

5. "Jane the Virgin" (CW Television Network, Oct. 13, 2014).

6. *See, e.g.*, Gladu v. Bos. IVF Inc., No. 98-4189, 1000 WL 177798, at *1–2 (Mass. State Ct. Jan. 30, 2004); Landgericht Dortmund Apr. 19, 2012, 4_O_320/10, https://www.justiz.nrw.de/nrwe/lgs/dortmund/lg_dortmund/j2012/4_O_320_10urteil20120419.html [https://perma.cc/TW5S-SFJY]; Haneen Dajani, *Sperm Theft Case Sent to Civil Court*, NAT'L UAE (Feb. 2, 2013), https://www.thenational.ae/uae/courts/sperm-theft-case-sent-to-civil-court-1.289394 [https://perma.cc/5WG9-LT4N]; Murray Wardrop, *Woman Had Two Children After Secretly Taking*

Ex-husband's Frozen Sperm, TELEGRAPH (May 29, 2011), https://www.telegraph. co.uk/news/uknews/8544783/Woman-had-two-children-after-secretly-taking-ex-husbands-frozen-sperm.html [https://perma.cc/G23B-3QPH].

7. Pressil v. Gibson, 477 S.W.3d 402, 405 (Tex. Ct. App. 2015).

8. *Id.* at 409–10. For similar cases from England and Canada, *see* ARB v. IVF Hammersmith, [2018] EWCA (Civ.) 2803; Keith Fraser, *Fertility Clinic Sued over Alleged Failure to Get Consent for Use of Surrogate Mom's Ovum*, VANCOUVER SUN (Nov. 9, 2017), http://vancouversun.com/news/local-news/fertility-clinic-sued-over-alleged-failure-to-get-consent-for-use-of-surrogate-moms-ovum [https://perma.cc/ 4CNY-93LV].

9. Pitre v. Opelousas Gen. Hosp., 530 So. 2d 1151, 1162 (La. 1988).

10. Christensen v. Thornby, 255 N.W. 620, 622 (Minn. 1934).

11. Shaheen v. Knight, 11 Pa. D. & C.2d 41, 45 (Lycoming Cty. 1957).

12. Cockrum v. Baumgartner, 447 N.E.2d 385, 388–89 (Ill. 1983) (citing Wilbur v. Kerr, 628 S.W.2d 568, 570 (Ark. 1982)); Public Health Trust v. Brown, 388 So.2d 1084, 1085–86 (Fla. App. 1980); Beardsley v. Wierdsma, 650 P.2d 288, 293 (Wyo. 1982).

13. Cockrum v. Baumgartner, 447 N.E.2d 385, 388–89 (Ill. 1983). *See also, e.g.*, O'Toole v. Greenberg, 477 N.E.2d 445, 448 (N.Y. 1985); Johnson v. Univ. Hosps. of Cleveland, 540 N.E.2d 1370, 1378 (Ohio 1989).

14. Terrell v. Garcia, 496 S.W.2d 124, 128 (Tex. Civ. App. 1973); Miller v. Johnson, 343 S.E.2d 301, 307 (Va. 1986); Girdley v. Coats, 825 S.W.2d 295, 298 (Mo. 1992) (en banc).

15. Philips v. United States, 508 F. Supp. 544, 549 (D.S.C. 1981).

16. Amy Norwood Moore, Note, *Judicial Limitations on Damages Recoverable for the Wrongful Birth of a Healthy Infant*, 68 VA. L. REV. 1311, 1320 (1982).

17. *See* ANNILY CAMPBELL, CHILDFREE AND STERILIZED: WOMEN'S DECISIONS AND MEDICAL RESPONSES 16–32, 113–40 (1999).

18. *See* Dianne Lalonde, *Regret, Shame, and Denials of Women's Voluntary Sterilization*, 32 BIOETHICS 281, 284 (2018).

19. *See* Dylan Ehman & Dustin Costescu, *Tubal Sterilization* in *Women Under 30: Case Series and Ethical Implications*, 40 J. OBSTETRICS & GYNECOLOGY CAN. 36, 37 (2018).

20. CAROL SANGER, ABOUT ABORTION: TERMINATING PREGNANCY IN TWENTY-FIRST CENTURY AMERICA 132–33 (2017).

21. Brief for the National Abortion Rights Action League et al. as Amici Curiae in Support of Appellees, Thornburgh v. Am. Coll. of Obstetricians & Gynecologists, 476 U.S. 747 (Nos. 84-495, 84-1379), 1985 WL 669630, at *28.

22. *See* Robin West, *Jurisprudence and Gender*, 55 U. CHI. L. REV. 1, 35 (1988).

23. *See* Khiara M. Bridges, *When Pregnancy Is an Injury: Rape, Law, and Culture*, 65 STAN. L. REV. 457, 477–79 (2013).

24. Boone v. Mullendore, 416 So. 2d 718, 724 (1982) (Faulkner, J., specially concurring).

25. Troppi v. Scarf, 187 N.W.2d 511, 518–19 (Mich. Ct. App. 1971), *rev'd on other grounds*, Taylor v. Kurapati, 600 N.W.2d 670 (Mich. Ct. App. 1999).

26. Lovelace Med. Ctr. v. Mendez, 805 P.2d 603, 609 (N.M. 1991).

27. *See, e.g.*, M.A. v. United States, 951 P.2d 851, 856 (Alaska 1998); Rouse v. Wesley, 494 N.W.2d 7, 10 (Mich. Ct. App. 1992); Hitzemann v. Adam, 518 N.W.2d 102, 107 (Neb. 1994); Emerson v. Magendantz, 689 A.2d 409, 413 (R.I. 1997).

28. *See* Custodio v. Bauer, 59 Cal. Rptr. 463, 477 (Ct. App. 1967); Lovelace Med. Ctr. v. Mendez, 805 P.2d 603, 612 (N.M. 1991); Zehr v. Haugen, 871 P.2d 1006, 1013 (Or. 1994); Marciniak v. Lundborg, 450 N.W.2d 243, 248 (Wis. 1990).

29. *See, e.g.*, Burke v. Rivo, 551 N.E.2d 1, 18 (Mass. 1990); Jones v. Malinowski, 473 A.2d 429, 436–37 (Md. 1984); Univ. of Ariz. Health Scis. Ctr. v. Superior Court, 667 P.2d 1294, 1299 (Ariz. 1983); Ochs v. Borrelli, 445 A.2d 883, 886 (Conn. 1982); Sherlock v. Stillwater Clinic, 260 N.W.2d 169, 176 (Minn. 1977).

30. RESTATEMENT OF TORTS § 920 & cmt. b. For discussion, *see* Michael B. Kelly, *The Rightful Position in "Wrongful Life" Actions*, 42 HASTINGS L.J. 505, 519–25 (1991).

31. Kathryn C. Vikingstad, *The Use and Abuse of the Tort Benefit Rule in Wrongful Parentage Cases*, 82 CHI.-KENT L. REV. 1063, 1099 (2007).

32. *See* Mahita Gajanan, *The Cost of Raising a Child Jumps to $233,610*, TIME (Jan. 9, 2017), http://time.com/money/4629700/child-raising-cost-department-of-agriculture-report/ [https://perma.cc/9S5V-N3J3].

33. LaPoint v. Shirley, 409 F. Supp. 118, 121 (W.D. Tex. 1976). *See also* Garrison v. Foy, 486 N.E.2d 5, 9 (Ind. Ct. App. 1985); Pitre v. Opelousas Gen. Hosp., 530 So. 2d 1151, 1154 (La. 1988).

34. Williams v. Univ. of Chi. Hosps., 688 N.E.2d 130, 134 (Ill. 1997).

35. Williams v. Rosner, 7 N.E.3d 57, 60–61 (Ill. App. Ct. 2014) (internal quotation marks omitted).

36. *Id.* at 69.

37. *See, e.g.*, Robak v. United States, 658 F.2d 471 (7th Cir. 1981); Walker v. Mart, 790 P.2d 735 (Ariz. 1990); Blake v. Cruz, 698 P.2d 315 (Idaho 1984); Smith v. Cote, 513 A.2d 341 (N.H. 1986); Procanik v. Cillo, 478 A.2d 755 (N.J. 1984); Jacobs v. Theimer, 519 S.W.2d 846 (Tex. 1975).

38. *See* Phillips v. United States, 575 F. Supp. 1309, 1320 n.10 (D.S.C. 1983); Arche v. United States Dep't of the Army, 798 P.2d 477, 486–87 (Kan. 1990); Garrison v. Med. Center of Delaware, Inc., 581 A.2d 288, 292 (Del. 1989); Kush v. Lloyd, 616 So. 2d 415, 422–24 (Fla. 1992); Arche v. United States Dep't of the Army, 798 P.2d 477, 486–87 (Kan. 1990).

39. *See* Jackson v. Bumgardner, 347 S.E.2d 743, 744–46 (N.C. 1986).

40. Paul Stokes, *Fertility Clinic Must Pay Couple for "Extra" Baby*, TELEGRAPH (Nov. 17, 2000), https://www.telegraph.co.uk/news/uknews/1374579/Fertility-clinic-must-pay-couple-for-extra-baby.html [https://perma.cc/679P-9VEZ]; Clare Dyer, *Payout to Triplet Parents in Landmark IVF Case*, GUARDIAN (Nov. 17, 2000), http://www.theguardian.com/uk/2000/nov/17/claredyer [http://perma.cc/2Q72-MU9E]. For similar cases, *see* G. & M. v. Armellin [2009] ACTCA 6, para. 4 (Austl.); Judith Mair, *Damages Claim for Wrongful Birth Due to a Systems Failure*, 41 HEALTH INFO. MGMT. J. 36, 36 (2012). *See also* Morgan v. Christman, No. 88-3211-O, 1990 WL 137405, at *1–2 (D. Kan. July 20, 1990); Assoc. Press, *Clinic Settles Malpractice Lawsuit by Parents Who Had Septuplets*, N.Y. TIMES (July 12, 1990), http://www.nytimes.com/

1990/07/12/us/clinic-settles-malpractice-lawsuit-by-parents-who-had-septuplets. html [https://perma.cc/WR2M-PF5Q].

41. *See* Andrew M. Kaunitz et al., *Abortions that Fail*, 66 OBSTET. & GYNECOL. 533 (1985); Rajesh Varma & Janesh K. Gupta, *Failed Sterilisation: Evidence-based Review and Medico-legal Ramifications*, 111 INT. J. OBSTET. & GYNECOL. 1322 (2004).

42. Ramirez v. Vintage Pharmaceuticals, Inc., 852 F.3d 324, 327 (3rd Cir. 2017); Allyson Chiu, *"Unintended Pregnancy": Nearly 170,000 Allergan Birth Control Packs Recalled*, WASH. POST (May 30, 2018), https://www.washingtonpost.com/news/morning-mix/wp/2018/ 05/30/nearly-170000-allergan-birth-control-packs-recalled-after-error-leaves-pills-out-of-order/?utm_term=.89e087a49595 [https://perma.cc/2NM5-Y3HM]; U.S. FOOD & DRUG ADMIN., QUALITEST PHARMACEUTICAL ISSUES A NATIONWIDE VOLUNTARY RECALL OF ORAL CONTRACEPTIVES (Sept. 15, 2011), http://www.fda.gov/Safety/Recalls/ ucm272199.htm [http://perma.cc/EUM5-4FCM].

43. *See* Brownfield v. Daniel Freeman Marina Hosp., 256 Cal. Rptr. 240 (Ct. App. 1989).

44. *See* Rees v. Darlington Mem'l Hosp. NHS Trust [2004] 1 AC 309 (HL) 317 (appeal taken from Eng.).

45. Troppi v. Scarf, 187 N.W.2d 511, 519 (Mich. Ct. App. 1971). *See also* Flowers v. District of Columbia, 478 A.2d 1073, 1077 (D.C. 1984).

46. Emerson v. Magendantz, 689 A.2d 409, 412, 413 (R.I. 1997) (citing Public Health Trust v. Brown, 388 So.2d 1084 (Fla. Dist. Ct. App. 1980), and Fassoulas v. Ramey, 450 So.2d 822 (Fla. 1984)).

47. Ziemba v. Sternberg, 45 A.D.2d 230, 234 (N.Y. 1974) (Cardamone, J., dissenting).

48. Girdley v. Coats, 825 S.W.2d 295, 297 (Mo. 1992) (en banc).

49. CHRISTINE OVERALL, WHY HAVE CHILDREN: THE ETHICAL DEBATE 9, 150 (2012).

50. Martinez v. Long Island Jewish Hillside Med. Ctr., 512 N.E.2d 538, 538 (N.Y. 1987).

51. *Id.*, Appellant's Opening Brief, at 54.

52. *In re* Quinlan, 355 A.2d 647 (N.J. 1976).

53. *Martinez*, 512 N.E.2d at 694 (Gibbons, J., dissenting); Appellant's Opening Brief, *supra* note 51, at 83, 71, 76, 84, 88, 69.

54. *Martinez*, 512 N.E.2d at 539.

55. Marciniak v. Lundborg, 450 N.W.2d 243, 247 (Wis. 1990).

56. Reva Siegel, *Reasoning from the Body: A Historical Perspective on Abortion Regulation and Questions of Equal Protection*, 44 STAN. L. REV. 261, 371–72 (1992).

57. Smith v. Gore, 728 S.W.2d 738, 752 (Tenn. 1987). *See also* Rieck v. Med. Protective Co., 219 N.W.2d 242, 244 (Wis. 1974); Beardsley v. Wierdsma, 650 P.2d 288, 292 (Wyo. 1982).

58. Catlin v. Hamburg, 56 A.3d 914, 917 (Pa. Super. Ct. 2012).

59. *Id.* at 924–26 (citations omitted).

Chapter 9

1. *See, e.g.*, D.D. v. Idant Labs., 374 F. App'x 319, 320 (3d Cir. 2010); Fruiterman v. Granata, 668 S.E.2d 127, 129 (Va. 2008); Doolan v. IVF Am. (MA), Inc., No. 993476, 2000 WL

33170944, at *1 (Mass. Super. Ct. Nov. 20, 2000); Paretta v. Med. Offices for Human Reprod., 760 N.Y.S.2d 639, 641 (Sup. Ct. 2003); Fruiterman v. Granata, 668 S.E.2d 127, 129 (Va. 2008); Wuth v. Lab. Corp. of Am., 359 P.3d 841, 846 (Wash. Ct. App. 2015); Editors, *Parents Reach Settlement with IVF Clinic after Sons were Born with Genetic Condition Fragile X Syndrome*, SYDNEY MORNING HERALD (Nov. 13, 2017, 9:25 PM), http://www.smh.com.au/nsw/parents-sue-ivf-clinic-after-sons-were-born-with-genetic-condition-fragile-x-syndrome-20171113-gzkdil.html [https://perma.cc/GW9W-KPR5]; Sharon Kirkey, *Switched Embryos and Wrong Sperm: IVF Mix-ups Lead to Babies Born with "Unintended Parentage,"* NAT'L POST (July 31, 2016, 9:42 AM ET), http://news.nationalpost.com/health/ivf-mix-ups-lead-to-babies-born-with-unintended-parentage?__lsa=f977-14ba [http://perma.cc/36LH-88WE]; David Klepper, *Couples Sue Fertility Clinic over Eggs with Genetic Defect*, ABS NEWS (Nov. 15, 2017, 5:32 PM ET), http://abcnews.go.com/Health/wireStory/couples-sue-fertility-clinic-eggs-genetic-defect-51179154 [https://perma.cc/P3TC-AXJ8]; Ilan Lior, *Gay Israeli Couple Received Wrong Baby from Surrogate Mother in Nepal*, HAARETZ (Jan. 8, 2016, 8:50 AM), http://www.haaretz.com/israel-news/.premium-1.696174 [https://perma.cc/8SKW-4BAS]. Spouse/stranger switches include Aschero v. Kao, No. CGC-09-492527, 2009 WL 2980676 (Cal. Super. Ct. Dec. 15, 2009); Robin Schatz, *New Questions in Sperm Case; Dreams Turn to Nightmares*, NEWSDAY, Apr. 22, 1990, at A4; Deborah Sharp, *Fla. Suit Highlights In Vitro Industry's Controversies*, USA TODAY, Nov. 15, 1996, at 3A. For cases outside the United States, *see* Sophie Arie, *Italian IVF Blunder Fuels Fertility Law Row*, GUARDIAN (Sept. 6, 2004, 7:00 PM EDT), http://www.theguardian.com/world/2004/sep/07/italy.sophiearie [http://perma.cc/ TZ9B-Z2X2]; A & B v. A Health & Soc. Servs. Tr. [2011] NICA 28 (Ir.); ACB v. Thomson Med. Pte Ltd. [2017] SGHC 20 (Sing.).

2. Andrews v. Keltz, 838 N.Y.S.2d 363, 365–66, 368 (Sup. Ct. 2007) (internal quotation marks omitted).

3. *Id.* at 367 (internal quotations marks omitted, citing Weintraub v. Brown, 470 N.Y.S.2d 634, 641 (Sup. Ct. 2007)).

4. Paretta v. Med. Offices for Human Reprod., 760 N.Y.S.2d 639, 648 (Sup. Ct. 2003).

5. Stephanie C. Chen & David T. Wasserman, *A Framework for Unrestricted Prenatal Whole-Genome Sequencing: Respecting and Enhancing the Autonomy of Prospective Parents*, 17 AM. J. BIOETHICS 3, 10–11 (2017).

6. Wendy F. Hensel, *The Disabling Impact of Wrongful Birth and Wrongful Life Actions*, 40 HARV. C.R.-C.L. L. REV. 141, 183 (2005).

7. Goldberg v. Ruskin, 499 N.E.2d 406, 411 (Ill. 1986) (Clark, C.J., dissenting).

8. Khadim v. Lab. Corp. of Am., 838 F. Supp. 2d 448, 452, 453–54 (W.D. Va. 2011). For similar facts, *see* Verdict and Settlement Summary, Sharad v. Sanghavi, No. 478265, 2006 WL 5346981 (N.J. Super. Ct. 2006).

9. Estrada v. Univ. of S. Fla. Bd. of Trs., No. 06-CA-000625, 2007 WL 4643824 (Fla. Cir. Ct. 2009).

10. Keel v. Banach, 624 So. 2d 1022, 1030 (Ala. 1993).

11. *See* Jeffrey R. Botkin, *Fetal Privacy and Confidentiality*, HASTINGS CTR. REP., Sept.–Oct. 1995, at 32, 37; Diane M. Korngiebel et al., *Generating a Taxonomy for Genetic*

Conditions Relevant to Reproductive Planning, 170 AM. J. MED. GENETICS 565, 571–73 (2016); Ingrid Lobo, *Same Genetic Mutation, Different Genetic Disease Phenotype*, 1 NATURE EDUC. 64, 65–66 (2008); Barbara Katz Rothman, Commentary, *Yes. Yes But*, 43 J. MED. ETHICS 11, 12 (2017).

12. *See* Dov Fox, *Parental Attention Deficit Disorder*, 25 J. APPLIED PHIL. 246, 254–55 (2008).

13. Carol Sanger, *The Lopsided Harms of Reproductive Negligence*, 117 COLUM. L. REV. ONLINE 1, 39 (2017), http://columbialawreview.org/content/the-lopsided-harms-of-reproductive-negligence/ [http://perma.cc/W5MD-27RC].

14. ANDREW SOLOMON, FAR FROM THE TREE: PARENTS, CHILDREN, AND THE SEARCH FOR IDENTITY 47 (2012).

15. Naccash v. Burger, 290 S.E.2d 825, 828 (Va. 1982).

16. *See* Marciniak v. Lundborg, 450 N.W.2d 243, 249 (Wis. 1990). For discussion, *see* DAN B. DOBBS, REMEDIES: DAMAGES, EQUITY, RESTITUTION 182–83 (1973).

17. Jones v. Malinowski, 473 A.2d 429, 436–37 (Md. 1984).

18. Hartke v. McKelway, 707 F.2d 1544, 1555 (D.C. Cir. 1983).

19. Smith v. Gore, 728 S.W.2d 738, 743 (Tenn. 1987).

20. Taylor v. Kurapati, 600 N.W.2d 670, 688 (Mich. Ct. App. 1999).

21. *Gore*, 728 S.W.2d at 744.

22. Grossbaum v. Genesis Genetics Inst., LLC, No. 07-1359 (GEB), 2011 WL 2462279, at *1–2 (D.N.J. June 10, 2011).

23. *NIH Fact Sheets—Cystic Fibrosis*, NAT'L INST. FOR HEALTH, https://report.nih.gov/NIHfactsheets/ViewFactSheet.aspx?csid=36 [https://perma.cc/ETH5-5K2N] (last updated Mar. 29, 2013).

24. Jen Gann, *Every Parent Wants to Protect Their Child. I Never Got the Chance*, N.Y. MAG. (Nov. 27, 2017), https://www.thecut.com/2017/11/raising-child-with-cystic-fibrosis.html [https://perma.cc/3YYH-S82Q].

25. *Grossbaum*, 2011 WL at *1–2; Grossbaum v. Genesis Genetics Inst., 489 Fed. Appx. 613 (3d Cir. July 24, 2012).

26. Atlanta Obstetrics & Gynecology Group v. Abelson, 398 S.E.2d 557, 561 (Ga. 1990); Grubbs v. Barbourville Family Health Ctr., 120 S.W.3d 682, 689 (Ky. 2003); Taylor v. Kurapati, 600 N.W.2d 670, 688 (Mich. Ct. App. 1999).

27. Harbeson v. Parke-Davis, Inc., 656 P.2d 483, 494 (Wash. 1983).

28. Marciniak v. Lundborg, 450 N.W.2d 243, 249 (Wis. 1990).

29. *See, e.g.*, Rowlette v. Mortimer, No. 4:18-cv-00143-DCN, 2018 WL 5305538, **10–12 (D. Idaho Oct. 25, 2018).

30. B.F. et al. v. Reprod. Med. Assoc. of New York, 92 N.E.3d 766 (N.Y. Ct. App. 2017).

31. *Id.* at 770, 773.

32. Erwei Zuo et al., *Cytosine Base Editor Generates Substantial Off-Target Single-Nucleotide Variants in Mouse Embryos*, SCIENCE, Feb. 28, 2019 (10.1126/science.aav9973); Yanfang Fu et al., *High-Frequency Off-Target Mutagenesis Induced by CRISPR-Cas Nucleases in Human Cells*, 31 NATURE BIOTECHN. 822 (2013).

33. *See* Sindell v. Abbott Labs., 607 P.2d 924, 936 (Cal. 1980).

34. Harnicher v. Univ. of Utah Med. Ctr., 962 P.2d 67, 72 (Utah 1998).

35. Grubbs v. Barbourville Family Health Ctr., 120 S.W.3d 682, 689 (Ky. 2003).

36. Greco v. United States, 893 P.2d 345, 349 (Nev. 1995).

37. *See* Edward A. Marshall, *Medical Malpractice in the New Eugenics*, 35 GA. L. REV. 1277, 1317–21 (2001).

38. *See* Adam C. Naj et al., *Common Variants at MS4A4/MS4A6E, CD2AP, CD33 and EPHA1 Are Associated with Late-onset Alzheimer's Disease*, 43 NATURE GENETICS 436, 441 (2011).

39. *See* U.S. v. Anderson, 669 A.2d 73, 78–79 (Del. 1995); DeBurkarte v. Louvar, 393 N.W.2d 131, 137 (Iowa 1986); *In re* Englert, 605 So. 2d 1349, 1351 (La. 1992).

40. *See* Petriello v. Kalman, 576 A.2d 474, 481–83 (Conn. 1990).

Chapter 10

1. *See* JOHN BELL, POLICY ARGUMENTS IN JUDICIAL DECISIONS 11–12 (1983); Farshad Ghodoosi, *The Concept of Public Policy in Law: Revisiting the Role of the Public Policy Doctrine in the Enforcement of Private Legal Arrangements*, 94 NEB. L. REV. 685, 726–29 (2016); James D. Hopkins, *Public Policy and the Formation of a Rule of Law*, 37 BROOK. L. REV. 323, 323 (1970); Robert J. Kaczorowski, *The Common-Law Background of Nineteenth-Century Tort Law*, 51 OHIO ST. L.J. 1127, 1143–50 (1990).

2. Cockrum v. Baumgartner, 447 N.E.2d 385, 388–89 (Ill. 1983) (citing Wilbur v. Kerr, 628 S.W.2d 568, 570 (Ark. 1982)).

3. Hartke v. McKelway, 707 F.2d 1544, 1552 n.8 (D.C. Cir. 1983).

4. Amy Norwood Moore, Note, *Judicial Limitations on Damages Recoverable for the Wrongful Birth of a Healthy Infant*, 68 VA. L. REV. 1311, 1329 & n.94 (1982).

5. Emerson v. Magendantz, 689 A.2d 409, 422 (R.I. 1997) (Bourcier, J., dissenting in part).

6. *See* Adrienne Asch & David Wasserman, *Where Is the Sin in Synecdoche?: Prenatal Testing and the Parent-Child Relationship*, *in* QUALITY OF LIFE AND HUMAN DIFFERENCE: GENETIC TESTING, HEALTH CARE, AND DISABILITY 172 (David Wasserman et al. eds., 2005); Alicia Ouellette, *Selection Against Disability: Abortion, ART, and Access*, 43 J.L. MED. ETHICS 211, 213 (2015); Michael E. Waterstone, *Disability Constitutional Law*, 63 EMORY L.J. 527, 550 (2014).

7. *See* SALLY BALDWIN, THE COSTS OF CARING: FAMILIES WITH DISABLED CHILDREN 141–42 (1985); Samuel R. Bagenstos, *Subordination, Stigma, and "Disability,"* 86 VA. L. REV. 397, 426–31 (2000); Mary Crossley, *The Disability Kaleidoscope*, 74 NOTRE DAME L. REV. 621, 655–58 (1999); Adam M. Samaha, *What Good Is the Social Model of Disability?*, 74 U. CHI. L. REV. 1251, 1270–71 (2007).

8. Plowman v. Fort Madison Cmty. Hosp., 896 N.W.2d 393, 406–07 (Iowa 2017).

9. *Id.* at 408 (citing Bader v. Johnson, 732 N.E.2d 1212, 1219–20 (Ind. 2000) (quoting Garrison v. Foy, 486 N.E.2d 5, 8 (Ind. Ct. App. 1985))).

10. Adrienne Asch & David Wasserman, *Reproductive Testing for Disability*, *in* ROUTLEDGE COMPANION TO BIOETHICS 417, 426 (Rebecca Kukla, John D. Arras, &

Elizabeth Fenton eds., 2015). *See also* Philip M. Ferguson, Alan Gartner, & Dorothy K. Lipsky, *The Experience of Disability in Families: A Synthesis of Research and Parent Narratives, in* PRENATAL TESTING AND DISABILITY RIGHTS 72, 73 (Erik Parens & Adrienne Asch eds., 2000).

11. *See* Parkinson v. St. James & Seacroft Univ. Hosp. NHS Tr. [2001] EWCA (Civ) 530 [90], [2002] QB 266 [293] (Eng.); Dov Fox, *Prenatal Screening Policy in International Perspective: Lessons from Israel, Cyprus, Taiwan, China, and Singapore*, 9 YALE J. HEALTH POL'Y L. & ETHICS 471, 478–79 (2009).

12. Melissa Healy, *Fertility's New Frontier*, L.A. TIMES (July 21, 2003), http://articles.latimes.com/2003/jul/21/health/he-pgd21 [https://perma.cc/MW4R-EEHD].

13. *See* David Wasserman, *Better Parenting through Biomedical Modification: A Case for Pluralism, Deference, and Charity*, 27 KENNEDY INST. ETHICS J. 217, 238 (2017); Faye Flam, *Designing the Family Tree a Road to Eugenics?*, BUFF. NEWS, June 25, 1995, at F7; Lindsey Tanner, *Some Ponder "Designer" Babies with Mom or Dad's Defective Genes*, USA TODAY (Dec. 21, 2006), http://www.usatoday.com/tech/science/genetics/2006-12-21-designer-disability_x.htm [http://perma.cc/H2SF-UJKP].

14. Gaby Hinsliff & Robin McKie, *This Couple Want a Deaf Child. Should We Try to Stop Them?*, OBSERVER (Mar. 9, 2008, 5:54 AM EDT), http://www.guardian.co.uk/science/2008/mar/09/genetics.medicalresearch [https://perma.cc/M7TR-8ZV3]. *See also* Darshak M. Sanghavi, *Wanting Babies like Themselves, Some Parents Choose Genetic Defects*, N.Y. TIMES, Dec. 5, 2006, at F5; Merle Spriggs, *Lesbian Couple Create a Child Who Is Deaf like Them*, 28 J. MED. ETHICS 283, 283 (2002); Sarah-Kate Templeton, *Deaf Demand Right to Designer Deaf Children*, SUNDAY TIMES (Dec. 23, 2007), http://www.timesonline.co.uk/tol/news/uk/health/article3087367.ece [http://perma.cc/6X6H-HD5L].

15. Dominic Lawson, *Of Course a Deaf Couple Wants a Deaf Child*, INDEPENDENT (Mar. 11, 2008, 1:00 AM GMT), http://www.independent.co.uk/opinion/commentators/dominic-lawson/dominic-lawson-of-course-a-deaf-couple-want-a-deaf-child-794001.html [https://perma.cc/5XF5-FSWG]. *See also* Clare Murphy, *Is It Wrong to Select a Deaf Embryo?*, BBC NEWS (Mar. 10, 2008, 1:34 GMT), http://news.bbc.co.uk/1/hi/health/7287508.stm [https://perma.cc/Z4XN-YPKT].

16. Liza Mundy, *A World of Their Own*, WASH. POST, Mar. 31, 2002, at W22; Gaby Hinsliff & Robin McKie, *This Couple Want a Deaf Child. Should We Try to Stop Them?*, OBSERVER (Mar. 9, 2008, 5:54 AM EDT), http://www.guardian.co.uk/science/2008/mar/09/genetics.medicalresearch [https://perma.cc/M7TR-8ZV3]. *See also* Darshak M. Sanghavi, *Wanting Babies like Themselves, Some Parents Choose Genetic Defects*, N.Y. TIMES, Dec. 5, 2006, at F5; Merle Spriggs, *Lesbian Couple Create a Child Who Is Deaf like Them*, 28 J. MED. ETHICS 283, 283 (2002); Sarah-Kate Templeton, *Deaf Demand Right to Designer Deaf Children*, SUNDAY TIMES (Dec. 23, 2007), http://www.timesonline.co.uk/tol/news/uk/health/article3087367.ece [http://perma.cc/6X6H-HD5L].

17. Faith McLellan, *Controversy over Deliberate Conception of Deaf Child*, 359 LANCET 1315, 1315 (2002).

18. Hernandez v. New York, 500 U.S. 352, 371 (1991).

19. *See* Alan Buchanan, Dan W. Brock, Norman Daniels, & Daniel Wikler, From Chance to Choice, Genetics and Justice 210 (2000); I. Glenn Cohen, *Beyond Best Interests*, 96 Minn. L. Rev. 1187, 1220 (2012); Eric Rakowski, *Who Should Pay for Bad Genes?*, 90 Cal. L. Rev. 1345, 1382 (2002).

20. John A. Robertson, *Procreative Liberty in the Era of Genomics*, 29 Am. J.L. & Med. 439, 450 (2003). *See also* Maher v. Roe, 432 U.S. 464, 478 (1977); Dov Fox, *Interest Creep*, 82 Geo. Wash. L. Rev. 273, 300–02 (2014).

21. Susannah Baruch, David Kaufman, & Kathy L. Hudson, *Genetic Testing of Embryos: Practices and Perspectives of U.S. In Vitro Fertilization Clinics*, 89 Fertility & Sterility 1053, 1055 (2008).

22. Russell Blackford, Humanity Enhanced: Genetic Choice and the Challenge for Liberal Democracies 27–28 (2014). *See also* Bonnie Rochman, The Gene Machine: How Genetic Technologies Are Changing the Way We Have Kids—And the Kids We Have 64 (2017).

23. Colin Gavaghan, Defending the Genetic Supermarket: Law and Ethics of Selecting the Next Generation 22 (Sheila A. M. McLean ed., 2007). *See also* Victoria Chico, Genomic Negligence 106–40 (2011).

24. Bergero v. Univ. of S. Cal. Keck Sch. of Med., No. B200595, 2009 WL 946874, at *1–4 (Cal. Ct. App. Apr. 9, 2009).

25. *See* Jaime King, *Predicting Probability: Regulating the Future of Preimplantation Genetic Screening*, 8 Yale J. Health Pol'y L. & Ethics 283, 294–95 (2008).

26. Barbara Miller, *Women Using IVF to Choose the Sex of Their Children Break Silence on "Gender Disappointment,"* ABC News (Feb. 16, 2017, 11:51 PM), http://www.abc.net.au/news/2017-02-07/women-using-ivf-to-choose-sex-of-their-babies/8234798 [https://perma.cc/BQ4R-FLMA].

27. Douglas Almond & Lena Edlund, *Son-Biased Sex Ratios in the 2000 United States Census*, 105 Proc. Nat'l Acad. Sci. 5681, 5681–82 (2008). *See also* Joseph G. Schenker, *Gender Selection: Cultural and Religious Perspectives*, 19 J. Assisted Reprod. & Genetics 400, 401–05 (2002).

28. Christina Farr, *Some Families Are Paying Thousands of Dollars to Choose Their Baby's Sex*, CNBC (Aug. 4, 2018, 10:37 AM ET), https://www.cnbc.com/2018/08/04/fertility-clinics-advertise-gender-selection-ethical-wuandary.html [http://perma.cc/RN25-PQS7] (quoting Dr. Jeffrey Steinberg).

29. *Family Balancing: Boy or Girl?*, Genetics & IVF Inst., http://www.givf.com/familybalancing/ [http://perma.cc/SJ3Q-K3Y4].

30. Kirsty Scott, *Bereaved Couple Demand Right to Baby Girl*, Guardian (Oct. 4, 2000, 9:20 PM EDT), http://www.theguardian.com/uk/2000/oct/05/humanrights.world1 [http://perma.cc/BJ9M-9TNG].

31. Jasmeet Sidhu, *How to Buy a Daughter*, Slate (Sept. 14, 2012, 3:30 AM), http://www.slate.com/articles/health_and_science/medical_examiner/2012/09/sex_selection_in_babies_through_pgd_americans_are_paying_to_have_daughters_rather_than_sons_.html [http://perma.cc/9U4T-QUVF]. *See also* Mara Hvistendahl, Unnatural Selection 10–15 (1st ed. 2011).

32. Sujatha Jesudason & Susannah Baruch, Editorial, *Sex Selection: What Role for Providers*, 86 Contraception 597, 597 (2012); Tamara Kayali Browne, *Why Parents Should Not Be Told the Sex of Their Fetus*, 43 J. Med. Ethics 4, 9 (2017); Emily W. Kane, The Gender Trap: Parents and the Pitfalls of Raising Boys and Girls 28 (2012).

33. Michael Boucai, *Is Assisted Procreation an LGBT Right?*, 2016 Wisc. L. Rev. 1065, 1122–23 (2016). *See also* Janet L. Dolgin, *Biological Evaluations: Blood, Genes, and Family*, 41 Akron L. Rev. 347, 348 (2008); Katharine K. Baker, *Bionormativity and the Construction of Parenthood*, 42 Ga. L. Rev. 649, 678–99 (2008).

34. Gay Becker, The Elusive Embryo: How Women and Men Approach New Reproductive Technologies 227 (2000); Gerald P. Mallon, Gay Men Choosing Parenthood 78 (2004).

35. Brief for Petitioner at 7172, Gartner v. Iowa Dep't of Pub. Health, 830 N.W.2d 335 (Iowa 2013) (No. 12-0243) (quoting Susan Frelich Appleton, *Presuming Women: Revisiting the Presumption of Legitimacy in the Same-Sex Couples Era*, 86 B.U. L. Rev. 227, 229 n.11 (2006)). For discussion, *see* Douglas NeJaime, *The Nature of Parenthood*, 126 Yale. L.J. 2260, 2331–35 (2017).

36. Michelle Harrison, *Social Construction of Mary Beth Whitehead*, 1 Gender & Soc'y 300, 302 (1987).

37. ACB v. Thomson Med. Pte Ltd. [2017] SGHC 4–5, 20, 210, 150, 133 (Sing.).

38. *Id.* at paras. 128, 130 (citing Dov Fox, *Reproductive Negligence*, 117 Colum. L. Rev. 149, 179, 174 (2017)).

39. *Id.* at paras. 125–27, 147, 134 (citing Fox, *Reproductive Negligence, supra* note 38, at 219–20).

40. *See id.* at paras. 86–101, 95, 87, 150.

41. *Id.* at paras. 6, 8, 134, 130, 132–33 (citing A & B v. A Health & Soc. Servs. Tr. [2011] NICA 28 (N. Ir.)); Andrews v. Keltz, 838 N.Y.S.2d 363, 367–68 (Sup. Ct. 2007).

42. *Woman Delivers 3 Black Children—The Truth Behind Them Moves the World to Tears*, Newsner (May 17, 2017), https://en.newsner.com/family/woman-delivers-3-dark-haired-children-the-truth-behind-them-moves-the-world-to-tears/ [https://perma.cc/T7KT-YBVF]; Astrid Indekeu, *Parents' Expectations and Experiences of Resemblance Through Donor Conception*, 34 New Genetics & Soc'y 398, 410 (2015).

43. *See* Maher v. Vaughn, Silverberg & Assocs., 95 F. Supp. 3d 999, 1003–04 (W.D. Tex. 2015).

44. Harnicher v. Univ. of Utah Med. Ctr., 962 P.2d 67, 68–69, 73, 72 (Utah 1998).

45. *Id.* at 74 (Durham, J., dissenting).

46. Ellen Herman, Kinship By Design: A History of Adoption in the Modern United States 7, 123–25, 150 (2008).

47. *See* Robert L. Burgess & Alicia A. Drais, *Beyond the "Cinderella Effect": Life History Theory and Child Maltreatment*, 10 Human Nature 373, 398 (1999); Martin Daly & Margo Wilson, *Is the "Cinderella Effect" Controversial? A Case Study of Evolution-Minded Research and Critiques Thereof*, in Foundations of Evolutionary Psychology 383, 383 (Charles Crawford & Dennis Krebs eds., 2008); Greg A.

Tooley et al., *Generalising the Cinderella Effect to Unintentional Childhood Fatalities*, 27 EVOLUTION & HUMAN BEHAV. 224, 230 (2006).

48. *See* Alicia Armstrong & Torie C. Plowden, *Ethnicity and Assisted Reproductive Technologies*, 9 CLINICAL PRAC. 651, 652 (2012); Molly Quinn & Victor Fujimoto, *Racial and Ethnic Disparities in Assisted Reproductive Technology Access and Outcomes*, 105 FERTILITY & STERILITY 1119, 1120 (2016).

49. Harnicher v. Univ. of Utah Med. Ctr., 962 P.2d 67, 72 (Utah 1998).

50. Marlise Simons, *Uproar over Twins, and a Dutch Couple's Anguish*, N.Y. TIMES, June 28, 1995, at A03. *See also* Mark Fuller, *Tube Twins from Different Sperm*, TIMES (London), June 20, 1995; Ronald Sullivan, *Sperm Mix-up Lawsuit Is Settled*, N.Y. TIMES, Aug. 1, 1991, at B4; Dareh Gregorian, *Fertility Clinic Is Sued on Egg Mixup*, N.Y. POST, Mar. 27, 1999, at 1; Michael Lasalandra, *Woman, Ex and Hospital Settle over Sperm Mixup*, BOSTON HERALD, Aug. 27, 1998, at 12.

51. Dorinda Elliot & Friso Endt, *Twins—With Two Fathers: A Fertility Clinic's Startling Error*, NEWSWEEK, July 3, 1995, at 38. For discussion, *see* Raizel Liebler, *Are You My Parent? Are You My Child? The Role of Genetics and Race in Defining Relationships After Reproductive Technological Mistakes*, 5 DEPAUL J. HEALTH CARE L. 15, 34–42 (2002); Kim Soffen, *In One Corner of the Law, Minorities and Women Are Often Valued Less*, WASH. POST: WONKBLOG (Oct. 25, 2006), http://www.washingtonpost.com/graphics/business/wonk/settlements/ [http://perma.cc/N2MN-DD3U].

52. Complaint for Wrongful Birth and Breach of Warranty at 5 Cramblett v. Midwest Sperm Bank, LLC, No. 2014-L-010159 (Ill. Cir. Ct. Sept. 29, 2014), 2014 WL 4853400.

53. *Id.* at 6–7. For discussion, *see* Joe Mullin, *White Woman Sues Sperm Bank—Again—After Getting Black Man's Sperm*, ARSTECHNICA (Apr. 25, 2016, 6:33 PM), https://arstechnica.com/tech-policy/2016/04/white-woman-sues-sperm-bankagainafter-getting-black-mans-sperm/ [https://perma.cc/4E2E-375P]; Meredith Rodriguez, *Lawsuit: Wrong Sperm Delivered to Lesbian Couple*, CHI. TRIB. (Oct. 1, 2014, 7:22 AM), http://www.chicagotribune.com/news/local/breaking/ct-sperm-donor-lawsuit-met-20140930-story.html [https://perma.cc/5U3D-9WQG].

54. Complaint at 5, Cramblett v. Midwest Sperm Bank, LLC, No. 1:16-cv-04553 (N.D. Ill. Apr. 22, 2016).

55. Ralph Richard Banks, *The Multiethnic Placement Act and the Troubling Persistence of Race Matching*, 38 CAP. U. L. REV. 271, 288–89 (2009).

56. *See* RITA J. SIMON & HOWARD ALTSTEIN, ADOPTION, RACE, AND IDENTITY: FROM INFANCY TO YOUNG ADULTHOOD 221–23 (2d ed. 2002); David D. Meyer, *Palmore Comes of Age: The Place of Race in the Placement of Children*, 18 U. FLA. J.L. & PUB. POL'Y 183, 202 (2007).

57. Complaint at 5, Cramblett, No. 1:16-cv-04553.

58. Order, Cramblett v. Midwest Sperm Bank, LLC, No. 2015 L 000282 (Ill. Cir. Ct. Sept. 3, 2015).

59. Kimani Paul-Emile, *When a Wrongful Birth Claim May Not Be Wrong: Race, Inequality, and the Cost of Blackness*, 86 FORDHAM L. REV. 2811, 2817–18, 2822 (2018); Robin Lenhardt, *The Color of Kinship*, 102 IOWA L. REV. 2071, 2085–86 (2017).

60. Palmore v. Sidoti, 466 U.S. 429, 432–33 (1984).

61. *Id.* at 433. For discussion, *see* Katie Eyer, *Constitutional Colorblindness and the Family*, 162 U. PA. L. REV. 537, 541–42 (2014).

62. *See* Dov Fox, *Racial Classification in Assisted Reproduction*, 118 YALE L.J. 1844, 1865–66, 1869–72 (2009).

63. Anderson v. Martin, 375 U.S. 399 (1964).

64. *Id.* at 402–03.

65. *See* Dov Fox, *Race Sorting in Family Formation*, 49 FAM. L.Q. 55, 62–65 (2015).

66. *See* RENE ALMELING, SEX CELLS: THE MEDICAL MARKET FOR EGGS AND SPERM 69–70 (2011).

67. Seline Szkupinski Quiroga, *Blood Is Thicker than Water: Policing Donor Insemination and the Reproduction of Whiteness*, 22 HYPATIA 143, 151 (2007).

68. CAMISHA A. RUSSELL, THE ASSISTED REPRODUCTION OF RACE, 129 (2018).

69. Suzanne Lenon & Danielle Peers, *"Wrongful" Inheritance: Race, Disability and Sexuality in* Cramblett v. Midwest Sperm Bank, 25 FEMINIST LEGAL STUD. 141, 160 (2017).

70. PATRICIA J. WILLIAMS, THE ALCHEMY OF RACE AND RIGHTS 186–87 (1991). *See also* Patricia J. Williams, *The Value of Whiteness: A Lawsuit Is Being Waged Against the "Wrongful Birth" of a Black Child*, NATION (Nov. 12, 2014), https://www.thenation.com/article/value-whiteness [https://perma.cc/22D6-HQMX].

71. Dorothy E. Roberts, *Why Baby Markets Aren't Free*, 7 U.C. IRVINE L. REV. 611, 617 (2017).

72. *Id.* at 614; DOROTHY E. ROBERTS, KILLING THE BLACK BODY: RACE, REPRODUCTION, AND THE MEANING OF LIBERTY 268 (1997).

73. *See* IAN F. HANEY-LÓPEZ, WHITE BY LAW: THE LEGAL CONSTRUCTION OF RACE 117 (1996); RANDALL KENNEDY, INTERRACIAL INTIMACIES: SEX, MARRIAGE, IDENTITY, AND ADOPTION 219–20 (2003).

74. Loving v. Virginia, 388 U.S. 1, 7 (1967) (internal quotation marks omitted, citing Naim v. Naim, 87 S.E.2d 749, 756 (Va. 1955)).

75. HERMAN, *supra* note 46, at 124, 130–33.

76. KENNEDY, *supra* note 73, at 235–36.

77. *See* Marco Jimenez, *Remedial Concilience*, 62 EMORY L.J. 1309, 1357–58 (2013).

78. *See* ANGELA ONWUACHI-WILLIG, ACCORDING TO OUR HEARTS: *RHINELANDER V. RHINELANDER* AND THE LAW OF THE MULTIRACIAL FAMILY 17–19 (2013); Clare Huntington, *Staging the Family*, 88 N.Y.U. L. REV. 589, 590–91 (2013).

79. Gleitman v. Cosgrove, 227 A.2d 689, 693 (N.J. 1967); Grubbs *ex rel.* Grubbs v. Barbourville Family Health Ctr., P.S.C., 120 S.W.3d 682, 690 (Ky. 2003); Dumer v. St. Michael's Hospital, 233 N.W.2d 372, 379 (Wis. 1975) (Hansen, J., dissenting). *See also* Azzolino v. Dingfelder, 337 S.E.2d 528, 535 (N.C. 1985); Atl. Obstetrics & Gynecology Grp. v. Abelson, 398 S.E.2d 557, 563 (Ga. 1990).

80. Taylor v. Kurapati, 600 N.W.2d 670, 688 (Mich. Ct. App. 1999).

81. *Id.* at 690; Williams v. Rosner, 7 N.E.3d 57, 68 (Ill. App. Ct. 2014).

82. Grubbs, 120 S.W.3d at 692–93 (Wintersheimer, J., concurring).

83. Nicholas Agar, Liberal Eugenics: In Defense of Human Enhancement 135 (2004). *See also* Joseph Fletcher, The Ethics of Genetic Control: Ending Reproductive Roulette 147–187 (1974); John Harris, Wonderwoman and Superman: The Ethics of Human Biotechnology 158–161, 168–175 (1992); Philip Kitcher, The Lives to Come: The Genetic Revolution and Human Possibilities 187–204 (1996); Glenn McGee, The Perfect Baby: Parenthood in the New World of Cloning and Genetics 125–140 (2000); Gregory E. Pence, Who's Afraid of Human Cloning? 168–180 (1998); Gregory Stock, Redesigning Humans: Our Inevitable Genetic Future 197–201 (2002).

84. *See* Dov Fox, *The Illiberality of "Liberal Eugenics,"* 20 Ratio 1, 3–4 (2007).

85. *See* Dov Fox, *Silver Spoons and Golden Genes: Genetic Engineering and the Egalitarian Ethos*, 33 Am. J.L. & Med. 567, 604–609 (2007); Rosalind McDougal, *Acting Parentally: An Argument Against Sex Selection*, 31 J. Med. Ethics 601, 603–604 (2005); Guido Pennings, *The Right to Choose Your Donor: A Step Towards Commercialization or a Step Towards Empowering the Patient?*, 15 Hum. Reprod. 508, 509–10 (2000); Sonia Mateu Suter, *The Routinization of Prenatal Testing*, 28 Am. J.L. & Med. 233, 251 (2002).

86. Michael J. Sandel, The Case Against Perfection: Ethics in the Age of Genetic Engineering 45, 85–87 (2007).

87. *See* Paul Ramsey, Fabricated Man: The Ethics of Genetic Control 138–45 (1970); Ted Peters, *"Playing God" and Germline Intervention*, 20 J. Med. & Phil. 365, 376–79, 385–86 (1995); John H. Evans, Playing God?: Human Genetic Engineering and the Rationalization of Public Bioethical Debate 125–35 (2002).

88. *See* Dov Fox, *Religion and the Unborn Under the First Amendment, in* Law, Religion, and Health in the United States 372, 380–81 (I. Glenn Cohen, Holly Fernandez Lynch, & Elizabeth Sepper eds., 2017).

89. *See* Cary Funk, Brian Kennedy, & Elizabeth Podrebarac Sciupac, *U.S. Public Wary of Biomedical Technologies to "Enhance" Human Abilities*, Pew Research Ctr. (July 26, 2016), http://www.pewinternet.org/2016/07/26/u-s-public-wary-of-biomedical-technologies-to-enhance-human-abilities/ [https://perma.cc/7PWY-FB2R].

90. Stephanie C. Chen & David T. Wasserman, *A Framework for Unrestricted Prenatal Whole-Genome Sequencing: Respecting and Enhancing the Autonomy of Prospective Parents*, 17 Am. J. Bioethics 3, 13 n.12 (2017).

91. Henry T. Greely, The End of Sex and the Future of Human Reproduction 226–27 (2016).

92. Frances M. Kamm, *Is There a Problem with Enhancement?*, 5 Am. J. Bioethics 5, 10 (2005).

93. *See* Dov Fox, *Parental Attention Deficit Disorder*, 25 J. Applied Phil. 246, 258 (2008). For analysis of these competing views, *see* I. Glenn Cohen, *What (If Anything) Is Wrong with Human Enhancement? What (If Anything) Is Right with It?*, 49 Tulsa L. Rev. 645, 669–72 (2014).

Conclusion

1. Christine Van Dusen, *A Georgia Sperm Bank, a Troubled Donor, and the Secretive Business of Babymaking*, ATLANTA MAG. (Feb. 13, 2008), http://www.atlantamagazine.com/great-reads/georgia-sperm-bank-troubled-donor-secretive-business-babymaking/ [https://perma.cc/252G-TTS9].

2. *See* Order on Def.'s Mot. Dismiss, Norman v. Xytex Corp., No. 2017CV298536 (Fulton County Sup. Ct. June 13, 2018); Zelt v. Xytex Corp., No. 1:17-CV-4851-TWT, 2018 U.S. Dist. LEXIS 28383, at *1–*2 (N.D. Ga. Feb. 22, 2018); Final Order, Collins v. Xytex Corp., No. 2015CV259033 (Fulton County Sup. Ct. 2015); Order Granting in Part and Den. in Part Def.'s Mot. Dismiss, Doe v. Xytex Corp., 2017 WL 1112996 (N.D. Cal. Mar. 24, 2017); Order Dismiss without Prejudice, Doe v. Xytex Corp., 2017 U.S. Dist. LEXIS 124358 (C.D. Cal. Aug. 7, 2017); Doe v. Xytex Corp., No. C 16-02935 WHA, 2016 WL 3902577 (N.D. Cal. July 19, 2016); Order Granting Defs' Mot. Dismiss, Doe v. Xytex Corp., 2017 U.S. Dist. LEXIS 38501* (N.D. Ga. Mar. 17, 2017); Order Granting Defs' Mot. Dismiss, Doe v. Xytex Corp., 2017 U.S. Dist. LEXIS 38500 (N.D. Ga. Mar. 17, 2017); Rebecca Lindstrom, *Sperm Bank Settles Negligence Lawsuits*, 11 ALIVE ATLANTA (Oct. 6, 2017), http://www.11alive.com/news/investigations/sperm-bank-settles-negligence-lawsuits/481397639 [https://perma.cc/2DJV-LWV6].

3. Order at *8, Doe, 2017 U.S. Dist. LEXIS 38500 (emphasis added).

4. Order at *4, Norman, No. 2017CV298536 (quoting Atl. Obstetrics & Gynecology Grp. v. Abelson, 398 S.E.2d 557, 561 (Ga. 1990); Azzolino v. Dingfelder, 337 S.E.2d 528, 534 (N.C. 1985)).

5. *Id.*

6. Rene Zelt, et al. v. Xytex Corporation, et al., No. 18-11164, at 3, 5, 13–15 (11th Cir. Feb. 4, 2019) (quoting *Abelson*, 398 S.E. 2d at 563).

7. *See, e.g.*, Larsen v. Banner Health Sys., 81 P.3d 196, 206 (Wyo. 2003); Mallette v. Children's Friend & Serv., 661 A.2d 67, 72 (R.I. 1995); Gibbs v. Ernst, 647 A.2d 882, 884 (Pa. 1994); Roe v. Catholic Charities, 588 N.E.2d 354, 365 (Ill. App. Ct. 1992); Meracle v. Children's Serv. Soc'y of Wis., 437 N.W.2d 532, 535 (Wis. 1989); Jackson v. State, 956 P.2d 35, 43 (Mont. 1998). For discussion, *see* Marianne Brower Blair, *Getting the Whole Truth and Nothing but the Truth: The Limits of Liability*, 67 NOTRE DAME L. REV. 851, 915–52 (1992).

8. Mohr v. Com., 653 N.E.2d 1104, 1112 (Mass. 1995).

9. *Id.* at 1113

10. Harshaw v. Bethany Christian Services, 714 F. Supp. 2d 771, 794 (W.D. Mich. 2010). Some states require even more. In Georgia, adoption agencies must "make a complete and thorough investigation and report" of a child's medical condition and the genetic, social, and health histories of his birth parents. GA. CODE ANN. § 19-8-23 (West 2017).

11. ANDREW SOLOMON, FAR FROM THE TREE: PARENTS, CHILDREN, AND THE SEARCH FOR IDENTITY 302 (2012).

12. *See* Karen S. Yeiser, Flight from Reason: A Mother's Story of Schizophrenia, Recovery, and Hope 109–13 (2014).

13. *See* Randye Kaye, Ben Behind His Voices: One Family's Journey from the Chaos of Schizophrenia to Hope 288 (2011).

14. Solomon, *supra* note 11, at 329.

15. *See* Kim T. Meuser & Susan Gingerich, The Complete Family Guide to Schizophrenia 92–96 (2006).

16. *See* Michael Schofield, January First: A Child's Descent into Madness and Her Father's Struggle to Save Her 232–35 (2011).

17. *See* Solomon, *supra* note 11, at 316.

18. Ashifa Kassam, *Sperm Bank Sued as Case of Mentally Ill Donor's History Unfolds*, Guardian (Apr. 14, 2016, 3:18 PM EDT), http://www.theguardian.com/world/2016/apr/14/sperm-donor-canada-families-file-lawsuit [http://perma.cc/HP74-ZN88].

19. *See* Daniel J. Solove & Danielle Keats Citron, *Risk and Anxiety: A Theory of Data Breach Harms*, 96 Tex. L. Rev. 737, 764–74 (2018).

20. Van Dusen, *supra* note 1.

21. *See* Solove & Citron, *supra* note 19, at 756–64.

Index

For the benefit of digital users, indexed terms that span two pages (e.g., 52–53) may, on occasion, appear on only one of those pages.